M.

THE STRUCTURE OF THE DEFENSE MARKET, 1955–1964

THE STRUCTURE OF THE DEFENSE MARKET 1955—1964

William L. Baldwin

Duke University Press
Durham, N. C.   1967

Printed in the United States of America
by Kingsport Press, Inc., Kingsport, Tenn.

Preface

This study deals with the structure of the defense market in a decade of cold war when neither escalation nor disarmament were significant features. By FY (Fiscal Year) 1955 the defense market had virtually completed its adjustment to the end of hostilities in Korea, and the Vietnamese build-up did not begin until late in FY 1965. The intervening decade may therefore prove to be characterized by far different circumstances than those which will prevail in the future. Yet the period is of interest precisely because it was one of rather high and rather steady spending on national defense, and hence a period in which the market structure could evolve and respond in a fairly orderly manner to the demands of national defense in an age of great technological change and an almost unimaginable potential for destruction.

Most of the material embodied herein was gathered during the academic year 1963–1964, while I held a Brookings Research Professorship. Subsequent preparation of the manuscript and some updating have been facilitated by grants from the Faculty Research Committee at Dartmouth College. I am grateful for advice, criticism, and stimulation to so many members of the staff of the Brookings Institution and colleagues at Dartmouth that deserved acknowledgements would run to excessive, indeed embarrassing, length. But I must acknowledge my particular debt to Charles H. Berry and Clarence H. Danhof for helpful comments and encouragement while I was at Brookings, and to Ian A. Stewart for his invaluable assistance on data problems and computer programing following my return to Dartmouth.

While I was in Washington, D.C., I made extensive use of the facilities of the library of the Industrial College of the Armed Forces. My thanks are due to the commandant of ICAF for permission to use the library and to its staff for generous assistance. Mr. Carrol I. Tod of the Office of the Assistant Secretary of Defense (Comptroller) was most helpful in providing me with data prepared by the Directorate for Statistical Services and in discussing with me problems of interpreting and using the material. Subsequently, Mr. Tod read an early draft of several chapters and offered very helpful suggestions and criticisms.

Portions of earlier drafts were also read and commented upon by Professors Murray L. Weidenbaum, then with Stanford Research Institute, Lee E. Preston of the University of California at Berkeley, Sumner Marcus of the University of Washington, and Daniel Marx, Jr., of Dartmouth College.

The customary stricture about the author's bearing complete responsibility holds in full for this study, if for no other reason than that I have not accepted all the suggestions made to me and have thereby no doubt rejected some very sound and useful advice.

I received diligent and competent research assistance from Mr. David B. Leahy in Washington, Mr. J. K. Sharma at Berkeley, and Mr. John Rapoport at Dartmouth. I am indebted to Mrs. Dorothy H. Bower for furnishing me with financial figures from the COMPUSTAT tapes and converting them into the forms in which they are presented in Chapter VIII.

My wife, Marcia Hurt Baldwin, has read the entire manuscript and is responsible for numerous corrections and improvements in form and style.

Hanover, New Hampshire
March 1, 1966

Contents

THE STRUCTURE OF THE DEFENSE MARKET, 1955–1964

I. INTRODUCTION

Large-scale military procurement, sustained over a protracted period of cold war, has given rise to a uniquely organized market in which the defense establishment purchases goods and services. Since the end of the Korean War much has been done to improve procurement policies and practices of the Department of Defense and to adapt these policies and practices to the perpetuation of a high level of peacetime military strength in an era of costly, technically complex, and rapidly changing weapon systems. Simultaneously, the supply side of the defense market has been evolving to meet conditions imposed by advanced and shifting technology and by the singular buying habits of the customer. Despite the emphasis on support of forces actually engaged in combat in Vietnam during 1965, the basic objective of this nation's military spending remains preparedness rather than active prosecution of hostilities.

Military procurement and the behavior of suppliers have come under intensive and repeated scrutiny from Congress,[1] the General Accounting Office, the Bureau of the Budget, industrial associations, both trade and general press, and academic researchers, as well as from within the Department of Defense itself; but most of the resulting analyses, criticisms, and recommendations for change have paid little or no systematic attention to the structure of the market. It would appear that more intensive investigations of structural factors are warranted, since structure, along with behavior, exerts a powerful influence on economic performance. Indeed, many students of industrial organization regard structure as a far more

1. In 1956, Secretary of Defense Charles E. Wilson, testifying before the House Subcommittee on Department of Defense Appropriations, stated, "I would like to remind you that we have approximately 80 congressional investigations, both major and minor, going on in the Department of Defense and our people get a little confused over the things sometimes." Later, when asked to furnish a list for the record, the Department of Defense enumerated 57 such investigations, assistance to two congressional commissions, and "a large number of investigations or requests for information involving the case of only one individual, an isolated procurement complaint, or lesser operational problem." The list ran from July 1, 1955, to Feb. 15, 1956. U.S. Congress, House Committee on Appropriations, Subcommittee on Department of Defense Appropriations, *Hearings: Department of Defense Appropriations for 1957, Procurement Policies and Practices of the Department of Defense* (Washington: Government Printing Office, 1956), pp. 158, 190–194.

important explanatory factor than behavior.[2] Further, the Department of Defense, as the sole customer, inevitably plays a major role in shaping the structure of the military market, its only real choice being whether to exert its influence through policy or inadvertence.

Market structure has many dimensions. It is employed as an analytical device, along with conduct or behavior, to explain the performance of firms in a given industry or market. It is also used as an aid to public policy. A major issue in antitrust enforcement, for example, has been whether remedial action designed to improve performance should focus on structural changes such as dissolution of specific firms and prohibition of certain mergers, or on regulation of conduct such as forbidding price agreements and misrepresentation. As a determinant of economic performance, structure embraces all elements of the environment within which firms operate and which conceivably might either restrain or give latitude to their behavior. In describing the structure of a specific industry or market in a manageable, comprehensible, and useful manner, it is necessary to discriminate and concentrate on selected features of the environment. Due regard must be given to the aspects of performance considered relevant, the structural elements which are believed to be important influences on these aspects of performance, and—if the exercise is to have any significance for public policy—the structural conditions which can and should be altered or preserved by the actions of public bodies.

The issues raised by structure and behavior in relation to performance are as highly relevant to procurement policy as they are to antitrust issues. It might be argued with some force that if the structure of the defense market could be altered so as to establish a more truly competitive environment, then regulation of contractors' behavior and attempts to influence performance directly would become unnecessary.

This study first examines some aspects of the structure of the defense market for which quantitative data are available and which can therefore be presented in numerical form. These are the concentration of prime contracts, the stability of the market, the industrial

2. See, for example, J. S. Bain, *Industrial Organization* (New York: Wiley, 1959); George W. Stocking, *Basing Point Pricing and Regional Development* (Chapel Hill: University of North Carolina Press, 1954); and Richard E. Caves, *American Industry: Structure, Conduct, Performance* (Englewood Cliffs, N.J.: Prentice-Hall, 1964).

mix of the largest producers of military products and services, and the degree to which the major defense contractors have specialized in military sales or have diversified into commercial markets. It will be argued below that, since the defense market is unique in certain crucial respects, comparisons with other markets or industries are quite apt to be misleading or meaningless. Therefore, changes in structure are considered of more interest than the cross-sectional profile at any one point in time. The study of measurable aspects of market structure is followed by a more discursive treatment of certain other vitally important subsurface structural features, namely the nature of the government's demand for military products, the technological base of the market, and conditions of entry. Next, there is a brief analysis of financial conditions among the major defense contractors. The study concludes with a discussion of the public policy implications of the structural material which has been developed.

The limitations of the approach used here should be noted and kept in mind while reading this study. The objective is to describe certain important structural aspects of the national defense market and to discuss the implications of market structure for military procurement policy. It is most certainly not contended that structural analysis provides a magic or scientific formula yielding the single optimal set of policy prescriptions. Indeed, military procurement policy cannot and should not be based entirely on the concepts of economic efficiency that underlie the performance norms to which structure is related. Perfectly valid political and strategic factors and ethical considerations peculiar to the munitions field must be taken into consideration.[3] Also, alleged improper political pressures and inefficient bureaucratic processes may have an extremely important influence on performance of the military market but are beyond the scope of this study. However, just as structural considerations alone cannot determine a correct line of procurement policy, a

3. This sentence was written before I had the opportunity to read the Preface to F. M. Scherer, *The Weapons Acquisition Process: Economic Incentives* (Boston: Division of Research, Graduate School of Business Administration, Harvard University, 1964). In his Preface, Scherer observes, "I am troubled more directly by a basic policy premise of this book: that efficiency is a desirable objective in the conduct of advanced weapons development and production programs. It is by no means certain that this is true. The weapons acquisition process may be too efficient already. To be sure, there are gross inefficiencies. But despite them, the process has given mankind all too much power for its own annihilation" (p. ix).

policy which ignores the structure of the market at which it is directed will, except by pure luck, be decidedly inferior to one which takes structure explicitly into account.

Table I–1 is designed to put the magnitude of military procurement into perspective. Procurement awards during the cold war period consumed somewhat more than one half of total appropriations made for the DOD (Department of Defense), absorbing roughly 5 per cent of the nation's total output of goods and services.

Table I-1: Total DOD procurement awards, except governmental

Fiscal year	Amount ($ millions)	Percentage of GNP	Fiscal year	Amount ($ millions)	Percentage of GNP
1951	$31,585	10.2	1958	23,666	5.4
1952	42,801	12.7	1959	24,554	5.3
1953	31,240	8.7	1960	22,908	4.6
1954	12,859	3.6	1961	24,703	4.9
1955	16,041	4.3	1962	28,099	5.2
1956	19,156	4.7	1963	29,032	5.1
1957	20,996	4.8	1964	28,234	4.7

Sources: OSD (Office of the Secretary of Defense), Military Prime Contract Awards and Subcontract Payments, July 1962–June 1963, p. 35, and July 1963–June 1964, p. 37; U.S. Department of Commerce, Office of Business Economics, Survey of Current Business, various issues.

II. THE STRUCTURE OF THE MILITARY MARKET AS DEPICTED BY ANNUAL CONTRACT AWARDS

A. Measurable Aspects of Market Structure

Each year, beginning with fiscal year 1957, the Department of Defense has published a list of *100 Companies and Their Subsidiaries* [or *Affiliates*] *Listed According to Net Value of Military Prime Contract Awards*. The lists rank companies in descending order by dollar value of contract awards received, indicate both parent and subsidiary companies by name, show the dollar value of contracts awarded to each firm with breakdowns by subsidiaries where necessary, and present the percentage of the total awards made to United States concerns accounted for by each firm on the list.[1] Prior to FY 1957, similar lists were prepared on irregular occasions and for various periods of time, generally in response to specific inquiries from congressional investigators.

There are several aspects of concentration and market structure which are amenable to investigation from lists of the largest firms in some defined group. In 1932 Berle and Means used data on the 200 largest non-banking corporations to indicate the extent of concentration of over-all economic activity. They showed the percentages of total corporate assets held by these giant corporations singly and in sum; through a comparison of holdings in 1928 with holdings in the years 1909, 1919, 1921, 1924, and 1926, they attempted to measure and predict the rate at which this type of concentration had increased and threatened to increase in the future.[2] In 1954 Kaplan pointed out that if we are interested in the intensity of competition in the United States economy, we should be concerned with the stability of the membership of such a list as well as with the percentage of total

1. The procurement totals on which the company percentages are based are somewhat smaller than the totals shown in Table I-1, which includes all procurement except from other governmental agencies. The percentages reported by the Department of Defense in its annual lists, and used throughout this chapter, are percentages of total prime contract awards going to United States firms only.

2. A. A. Berle and G. C. Means, *The Modern Corporation and Private Property* (New York: Macmillan, 1932).

assets, sales, or employment accounted for by whatever firms happen to comprise the largest 100 or 200 at a certain time.[3] From examination of various lists of the 100 largest firms, Kaplan found the turnover to be substantial and concluded that competitive forces in the United States appeared to be quite strong and effective enough to drive inefficient and unprogressive giant firms from their positions of dominance. In a 1957 article Friedland investigated what had happened to the firms which had dropped out of the largest 50 and from what positions the successors of these firms had come.[4] Friedland examined mergers and dissolutions and determined how far below the fiftieth rank the disappearing firms had dropped, and the ranks from which their successors rose. His interpretation of the significance of competitive forces in generating turnover among the giant firms substantially disagreed with Kaplan's. Finally, in 1961, Collins and Preston noted that there were aspects of stability and concentration worthy of analysis among those firms which remained in the lists of the largest,[5] as well as among those leaving and their replacements. Pursuing this observation, they examined the size-distribution of firms on the lists at various times and stability of both rank and size of the survivors from list to list. These earlier works, then, suggest at least three major aspects of concentration and market structure which might be examined using the data contained in the Department of Defense's annual lists of the largest prime contractors: (a) Over-all concentration of prime contract awards, showing the percentages of the total accounted for by various numbers of the largest contractors. (b) Stability among the largest contractors, in terms of both exit from and entry to the group and the positions of the firms remaining within the group from one list to the next. (c) Internal concentration, or the degree of inequality of contract awards within the group.

B. Over-all Concentration in the Defense Market

Table II-1 shows the percentages, for various periods, of total military prime contract awards received by all United States busi-

3. A. D. H. Kaplan, *Big Enterprise in a Competitive System* (Washington: Brookings Institution, 1954).
4. Seymour Friedland, "Turnover and Growth of the Largest Industrial Firms, 1906–1950," *Review of Economics and Statistics*, XXXIX (Feb., 1957), 79–83.
5. N. R. Collins and L. E. Preston, "The Size Structure of the Largest Industrial Firms," *American Economic Review*, LI (Dec., 1961), 986–1011.

ness firms which were awarded to the 100 largest contractors, the 50 largest, and to small business concerns. The percentages are of dollar value, not number, of awards. There are several features of this table to be noted.

First, the table indicates that if attention is directed to changes in concentration rather than its absolute levels, it makes little difference whether the percentages accounted for by the 100 largest or the 50 largest are used as indicators. One reflects the other quite accurately, since the share of contract awards going to firms ranking 51 through 100 has varied only slightly in comparison with the total, especially since 1950. However, the figures do not reflect stability so much as the comparative unimportance of the lower half of the list. The percentage of awards received by firms ranking 51 through 100 has ranged since World War II from a low of 7.3 per cent in FY 1958 to a high of 8.9 per cent in FY 1962. While only 1.6 per cent of

Table II-1: Distribution of U.S. military prime contract awards

	Percentage of total accounted for by			
Period	Largest 100	Largest 50	51–100	Small business
June 1940–Sept. 1944 (WWII)*	67.2	57.6	9.6	
July 1950–June 1953 (Korean War)	64.0	56.3	7.7	
Jan. 1955–June 1957	67.4	59.5	7.9	
FY 1957	68.4	59.8	8.6	19.8
FY 1958	74.2	66.9	7.3	17.1
FY 1959	73.8	65.3	8.5	16.6
FY 1960	73.4	64.8	8.6	16.1
FY 1961	74.2	65.8	8.4	15.9
FY 1962	72.3	63.4	8.9	17.7
FY 1963	73.9	65.6	8.3	15.8**
FY 1964	73.4	65.8	7.6	17.2**
FY 1965	68.9	61.2	7.7	19.6**

* The figure for World War II is based on prime contracts of $50,000 or more and excludes procurement of food. The more recent series are based on contracts of $10,000 or more, including food procurement. Thus, neither coverage nor base are strictly comparable.

** Because of a change in reporting coverage, the ratios starting with FY 1963 are not comparable with those for prior years. On a comparable basis, the FY 1963 ratio is 16.5 per cent; those for FY 1964 and FY 1965 are not available.

Sources: For World War II, Smaller War Plants Corporation, *Report to U.S. Senate Special Committee to Study Problems of American Small Business, Economic Concentration and World War II* (Washington: Government Printing Office, 1946), pp. 30–31.

For the Korean War, U.S. Congress, Senate Committee on Armed Services, Preparedness Investigating Subcommittee, *Investigation of the Preparedness Program, Second Report, Report on Concentration of Defense Contracts* (Washington: Government Printing Office, 1955), pp. 8–14.

For FY 1957–65, OSD, *100 Companies and Their Subsidiaries Listed According to Net Value of Military Prime Contract Awards*, various years; OSD, *Military Prime Contract Awards and Subcontract Payments, July 1964–June 1965*, p. 12.

total awards, this change represents an increase of nearly 22 per cent for the size class involved, followed by a subsequent sharp decline. Other reasons will be given below for concentrating attention on firms appearing among the 50 largest rather than the 100 largest prime contractors. At this point it is merely noted that since these firms account for nearly two-thirds of the prime contract awards, it is not surprising that they also account for the bulk of the changes in the over-all level of concentration.

Second, the share of prime contracts going to small business (generally defined as consisting of firms of five hundred or fewer employees, independent, and not dominant in their markets) decreased steadily from FY 1957 through FY 1961, rose sharply in FY 1962, fell off again, and then evidently recovered. Congress and the Department of Defense have long been concerned with increasing the participation of small business in defense contracting. The Armed Services Procurement Act of 1947 requires that "a fair proportion of the purchases and contracts made under this chapter be placed with small business concerns." [6] Congress has inserted similar language in several other statutes, including the Defense Production Act of 1950, the National Aeronautics and Space Act of 1958, and the Communications Satellite Act of 1962.[7] In response to this direction from Congress, plus continuing pressure especially from the Small Business Committees of both the House and Senate, the Department of Defense has for several years had in force a very elaborate program, including small business advisors at all major procurement offices, set-asides under which certain purchases are restricted to small vendors, and waiver of procurement offices' responsibilities to determine the capabilities of small firms which are certified as responsible bidders by the Small Business Administration. The decline in percentage of awards going to small firms through FY 1961 occurred in spite of these requirements, pressures, and devices. On March 15, 1961, President Kennedy instructed the Department of Defense "to set a goal increasing individually in the fiscal year 1962 small business participation by 10 percent over the year for fiscal 1960. Contracts for small business in fiscal year 1960," he added, "amounted to $3,440 million, or 16 percent. We

6. U.S. Congress, House Select Committee on Small Business, *Small Business and Government Procurement: A Report of the Select Committee on Small Business* (Washington: Government Printing Office, 1962), p. 1.

7. *Ibid.*, pp. 1–3.

are going to try to increase that by 10 percent." [8] In response to this directive, the Department of Defense launched "Operation Booster"; and in testifying on appropriations for FY 1964, Thomas D. Morris, Assistant Secretary of Defense (Installations and Logistics), spoke of its success:

> Sir, as you know, one of President Kennedy's earliest memorandums to the Secretary of Defense was one calling his attention to his personal interest in, and concern with, the small business program in the Department of Defense. In fiscal year 1962 the Secretary set an objective of increasing the percentage of our prime contract awards to small business by 10 per cent. This goal was met and resulted in awards to small business to the extent of 18 percent of our total procurement, including civil works procurement. This amounted to about $4.5 billion of prime contract awards. . . .
>
> For fiscal 1963 we set a target of sustaining that performance obtained in 1962 and, if possible, bettering it in terms of total dollars. Through the first six months of 1963, we were at approximately the same dollar level as we had been in the first six months of 1962. Percentagewise we had slipped slightly. We are currently giving renewed emphasis throughout the Department so that the last six months, hopefully, will overcome that slight slippage.[9]

Yet the final figure for FY 1963 showed that on a comparable basis two-thirds of the percentage gain of the previous year had been wiped out. Despite a lack of comparability between the FY 1964 figure and that for FY 1962, it would appear that the lost ground was regained, but that there was little if any new advance before FY 1965 and the Vietnamese build-up. In Chapter VII, which discusses barriers to entry into the defense market, several difficulties facing small firms will be noted, and it will be argued that there are structural and institutional reasons for expecting at best only a moderate long-run increase in the participation of independent small businesses in prime contract awards.

Table II–1 shows that the concentration of total defense contracts increased during the cold war years. From FY 1958 through FY 1964 concentration of prime contracts, whether for the top 50 or top 100, was substantially above the levels of World War II and the Korean War. It is not surprising that concentration was higher during the

8. *Ibid.*, p. 3.

9. U.S. Congress, House Committee on Appropriations, Subcommittee on Department of Defense Appropriations, *Hearings: Department of Defense Appropriations for 1964, Part 5, Procurement* (Washington: Government Printing Office, 1963), p. 131.

cold war situation than it was during major shooting conflicts, or that it rose with the cutbacks accompanying the end of the Korean War. In World War II, and to a lesser extent in the Korean War, the government exercised direct controls over industry. Through devices such as assignment of priorities, allocation orders, price ceilings, and rationing, governmental agencies were able to put a damper on commercial operations and stimulate the shift of resources into military production. Such controls, the need to draw on a wide industrial base when a substantial portion of the nation's economic activity was committed to the war effort (very roughly, twice the percentage in World War II as in the Korean War and again twice the percentage in the Korean War as in the post-Korean cold war period), plus patriotic motivations among the business community—all drew commercially-oriented firms into the military market on a temporary basis. Even in the years between World War II and the Korean War it appears that industrial firms typically thought that "Government business was just *plus* business—business that was only temporary and relatively unimportant in long-range planning."[10] Today the situation is quite different, as described in a report prepared by Stanford Research Institute for an agency of the Department of Defense:

In contrast to the situation in World War II, and even with that during the Korean War, a larger share of defense production today is performed by highly specialized defense contractors, many of whose products bear little resemblance to any civilian items, and who have had. little experience outside defense production. For many of these companies, there is no reconversion problem as such, because they have never "converted" from civilian production in the first place.[11]

The fact that procurement awards were more highly concentrated in World War II than in the Korean War requires further explanation if there is any validity to the argument that controls on civilian production, priorities for defense or war work, and the need to mobilize a greater part of the country's productive capacity all tend to reduce concentration, for these features were obviously more in-

10. National Security Industrial Association, *Problems in Military Contracting: Papers Presented at NSIA's Ninth Annual Meeting, October 1, 1952* (New York: National Security Industrial Association, 1952), p. 4.

11. Stanford Research Institute, "Industrial Adjustments to Shifts in Defense Spending," in Senate Committee on Labor and Public Welfare, *Selected Readings in Employment and Manpower* (Washington: Government Printing Office, 1964), II, 700.

fluential in World War II than during the Korean War. Perhaps the explanation lies in the account of Donald M. Nelson, who became chairman of the War Production Board in 1942. He noted that in the early months of the war, "The awful realization was slowly coming over the country that America was losing a war, the greatest in history, one upon which our national existence depended." [12] He pointed to the administrative ease and speed, when speed was of overriding importance, of dealing with only a few large prime contractors who could in turn subcontract fairly quickly because of their established commercial relations. "We cut a wide, rakehelly swath through the economy," he wrote, "knowing that any damage done could be corrected later but if we didn't succeed there would be no economy and no country." [13]

There is no work on the Korean War period comparable to Nelson's description of attitudes among civilian and military leaders during World War II. We may assume that during the Korean War there was less of a sense of urgency and no fear for the immediate survival of the nation, as well as an awareness among procurement officials that there would be no wholesale demobilization at the end of active hostilities and hence a concern over the ability of the defense establishment to live on a permanent basis with the market patterns being established. The Smaller War Plants Corporation had submitted a report to the Senate Special Committee to Study Problems of American Small Business which was harshly critical of the concentration of procurement during World War II, [14] and the Congress as a whole had made its interest in small business clear in passage of the Armed Services Procurement Act of 1947. The Administration's concern was made known when President Truman, commenting on his signing of the Armed Services Procurement Act, wrote in February of 1948:

This bill grants unprecedented freedom from specific procurement restrictions during peacetime. That freedom is given to permit the flexibility and latitude needed in present day national defense activities. . . . There is danger that the natural desire for flexibility and speed in

12. Donald M. Nelson, *Arsenal of Democracy: The Story of American War Production* (New York: Harcourt, Brace, 1946), p. 3.

13. *Ibid.,* p. 278.

14. Smaller War Plants Corporation, *Report to the U.S. Senate Special Committee to Study Problems of American Small Business: Economic Concentration and World War II* (Washington: Government Printing Office, 1946).

procurement will lead to excessive placement of contracts by negotiation and undue reliance upon large concerns, and this must not occur.[15]

Thus, procurement officials had both greater opportunity and greater encouragement to seek to hold down concentration during the Korean War than had been the case in World War II.

In FY 1958 concentration rose suddenly and substantially to a level which remained quite constant through FY 1964. In commentary accompanying the FY 1958 list, the Department of Defense explained:

> The increase in the percent of total awarded to the first two companies on the list, Boeing Airplane Co. and General Dynamics Corporation, was as large as the net increase in the entire list of 100. Contracts with Boeing increased from $907 million in Fiscal Year 1957 to $2,131 million in Fiscal Year 1958. Practically all of the Boeing awards were in the programs for B-52 bombers, KC-135 jet tankers, and the Bomarc missile. Most of the General Dynamics awards, which increased from $1,018 million to $1,383 million, were for work of the Convair Division on the Atlas Missile program, certain Navy missiles, the F-102 and F-106 fighter aircraft, and the B-58 bomber, with smaller amounts going to Electric Boat and other divisions for submarines and other products. The percent of total awarded to these two companies increased from 10.2% in Fiscal Year 1957 to 16.2% in Fiscal Year 1958.[16]

The 6 per cent of the total gained by Boeing and General Dynamics was not at the expense of the other firms among the 50 largest, for the share of this group in fact rose by 7.1 per cent of the total at the same time. Neither did the increased share of the first two firms seriously cut into the share of the 100 largest, which increased by 5.8 per cent. The major offset to Boeing's and General Dynamics' gains was clearly the decline of 5.8 per cent in the share going to firms below the top 100, including the drop of 2.7 per cent in small business's portion of the total.

The more interesting aspect of the figures for FY 1958 through FY 1964 is that the FY 1958 rise in concentration was not subsequently reversed until FY 1965. Awards going to Boeing and

15. Quoted in U.S. Congress, House Committee on Armed Services, Special Subcommittee on Procurement Practices of the Department of Defense, *Report Pursuant to Section 4, Public Law 86–89* (Washington: Government Printing Office, 1960), p. 11.

16. Department of Defense, Office of the Secretary of Defense (hereafter cited as OSD), *100 Companies and Affiliates Listed According to Net Value of Military Prime Contract Awards*, 1 July 1957–30 June 1958, p. 1.

General Dynamics cannot explain the continuation of the new level, since by FY 1964 these two firms between them received only 9.3 per cent of the total awards, down almost 1 per cent from their combined position in FY 1957 and down nearly 7 per cent from their FY 1958 share. More basic and fundamental forces than the temporary fortunes of two firms were at play among the top 50 as a group, offsetting the reduction which otherwise would have occurred after FY 1958 as the shares of Boeing and General Dynamics declined. The explanation appears to lie primarily in the impact of "space age" technology. As Table II-2 shows, the share of experimental, development, test, and research (EDTR) work rose sharply from FY 1956 to FY 1960 and FY 1961 and thereafter declined slowly through FY 1964. The table also indicates a similar pattern for missile systems and shows that only very small percentages of the awards for EDTR and missile systems go to small firms. It will be argued later that the nature of these types of work favors quite large firms specializing in defense projects.

In interpreting this table, it should be kept in mind that the figures given for EDTR and missile systems are not additive but overlap, since a substantial portion of missile system awards were for EDTR. From FY 1960 through FY 1964 the percentages of total missile systems awards which were for EDTR were respectively 65.3, 57.9, 51.9, 53.6, and 55.8.[17]

The decline in concentration and the increasing share of prime

17. OSD, *Military Prime Contract Awards and Subcontract Payments, July 1963– June 1964*, p. 27.

Table II-2: EDTR and missile systems procurement, FY 1956–64

Fiscal Year	EDTR as percentage of total procurement	Percentage of EDTR awards to small business	Missile systems as percentage of total procurement	Percentage of missile systems awards to small business
1956	13.5	5.7	5.6	2.1
1957	16.8	4.3	9.8	1.9
1958	18.1	3.7	13.0	1.5
1959	22.6	3.5	19.7	1.4
1960	25.6	3.4	23.4	1.2
1961	25.7	2.9	25.6	1.2
1962	22.9	3.5	25.6	1.4
1963	22.4	3.5	24.6	1.6
1964	21.4	3.7	21.3	1.6

Source: OSD, *Military Prime Contract Awards and Subcontract Payments,* various years.

contract awards going to small business firms in FY 1965 are primarily attributable to two factors. Awards for missiles fell by over $1.3 billion between FY 1964 and FY 1965, signaling the end of the missile build-up. There were less dramatic but substantial declines in the aircraft and electronics procurement programs. On the other hand, with the increasing involvement of armed forces of the United States in Vietnam, procurement awards rose in the ships, tank-automotive, weapons, fuels, ammunition, and services programs. This shift in emphasis clearly favored firms with diversified military and civilian interests at the relative expense of heavily defense-oriented aerospace firms higher on the lists of prime contractors. Small business benefited in particular from substantial rises in procurement awards for subsistence goods, textiles, commercial-type hard goods, construction, and purchases of less than $10,000.

In light of the circumstances which distinguish FY 1965 from the decade which preceded it, and in the hope that the need to support actual combat operations will prove temporary, it seems most appropriate to exclude FY 1965 from an analysis of developments in the structure of the defense market which may be attributed to the conditions of the cold war.

C. Stability among the Largest Contractors

The second aspect of market structure reflected in the lists of 100 largest prime contractors is stability. The concept of stability involves two observable phenomena, differing not in their nature but rather as a result of the arbitrary selection of cut-off points of 50 or 100 firms. First, there is turnover, or exit from and entry to the lists; and second, there is stability of both rank and dollar value of contract awards for all of the firms comprising the lists.

Table II-3 illustrates certain aspects of annual turnover.

If one's attention is directed exclusively to the number of firms dropping out of the 100 largest each year, the market appears to be extremely unstable. Writers wishing to emphasize the instability of defense contracting and the resulting risk to defense contractors have noted the twenty or so firms vanishing from the list from year to year. A Rand Corporation study by F. T. Moore notes the "volatility of the list of major firms in the industry," and adds, "This

kind of rapid entry to and exit from the 'industry' is unique." [18]
Moore notes that most of the firms in the defense "industry" also
produce commercial goods and attributes much of the instability
to variations in the division between defense and civilian business.
Two features of this sort of interpretation of the data should be
noted at the outset of a discussion of stability. First, any comparison
with other industries which would justify such a description as
"unique" would require an annual list of the 100 or so largest firms
in these industries and, to the best of my knowledge, no such lists
have ever been assembled. Second, the comparison would be meaningless if made, since the defense market can hardly be described as
one industry, a problem which was recognized by Moore when he
put the word within quotation marks. A more detailed examination
of Table II-3 and a brief survey of the firms which dropped
out and their replacements suggest that impressions of instability
gained from merely looking at annual exits from the top 100 are
grossly exaggerated.

18. F. T. Moore, *Military Procurement and Contracting: An Economic Analysis,*
Memorandum RM–2948–PR (Santa Monica: Rand Corp., 1962), p. 109.

Table II-3: Disappearances from DOD lists of 100 largest prime
contractors

Fiscal years	In earlier year, among largest			Disappearances, using only top 50 in both years
	100	75	50	
	A. Unadjusted			
1957–58	19	8	2	7
1958–59	22	9	1	10
1959–60	18*	7	2	6
1960–61	23	8	3	7
1961–62	19	7	2	7
1962–63	17	6	0	6
1963–64	19	5	3	6
(1957–64)	(39)	(21)	(8)	(18)
	B. Adjusted for mergers, joint ventures, and transfer of assets			
1957–58	18	8	2	7
1958–59	19	6	1	10
1959–60	11*	4	1	5
1960–61	17	5	1	5
1961–62	11	4	0	5
1962–63	14	4	0	6
1963–64	15	2	1	4
(1957–64)	(29)	(15)	(4)	(13)

* Disappearances out of 99 rather than 100, if Shell Caribbean Co. and Asiatic
Petroleum Corp., both subsidiaries of Royal Dutch Petroleum, are counted as one
concern.

In the first place, some of the entries and exits are accounted for by merger. A firm may vanish because it is acquired in whole or in part by another firm, and the acquiring firm may appear on the list for the first time solely by virtue of the continued defense orders of its new division or subsidiary. The implications for stability and risk of mergers and acquisitions of defense-oriented plant and equipment are ambiguous. A firm's being acquired because it is failing might be viewed as just as indicative of instability and risk as one's vanishing from the list as a result of bankruptcy or decline in defense orders. On the other hand, firms desiring to enter the defense business or wishing diversification of existing defense orders may acquire successful defense contractors on terms favorable to the acquired firms' owners; and such mergers should most certainly not be interpreted as failures to meet the challenges of a risky market or as indications of harsh competitive conditions. The only way to evaluate the significance of mergers and acquisitions in turnover figures would be to examine the circumstances surrounding each one, including the expectations of those promoting the merger as well as the past histories of the companies involved.

Each year, several joint ventures appear on the list, only to disappear in almost every case by the following year. These joint ventures are composed of construction firms and are formed to bid for contracts on major construction projects. Unless there are substantial increases in the original contract resulting from subsequent change orders, or unless the same group is awarded additional contracts, the joint venture appears on the list only in the year the contract is awarded, even though the project may take several years to complete. There are a number of construction companies which appear frequently among the participants in these joint ventures, in differing combinations, year after year. Unfortunately, data are not available on the shares of the separate participants in these joint ventures so that shifts in the defense business of the individual construction firms involved cannot be isolated.

Finally, one disappearance resulted from the fact that in 1959 a non-profit corporation, Jet Propulsion Laboratories, was transferred from nominal ownership by California Institute of Technology to the National Aeronautics and Space Administration.

The adjusted portion of Table II-3 shows disappearances net of mergers and acquisitions, joint ventures, and Jet Propulsion Laboratories. Some of the disappearances of merged firms may be analogous to other disappearances. Construction projects are generally let on sealed bids subject to precise specifications and are among the most competitive of defense programs. Thus it is not contended that the adjusted portion of Table II-3 is superior to the unadjusted, but only that unadjusted turnover figures are undoubtedly too high. Similarly, the adjusted turnover is too low to give an accurate measure.

Table II-3 shows that most of the disappearances, whether unadjusted or adjusted, from the 100 largest are from the lower end of the list, and that most of the firms which disappear re-enter the list shortly thereafter. To use the years with the largest number of unadjusted disappearances between them as an example, of the 23 firms which vanished between FY 1960 and FY 1961, only 8 had been in the top 75 in FY 1960; or, 15 of the 23 had been among the 25 firms receiving the smallest value of contracts listed. Three firms which had been among the top 50 in FY 1960 were not among the top 100 in FY 1961, but one of these disappearances is accounted for by a merger and another by a joint venture of construction firms. The third such disappearance was of Merritt-Chapman and Scott Corporation, which appears on the lists as it receives major shipbuilding contracts. This firm ranked 32 in FY 1957, was not on the list in FY 1958, reappeared with ranks of 31 and 38, respectively, in FY 1959 and FY 1960, then disappeared for FY 1961 and FY 1962, only to re-enter as number 34 in FY 1963 and vanish again in FY 1964. If the length of time involved in ship construction is considered, it would be highly misleading to assume that Merritt-Chapman and Scott's sales revenue from defense sources fluctuated as severely as its annual contract awards.

If annual unadjusted disappearances from the lists of the 100 largest are summed for each pair of years between FY 1957 and FY 1964, the total number of disappearances is 137. Yet when the FY 1957 list is compared directly with that for FY 1964, there are only 39 firms on the former that are not also on the latter; or 98 of those which disappeared reappeared later. Of these 39 disappearances, 10 are the result of mergers, transfer of assets, or joint ventures, and the published list for FY 1964 gives no indication of how many of the remaining 29 would appear among the top 150 or 200 prime contractors.

The fact that some of the disappearing firms may rank only slightly below the 100 largest contract recipients suggests an advantage of concentrating on the top 50 firms. By so doing, it is possible to use the lists of largest 100 to show what happened to most of the firms vanishing from the top 50 and to indicate the previous ranks of most of their replacements. There are additional advantages to limiting the study to those firms which were among the largest 50 contractors in at least one year. All but a few of the joint ventures and most of the non-profit institutions are eliminated by this procedure. We are left with lists made up almost solely of the major permanently organized and profit-oriented defense firms which, as a group, have been receiving well over seven times the contract dollars that have gone to the organizations omitted. The group being left out is a heterogeneous collection of private firms, universities, non-

Table II-4: Firms on the list of 50 largest prime contractors in FY 1957 but not in FY 1964

FY 1957 rank	Name of firm	Status in FY 1964
15	Chance Vought Aircraft	Merged with Ling-Temco to form Ling-Temco-Vought.
19	Curtiss-Wright	FY 1964 rank: 60.
21	Republic Aviation	FY 1964 rank: 51.
25	American Bosch Arma	FY 1964 rank: 87.
26	Bell Aircraft	Entire defense business sold to Textron.
28	Bethlehem Steel	FY 1964 rank: 85. Sold shipyard at Quincy, Mass., to General Dynamics in FY 1964.
32	Merritt-Chapman & Scott	Not on FY 1964 list.
34	Bath Iron Works	Not on FY 1964 list.
40	Burroughs	FY 1964 rank: 53.
41	Fairchild Engine & Airplane	FY 1964 rank: 93.
43	Olin Mathieson	FY 1964 rank: 52.
44	Garrett	Acquired by Signal Oil & Gas in FY 1964.
45	Hayes Aircraft	FY 1964 rank: 73.
46	Philco	Acquired by Ford.
47	Brown-Raymond-Walsh	A joint venture of Brown & Root, Raymond Pile, and Walsh Construction.
48	Cities Service	FY 1964 rank: 75.
49	Tidewater Oil	Not on FY 1964 list.
50	Morrison-Knudsen	Not on FY 1964 list in its own right, but a participant in two FY 1964 joint ventures.

Sources: OSD, *100 Companies and Their Subsidiaries Listed According to Net Value of Military Prime Contract Awards*, FY 1957 and FY 1964; *Moody's Industrial Manual; Standard & Poor's Corporation Register*.

profit management and research companies established by the armed services, joint construction ventures, and, in one year, even Blue Cross Association, Incorporated.

Table II-3 also shows that 18 firms among the top 50 in FY 1957 were not so listed in FY 1964. Merger accounted for the disappearance of 4 of the firms, 1 of those leaving the list was a joint venture, and of the remaining 13, 4 were not among the top 100 in FY 1964. The 18 firms and their status by FY 1964 are shown in Table II-4.

Of the 4 mergers, only Textron's purchase of Bell's defense group involved the acquisition of a firm whose position in the defense market was obviously considered unsatisfactory by its management. Also, 3 aircraft firms—Fairchild, Curtiss-Wright, and Republic —quite obviously lost position between FY 1957 and FY 1964 as a result of their failure to make the transition to the missile age as painlessly as their rivals.

The 18 firms which replaced those that dropped from the top 50 between FY 1957 and FY 1964 are comprised of 1 joint venture, 2 non-profit firms including one established by the Air Force, 4 firms entering as the result of mergers, 8 which were among the top 100 in FY 1957 (including one of the non-profits), and only 4 which were not on the FY 1957 list of 100 largest prime contractors. The 18 entrants are shown below.

The fact that Grumman Aircraft was not on the FY 1957 list is an oddity resulting from use of annual contract data and from the practice of the Department of Defense of showing net contract awards or new contracts minus cancellations and adjusted for change orders. Grumman is a defense contractor of many years' standing, having ranked 13 for the period from FY 1951 through FY 1957. Grumman suffered so many cancellations in FY 1957 that its net contract awards for that year were negative, but by FY 1958 it had rebounded to a rank of 21.

Thus it seems clear that the defense market is not nearly so unstable as it would appear to be from a simple numerical count of annual turnover in the ranks of the 100 largest recipients of prime contract awards, although the experiences of individual companies such as Curtiss-Wright, Fairchild, and Republic demonstrate that the market is neither stagnant nor riskless. Despite the lack of comparability with other markets, and with due regard to the inadequacies of annual contract data, descriptions such as "volatile" and "unique" in rapidity of entry and exit must be considered unwarranted and misleading.

Movement within the group, the second major aspect of stability to be discussed, involves both stability of rank and of contract awards. Here, a procedure of correlation analysis employed by Collins and Preston [19] is adopted. Normally, correlation coefficients are used to indicate the degree to which two or more variables are related, to measure the extent to which changes in one variable

19. "The Size Structure of the Largest Industrial Firms," *American Economic Review*, LI, 986-1011.

Table II-5: Firms on the list of 50 largest prime contractors in FY 1964 but not in FY 1957

FY 1964 rank	Name of firm	Comments
10	Newport News Shipbuilding & Dry Dock	FY 1957 rank: 69.
11	Grumman Aircraft Engineering	Not among top 100 in FY 1957.
20	Thiokol Chemical	FY 1957 rank: 67.
22	Ling-Temco-Vought	Entry through merger.
25	General Telephone & Electronics	Entry through merger.
26	Textron	Entry through merger.
28	Litton Industries	Entry through merger.
32	Pan American World Airways	FY 1957 rank: 55.
34	Kaiser Industries	Not among top 100 in FY 1957; subsidiary, Kaiser Jeep, acquired Studebaker manufacturing plant at South Bend, Indiana, in FY 1964.
35	FMC	Not among top 100 in FY 1957.
36	Hercules Powder	FY 1957 rank: 81.
38	General Precision Equipment	FY 1957 rank: 53.
40	Morrison-Utah-Perini-Leavell	A joint venture of Morrison-Knudsen, Utah Construction & Mining, Perini, and C. H. Leavell.
43	Massachusetts Institute of Technology	FY 1957 rank: 52.
45	Aerospace	Non-profit established by the Air Force in 1961, for purposes of providing the Air Force with technical analyses and recommendations.
46	Thompson Ramo Wooldridge	FY 1957 rank: 68.
48	Magnavox	Not among top 100 in FY 1957.
49	E. I. du Pont de Nemours	FY 1957 rank: 86.

Sources: OSD, *100 Companies and Their Subsidiaries Listed According to Net Value of Military Prime Contract Awards,* FY 1957 and FY 1964; *Moody's Industrial Manual; Standard & Poor's Corporation Register.*

"explain" or appear to account for changes in another (if causality in the relationship is assumed), and to help in determining whether the relation is statistically significant. But, as Collins and Preston note, the size of a company is obviously one important determinant of its size at a future date if the interval is fairly short; and the ranks of a given company on two lists separated by only a few years are similarly interdependent. Correlation coefficients, therefore, are not used as tests of the existence of relationships within such series, but as measures analogous to index numbers. Thus one would expect to find a high correlation between the ranks of firms listed among the top 50 in a given year and the ranks of the same firms the following year. Similarly, product-moment correlations between contract award amounts going to the same firms in two consecutive years should be high. While the absolute sizes of the correlation coefficients and tests of their individual levels of significance are considered of no explanatory importance, an increase in one or the other over a period of time indicates greater stability in ranking or in the dollar value of contracts received.

Table II-6 shows both the Spearman coefficient of rank correlation (r_s) and the product-moment correlation (r) for the logarithms of contract awards for each pair of consecutive fiscal years for which data are available. The number of firms appearing in the top 50 for both years, and hence the number of pairs correlated (n), is also shown.[20] To calculate the Spearman coefficients it was necessary to rerank the firms after eliminating those on one of the lists but not on both. The logarithms of contract awards are correlated, instead of the awards themselves, in order to reflect relative rather than abso-

20. Ling-Temco-Vought was considered a successor company to Chance Vought. Bell Aircraft and Textron were treated similarly, as were Ingalls Iron and Litton Industries, Sylvania and General Telephone and Electronics, and Garrett and Signal Oil and Gas. In each of these cases, a firm which had previously not been among the 100 largest prime contractors entered by acquiring a firm or a division of a firm which had been on the list. In each case, all of the defense business of the acquired firm was transferred to the acquiring firm. Chance Vought ranked 36 in FY 1961, the last year it appeared on the list. Therefore, treating Ling-Temco-Vought as a successor adds one to the number of firms which are considered among the 50 largest in both FY 1961 and FY 1962. For this reason, Table II-6 is not consistent with Table II-3 for FY 1961–62. Since Bell, Ingalls, Sylvania, and Garrett were not among the top 50 in their last years on the list, these firms pose no problems of reconciliation. Since both Ford and Philco were on the lists in their own right prior to Ford's acquisition of Philco, these firms have been treated separately and Philco has been considered a disappearing firm. Asiatic Petroleum and Shell Caribbean, both subsidiaries of Royal Dutch Petroleum, have been combined.

lute increases or decreases and thus avoid the difficulty of having, for example, a 20 per cent change in awards going to the largest contractor utterly obscure all changes in awards made to the lowest ten firms.

It does not seem possible to find any pattern in Table II-6, and the time period is probably too short for the word "trend" to be applicable even if there were some sort of smooth progression.[21]

Since the correlations involve only the top 50 firms, second-year data on contract awards are available for most of the firms disappearing, as well as first-year data on their replacements. Use of rank correlations including these firms would involve drastic reranking in some cases and could yield misleading results, but it was hoped that product-moment correlations of this type might shed additional light on the question of stability. The results, shown as Table II-7, appear to add little or nothing to Table II-6.[22] The most that can possibly be concluded from the Collins-Preston technique of using correlation coefficients as indexes, when it is applied to defense contracts on a year-to-year basis and for a period of eight years, is that there is no clear indication of increasing or decreasing stability among the major defense contractors.

21. The only product-moment correlation in Table II–6 which is significantly different, in a statistical sense, from those on either side of it is that for FY 1960–61. The difference between r for FY 1959–60 and r for FY 1960–61 is significant at the .05 level of probability of rejecting a true difference; the difference between the coefficients for FY 1960–61 and FY 1961–62 is significant at the .01 level of probability. No other differences are significant at the .05 level. Fisher's r to Z transformation was used to test the significance of the differences. The hypothesis tested is that the first of any pair of correlation coefficients is that for a sample drawn from a population whose true correlation is measured by the second coefficient. It should be noted that the validity of this test declines as the absolute sizes of the correlation coefficients being compared increase and as the number of observations on which the first is based decreases. See William L. Hays, *Statistics for Psychologists* (New York: Holt, Rinehart and Winston, 1963), pp. 529–532.

22. The coefficient for FY 1960–61 on line A of Table II-7 is significantly different from those on either side of it at the .01 level. There are no other differences in either line A or line B that are significant at the .05 level.

Table II-6: Rank and product-moment correlations for recipients of prime contract awards between pairs of years, for firms among the 50 largest recipients in both years

	FY 1957–58	FY 1958–59	FY 1959–60	FY 1960–61	FY 1961–62	FY 1962–63	FY 1963–64
r_s	.921	.922	.915	.962	.884	.923	.909
r	.962	.972	.972	.986	.961	.974	.965
n	43	40	44	43	44	44	44

D. Internal Concentration

The third and final aspect of market structure to be analyzed from information on the largest defense contractors is the concentration of awards within the group. Here, concern is with how the contract awards going to the 50 largest recipients, amounting to nearly two-thirds of the dollar value of all defense procurement contracts, are divided among these 50 firms from year to year. The measure chosen as an index of this sort of internal concentration is the Gini coefficient, which is an indicator of the degree of inequality of distribution of some factor among the members of a group. The Gini coefficient is best illustrated by a graph.

When the firms are ranked in order from the largest contract recipient to the smallest, a cumulative percentage distribution of

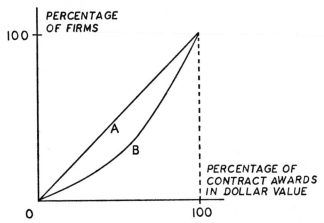

Table II-7: Product-moment correlations of the logarithms of prime contract awards between pairs of years, for firms among the 50 largest recipients in either year

		FY 1957–58	FY 1958–59	FY 1959–60	FY 1960–61	FY 1961–62	FY 1962–63	FY 1963–64
A.	r	.958	.958	.965	.986	.956	.955	.961
	n	48	49	48	48	49	50	47
B.	r	.964	.970	.973	.978	.962	.976	.961
	n	48	49	48	48	48	48	49

A. Eliminating only those of the largest 50 in the earlier year which were not among the largest 100 during the later year (i.e., including those that *disappeared* from the largest 50 but not from the largest 100).

B. Eliminating only those of the largest 50 in the later year which were not among the largest 100 during the earlier year (i.e., including those that *entered* the largest 50 from the group ranking 51–100).

contract awards received in any one year by the group may be plotted, as illustrated by the curved line on the graph. If all firms in the group received awards of equal value, the line plotted from the cumulative distribution would be identical with the straight line on the graph, intersecting the origin and having a slope of 45 degrees. The Gini coefficient compares the actual distribution with one of perfect equality. It is expressed as a ratio of areas $\frac{A}{A+B}$ where A and B are as shown on the graph. With perfect equality, A becomes zero, as does the ratio. As the distribution approaches perfect inequality, B approaches zero and the ratio approaches unity. The major difficulty with using the Gini coefficient is that it does not discriminate among numbers; the coefficient would be zero if two firms shared a market equally or if there were 200 firms with equal shares. However, this shortcoming is of no concern at the moment, since the coefficient is being used to measure concentration among the same number, 50, in each year. An increase in the Gini coefficient means that contracts are being less equally distributed among the top 50 recipients, and a decrease in the coefficient means that the distribution is becoming more nearly equal.

Table II-8 shows a perceptible decline in the Gini coefficient since the high point of FY 1958, the year in which the two largest contractors received 16.2 per cent of the dollar value of total contract awards or 24.2 per cent of that going to the top 50 firms. In FY 1962 and FY 1963 the distribution of contract awards among the top 50 was more nearly equal than it had been during World War II. In these two years and in FY 1964, despite a rise in the coefficient during the last year shown, contracts were spread among the major firms quite a bit more evenly than had been the case during the Korean War or from FY 1955 through FY 1961.

Table II-8: Gini coefficients of inequality for awards to the 50 largest prime contractors

Period	G	Period	G
June 1940–Sept. 1944	.46	FY 1960	.49
July 1950–June 1953	.49	FY 1961	.49
Jan. 1955–June 1957	.50	FY 1962	.45
FY 1957	.48	FY 1963	.45
FY 1958	.53	FY 1964	.47
FY 1959	.50		

E. Summary

Year-by-year analysis through FY 1964 indicates that defense contracts became more highly concentrated in terms of the percentage of total awards going to the 50 largest contractors as opposed to other firms; in general, the positions of the largest defense contractors are a good deal more stable than unadjusted annual turnover figures would suggest; correlation coefficients do not clearly indicate whether stability within the ranks of the top 50, in terms of both rank and dollar value of awards, increased or decreased; and awards became more evenly spread among the major contractors.

There are at least three serious objections to accepting conclusions such as those just expressed as final. First, the data deal only with prime contract awards made by military agencies, and a great deal of defense work is done on subcontract from other business firms. Second, since sales receipts lag behind contract awards and contracts may contain delivery and payment dates extending well beyond the year of award, annual contract figures can be misleading. Third, a very mixed group of firms have been lumped together as "prime contractors," including firms in different industries, working on different types of defense programs, and with different degrees of specialization in defense production. Such an aggregation may conceal more than it illuminates. The first two objections are dealt with in the next chapter, and the third comprises the subject matter of the chapter following that one.

III. MARKET STRUCTURE:
SUBCONTRACTING AND MULTI-YEAR
MEASURES

A. Subcontracting

The annual lists of contract awards put out by the Department of Defense are lists of prime contractors, including only those firms which sell their goods and services directly to military agencies. The lists give no information concerning the subcontracting firms in the military market which sell to each other and to the prime contractors. Many subcontractors produce highly specialized subsystems and components of little or no non-military use and are as thoroughly defense-oriented as the prime contractors. Table III-1 indicates the importance of subcontracting in the defense market.

In the absence of certain special features of defense procurement, subcontracting would pose a problem which is likely to be found in any study of market structure but which, more often than not, can safely be ignored after it is recognized. Essentially, whether or not to subcontract is a question of make or buy, similar to questions facing manufacturers of automobiles or refrigerators in civilian markets, who must decide whether to produce particular components or purchase them from other firms. The problem arises from the

Table III-1: Subcontracting as a percentage of prime contract payments

	Fiscal year						
Percentage of military contract payments by reporting prime contractors * paid to:	1957	1958	1959	1960	1961	1962	1963
All business concerns	54.8	51.6	48.9	50.6	47.5	47.3	48.2
Small business concerns	20.9	18.5	17.8	18.8	17.7	18.0	18.3

* The sample varies. Prior to January 1, 1960, subcontracting reports were submitted on a voluntary basis. At that time, reporting became mandatory for all prime contractors and subcontractors who obtained contracts of $1 million or more with substantial subcontracting possibilities. On January 1, 1962, the limitation was reduced to $500,000.

Source: OSD, *Military Prime Contract Awards and Subcontract Payments, July 1962–June 1963,* pp. 46–47, and *July 1963–June 1964,* p. 49.

fact that a firm's competitive position and its degree of market power are not independent of the extent to which it is vertically integrated. A firm which integrates forward to acquire a former customer excludes, or gains the power to exclude, its competitors from that particular portion of the market represented by the acquired firm. An integrated firm may exert a price squeeze on its non-integrated competitors in two ways: by maintaining relatively high prices for materials it supplies to them and relatively low prices for the finished goods it sells in competition with them, or by using its power to squeeze as a threat to limit price competition among producers of the final product. In terms of market structure, however, exclusion is a tactic used against competing suppliers, and a price squeeze requires some pre-existing degree of monopolistic power in the market in which competing non-integrated sellers must buy. In the short run, vertical integration in and of itself does not increase a seller's power over the price charged to the ultimate customer. In the long run, exclusion of competing suppliers of components might well affect prices and the rate of technological advance in the final market, and a price squeeze could affect the structure of the final market by eliminating or reducing the shares of non-integrated firms. But the effect on customers would be felt only after some observable structural change or increase of collusive behavior in the market in which they buy. It is possible to describe the current market for household refrigerators, for example, in a meaningful fashion without bothering to specify which firms produce their own motors and which do not. But one would want information on the degree of vertical integration before attempting to predict future changes in the market.

If predatory tactics such as exclusion or squeezing are disregarded, one finds that a firm in a civilian market normally will base its make or buy decisions on relative costs. If the market is competitive, firms will be forced to make the appropriate decisions, and lower costs will be reflected in lower prices to customers. When firms differ in such factors as geographical location, access to raw materials, product diversification, age of plants, and patent holdings, producers of identical products or close substitutes may quite rationally come to different make or buy decisions. The differing degrees of vertical integration should be of no particular interest to customers who presumably make their decisions on the basis of price and quality of the final products offered for sale. In the military market, on the other hand, contractors' make or buy decisions are of great interest to the sole customer, the Department of Defense. These decisions may very well influence aspects of performance which the customer deems important. Some of these performance criteria are peculiar to the Department of Defense and would be of no concern to a normal commercial buyer or a rational consumer.

There are incentives to perform defense work internally which are not so powerful in or are absent from civilian markets. In order to develop his own facilities and experience in a new technical field with the hope of thereby being in a better position to bid success-fully on future contracts, a contractor may seek to undertake a cer-tain task which he knows could be performed more economically on subcontract in terms of the total costs of the project under considera-tion. Thus an aircraft firm might greatly prefer to develop its own capabilities in certain branches of electronics rather than subcon-tract complex and vital new electronic subsystems to established electronics concerns.[1] Defense firms are certainly not unique in tak-ing consideration of future capabilities into account in weighing the long-run costs and benefits involved in make or buy decisions, but the incentives to acquire diversified technological capabilities are particularly strong in the defense market in which success is based on adaptation to an extremely complex and rapidly changing tech-nology. The defense market is, however, quite singular in the extent to which the customer makes use of cost-plus contracts in his pur-chasing.[2] Under a cost-plus contract, whether with a fixed fee or an incentive fee, the costs of developing know-how in a new field may be borne totally or in large part by the government, depending on what cost items are and are not considered reimbursable in the con-tract. Although to a far greater extent in the past than in the present,

1. The prevalence of such preferences in the aircraft industry has been noted in M. J. Peck and F. M. Scherer, *The Weapons Acquisition Process: An Economic Analy-sis* (Boston: Division of Research, Graduate School of Business Administration, Har-vard University, 1962), p. 388.

2. In recent years the use of cost-plus contracts has been curtailed. In FY 1960, 31.4 per cent of procurement contracts, by dollar volume, were firm fixed price. By FY 1964, the figure had risen to 46.3 per cent. During the same period, cost plus fixed fee contracts declined from 36.8 per cent to 12.0 per cent of total contracts. However, cost plus incentive fee contracts increased from 3.2 per cent to 14.1 per cent of the total. OSD, *Military Prime Contract Awards and Subcontract Payments, July 1963–June 1964*, p. 47.

the government might be willing to furnish the plant and equipment required, particularly if what was needed was highly specialized and had little potential for other uses. Even if costs are not covered, the knowledge and experience gained from a research and development contract frequently put a firm in a highly advantageous position to bid on the ensuing production contract, which in most cases will be larger and have a greater potential for profit. Finally, although cost-plus-a-percentage-of-cost contracts are now forbidden by law, the fees which are negotiated will vary with the estimated costs and difficulties connected with different projects. In order to reduce the abuses of profit pyramiding, under which the prime contractor pays the subcontractor enough to yield him a profit and the government in turn pays the prime contractor an amount which includes a profit on the entire project, fees are now frequently higher on those portions of the job which the prime contractor proposes to do himself than on those which are to be subcontracted. The Department of Defense's current policy on this matter was described in a statement on pyramiding of profits supplied to the House Subcommittee on Department of Defense Appropriations in connection with hearings on the appropriations for FY 1963. When subcontracting results in a reduction in the technical and managerial effort required of the prime contractor, or when the prime contractor reduces his risk and responsibility by subcontracting, the fee on the subcontracted portion of the work is reduced to less than it would be if the work were performed internally. On the other hand, the statement continues, as long as the contractor supplies managerial and technical contributions and accepts some responsibility for the subcontractor's performance, he is entitled to a reasonable profit and pyramiding is justified.[3] But the net effect of concern over pyramiding is undoubtedly to discourage subcontracting.

The Department of Defense, on the other hand, has several reasons for attempting to increase the amount of subcontracting. In the first place, if the contract is of a cost-reimbursable type, the procurement agency has a responsibility and the authority to assure itself that various aspects of the project are carried out as efficiently

3. U.S. Congress, House Committee on Appropriations, Subcommittee on Department of Defense Appropriations, *Hearings: Department of Defense Appropriations for 1963, Part 4, Procurement* (Washington: Government Printing Office, 1962), pp. 637–638.

and competently as possible, and at the lowest cost to the government. If cost and efficiency were the only concerns of the Department of Defense, the objective of the contract negotiators would be merely to offset the prime contractor's desire to obtain work he could perform only at additional cost and therefore to encourage make or buy decisions such as those at which rational civilian-oriented firms would arrive in competitive markets. However, the Department of Defense has still other objectives in encouraging subcontracting. Although forbidden by law to pay a premium for these purposes, defense agencies are expected to encourage the maximum amount of both prime and subcontract placement with small business and in depressed areas. The department is also concerned with geographic dispersal of defense facilities for strategic purposes. There is a program designed to maintain an industrial reserve to meet the needs of mobilization or a sharp increase in defense requirements; and occasionally a contract or subcontract is placed with a certain firm because the order is deemed essential to the firm's survival and the firm's survival, in turn, is considered beneficial to the government. Finally, since the Department of Defense is the sole customer, it has an opportunity which few other buyers possess of influencing both the degree of future competition among its suppliers and their abilities to meet its anticipated needs through the judicious placement of both prime and subcontract awards.

Thus defense contractors have greater incentives to perform work internally than they would have in civilian markets, and the Department of Defense has reasons for encouraging more subcontracting than would result from a pure business rationale of weighing costs and savings to the firm. It is not clear whether the net result of these opposing forces is more or less subcontracting than would exist in their absence.

Until quite recently, the Department of Defense did not seem to be exercising the powers granted to it by law and its own regulations to compel a larger volume of subcontracting than its prime contractors might desire. In a 1956 study, J. S. Day concluded that the procurement policies of the Department of Defense and congressional pressures favoring small business had far more influence on the selection of the firms with which subcontracts were placed than they did on the volume or nature of the work subcontracted by prime contractors in the airframe industry.[4] In 1962, Peck and Scherer noted that procurement officers were generally reluctant to substitute their judgment in such matters for the presumably better-informed decisions of the prime contractors.[5] However, the field work for the Peck and Scherer study was completed before the Kennedy Administration was installed, and the Foreword to their book warns, "The present volume takes little note of changes that have occurred since January 1961." [6]

There has been a marked change in the attitude of the Department of Defense toward subcontracting. The shift is perhaps best illustrated by comparing testimony of Department of Defense officials under the Eisenhower Administration with that of Assistant Secretary of Defense T. D. Morris on FY 1963 defense appropriations. The two following statements are quoted from hearings before the House Subcommittee on Department of Defense Appropriations in 1957, during testimony on the appropriation for FY 1958. The first is from a statement of Secretary Morris' predecessor, Perkins McGuire, and the second from a statement submitted for the record by the Department of the Army.

With respect to subcontracting, the basic responsibility rests with the prime contractor for the selection of subcontractors, determination of prices, and the assurance of performance and quality. However, the regulation requires that the military contracting officer have adequate knowledge of all of these matters and their effects on prime contract prices. The contracting officer is also expected to review major subcontracts prior to placement, when the prime contract is subject to price or cost redetermination. Since in these cases the ultimate cost to the Government depends in part on subcontract prices and performance. In such cases the prime contractor must also reserve to the Government the right to audit the books of the subcontractor.[7]

The Army has always followed the policy that when it contracts with industry for an item it is contracting for everything which is required to produce the item. This includes not only the material and facilities but management in its broadest terms, which includes the techniques of

---

4. J. S. Day, *Subcontracting Policy in the Airframe Industry* (Boston: Division of Research, Graduate School of Business Administration, Harvard University, 1956).

5. *The Weapons Acquisition Process: An Economic Analysis,* esp. pp. 399–404.

6. *Ibid.,* p. xiii.

7. U.S. Congress, House Committee on Appropriations, Subcommittee on Department of Defense Appropriations, *Hearings: Department of Defense Appropriations for 1958, Procurement Policies and Practices of the Department of Defense* (Washington: Government Printing Office, 1957), p. 89.

subcontracting. Furthermore, the Army takes the position that the prime contractor is responsible for the full performance of the contract, and that when it has directed a contractor's subcontracting activities it has relieved the contractor of his responsibility for the subcontractor's performance under the contract. Thus, while the Army encourages subcontracting for the benefit of small business, it discourages the control of subcontracting.[8]

Two years later, in response to a question about the position of subcontractors under the weapon system concept, Secretary McGuire replied:

As you understand, this is a very difficult area. . . .

When you have a contractor who has a responsibility to deliver a weapons system, you are in effect also buying a substantial amount of his judgement as to how that will be developed and made, so you get into that kind of an area here.

There is a tendency, and I want to be frank about this, that the contractor will seek to make his product as much as he can within his own plant. . . .

I do not think we can take an arbitrary position on this, Mr. Ford, and still have the contractor responsible for all of the things we put on him to do in the form of performance.[9]

In contrast, in 1962 Secretary Morris made the two following statements on the subcontracting policies which had been initiated under the direction of Secretary McNamara.

It is estimated that half of our procurement dollars are spent by prime contractors with subcontractors. Thus, if we are to assure that the best results are being obtained, we must be concerned with the efficiency and economy of prime contractors' purchasing systems and practices. We now require our contracting officers to review the subcontracting plans of prime contractors and to approve large subcontracts before they are awarded; the Air Force has inaugurated a very effective program of surveying in detail the purchasing systems of prime contractors.

During the coming year we expect to work even more closely with our principal prime contractors to assure that they obtain maximum price competition and give proper emphasis to small business and distressed labor area awards in order to fully support the objectives of defense procurement programs.[10]

8. *Ibid.*, p. 33.

9. U.S. Congress, House Committee on Appropriations, Subcommittee on Department of Defense Appropriations, *Hearings: Department of Defense Appropriations for 1960, Part 5, Procurement* (Washington: Government Printing Office, 1959), p. 55.

10. U.S. Congress, House Committee on Appropriations, Subcommittee on Department of Defense Appropriations, *Hearings: Department of Defense Appropriations for 1963, Part 4, Procurement*, p. 498.

Under the armed services procurement regulations we have a requirement that our contracting officer examine with the prime contractor his make-or-buy program, that which he will make inhouse and that which he will subcontract. We have recently strengthened our regulation to require a maximum of subcontracting where it is not more economic for the prime to make the material inhouse. This opens up and spreads the competitive base.

Secondly, we require the contracting officers to examine proposed buys of large size to be made by the primes to be sure that good competitive procurement practice was applied.

Thirdly, as of just this week we have further amended ASPR [*Armed Services Procurement Regulation*] to insert a clause in principal contracts with primes requiring that they seek to the maximum extent to obtain competitive procurements.[11]

It is extremely difficult to ascertain the extent to which such a shift in policy has been or can be implemented in actual contract negotiations. An observation by J. S. Day seems as pertinent now as it was in 1956: "That pressures to select certain subcontractors are sometimes levied upon the prime contractor by the Armed Services seems unquestionable. How these pressures operate and how strong they are is a different matter, and any attempt to measure them faces the insurmountable industry belief that such an analysis will react to the detriment of good customer relationships." [12] A policy change cannot alter certain difficulties facing a negotiator. Peck and Scherer point out that bargaining rather than arbitrary orders must precede the signing of a contract regardless of the powers that contractors are required by procurement law and the *Armed Services Procurement Regulation* to grant to the government in contract clauses. The government's procurement personnel, Peck and Scherer also observe, are not in possession of adequate technical information nor do they usually possess the technical skills to challenge a contractor's conclusions effectively, particularly in cases in which early estimates are uncertain and the contractor has stated his preferences strongly.[13]

Two other aspects of procurement policy changes have tended to reduce subcontracting. First, under Secretary McNamara the Department of Defense has greatly increased the amount of incentive contracting, in which the prime contractor's fee is not fixed but

11. *Ibid.*, p. 553.
12. *Subcontracting Policy in the Airframe Industry*, p. 58.
13. *The Weapons Acquisition Process: An Economic Analysis*, p. 401.

varies with final cost, delivery dates, and performance characteristics of the final product. Day pointed out that in theory incentive contracts do not favor subcontracting since the prime contractor's fee depends in part on the performances of others over whom he presumably has no control. In fact, Day found that in the airframe industry the prime contractors were able to exert considerable control over the performance of subcontractors through such devices as engineering assistance, plant inspections, and the writing of specifications.[14] Further, many small subcontractors are completely dependent on continued orders from one prime contractor. Nevertheless, the bargaining position of a contract negotiator seeking to increase subcontracting and to influence selection of subcontractors is weakened if he is negotiating an incentive fee contract.

Second, as pointed out by Murray L. Weidenbaum, there has been a shift from weapon system contracting to use of associate contractors. Under the weapon system concept, a prime contractor is given responsibility for production of an entire system, e.g., a bomber. The prime contractor then subcontracts components and subsystems such as communications, powerplant, and armament, but assumes the managerial functions of co-ordinating production schedules and determining specifications so that the subsystems and components will mesh properly into the final weapon system. Under the associate contractor system, the government signs contracts directly with a number of subsystem and component manufacturers and supplies items produced by others, as government-furnished equipment, to the contractor who is producing the final product. The system engineering and technical direction (SETD) functions are in large part carried out by non-profit SETD firms established by the armed services, or by government arsenals and laboratories when the associate contractor system is used. As Weidenbaum observes, such a shift makes no real difference in the structure of the military market but does have an effect on the statistics. The amount of subcontracting reported is reduced since the associate contractors who would have been subcontractors under a weapon system procurement receive direct contracts and are reported as prime contractors.[15]

While increased use of associate contractors has no effect on total

14. *Subcontracting Policy in the Airframe Industry*, pp. 84–85.
15. Murray L. Weidenbaum, "The U.S. Aircraft Industry," *Financial Analysts Journal*, XIX (March-April, 1963), 49–53.

procurement reported by the Department of Defense, it does result in the reporting of awards to the associate contractors and in lower dollar amounts shown as awards to the firms delivering the final products. Consequently, it tends to reduce reported concentration. The stability apparently indicated by the rather constant percentage of total contract awards going to the 50 and 100 largest prime contractors from FY 1958 through FY 1964, as shown in Chapter II, must be viewed in light of this change in contract management, a view which reinforces the conclusion drawn in that chapter that concentration was increasing. At least a part of the observed reduction in inequality of award distribution among the 50 largest prime contractors must also be attributed to increased use of associate contractors.

Table III-1 indicates a slight decline in subcontracting as a percentage of total procurement awards, but shows a fairly steady percentage of this total going to small business firms since FY 1958. The percentage of all subcontracting payments received by small business from prime contractors has, therefore, increased somewhat since FY 1958, as shown in Table III-2.

The figures of Tables III-1 and III-2 are perfectly consistent with, although hardly positive evidence for, the major conclusions drawn about subcontracting in the above discussion. The increasing use of incentive contracts and associate contracting may, in part, explain the slight decline in subcontracting. The more active subcontract policy of the Department of Defense under Secretary McNamara has not reversed this decline, perhaps for the reasons noted by Peck and Scherer as well as those given by Day in his earlier study. Under the new and more vigorous policies and regulations, procurement officials have been able to continue the increase in the share of sub-

Table III-2: Percentage of total reported subcontract payments paid to small business concerns

Fiscal year	Percentage	Fiscal year	Percentage
1957	38.2	1961	37.2
1958	35.9	1962	38.0
1959	36.5	1963	38.0
1960	37.1		

Source: OSD, *Military Prime Contract Awards and Subcontract Payments, July 1963–June 1964*, p. 49.

contracting directed to small business. Thus, it is far from proven that subcontracting decisions are closely analogous to commercial make or buy decisions, subjected as they are to conflicting forces, or that patterns of subcontracting pose no more serious problems for a description of market structure than do the degrees of vertical integration in other industries. Nevertheless, these assumptions do seem preferable to alternatives positing a strong net bias either in favor of subcontracting or against it.

Another approach to the evaluation of subcontracting in the structure of the defense market is to compare value added by prime defense contractors with value added by civilian-oriented firms. Earlier works show, in general, that defense firms perform internally, relative to their sales, as much work as or more than is typical in the industries with which comparisons were made. Peck and Scherer broke a sample of sixty-one major prime contractors into three subgroups: electrical control apparatus, aircraft, and aircraft engines. For each of these subgroups, the percentage of business receipts paid to other firms was computed, and then compared with similar percentages computed for twelve commercial non-defense industries for the year 1958. Peck and Scherer found "about the same range of distribution" for the defense subgroups and the civilian industries.[16]

In 1963 two large contract research institutions, Stanford Research Institute and Arthur D. Little, Incorporated, published separate studies dealing with the defense market. The Stanford Research Institute study, confined to the "aerospace industry," found that over the fourteen-year period from 1948 to 1961, value added for 22 aerospace firms came to 52 per cent of total costs and expenses, on a weighted average basis. The comparable figure for all manufacturing for the same period, the study continued, was only 44 per cent.[17] The Arthur D. Little study took the same figures as shown in Table III-1 and calculated an average for the period from FY 1957 through 1962, arriving at a figure of 49.9 per cent of total receipts being paid out to other business firms by reporting prime contractors. This figure of 49.9 per cent was compared with 54 per cent of total receipts being paid out to other firms for 12 selected non-de-

16. *The Weapons Acquisition Process: An Economic Analysis*, p. 150.
17. Stanford Research Institute, *The Industry-Government Aerospace Relationship: Prepared for Aerospace Industries Association of America, Inc.* (Menlo Park, Calif.: Stanford Research Institute, 1963), I, 45.

fense industries in 1958.[18] Or, to reverse the figures, value added by the defense group amounted to 50.1 per cent of total receipts and that by the non-defense group came to 46 per cent.

Table III-3 shows weighted averages of value added as a percentage of value of shipments for the same civilian-oriented industries as those selected by Peck and Scherer and compares these with value added figures for reporting defense contractors derived from Table III-1.

Table III-3 does not show quite such dramatic contrasts as do the Stanford Research Institute and Arthur D. Little studies. However, the table certainly supports the conclusion of all three earlier investigations that defense contractors as a group do not stand out from non-defense firms in terms, relative to their sales, of the dollar value of their purchases from other companies.

18. Arthur D. Little, Inc., *How Sick Is the Defense Industry?* (Cambridge: Arthur D. Little, Inc., 1963), pp. 16–17.

Table III-3: Value added as percentage of prime contract payments and value of shipments for defense and non-defense firms

| | Value added (percentage) | |
Fiscal year	Reporting defense contractors	Eleven non-defense industries *
1957	45.2	–
1958	48.4	47.3
1959	51.1	47.9
1960	49.4	47.4
1961	52.5	48.0
1962	52.7	48.2
1963	51.8	48.2

* Two of the industries used by Peck and Scherer were farm machinery (except tractors), and tractors. Since the 1957 revisions of the Standard Industrial Classification Manual, all farm machinery, including tractors, is in SIC 3522, farm machinery and equipment. Non-farm tractors are in other industrial classifications. Thus SIC 3522 combines most of two industries used by Peck and Scherer. The other industries, in addition to SIC 3522, are:

SIC	2033	canned fruits and vegetables	SIC 3011	tires and inner tubes
	2311	men's and boys' suits and coats	3141	footwear, except rubber
	2431	millwork plants	3251	brick and structural tile (not available for 1963)
	2819	inorganic chemicals, n.e.c.	3323	steel foundries
	2851	paints and varnishes	3552	textile machinery

Sources: Table III-1; M. J. Peck and F. M. Scherer, *The Weapons Acquisition Process: An Economic Analysis* (Boston: Division of Research, Graduate School of Business Administration, Harvard University, 1962), p. 151; U.S. Department of Commerce, *1958 Census of Manufactures* (Washington: Government Printing Office, 1961); U.S. Department of Commerce, *Annual Survey of Manufacturers, 1959, 1960, 1961,* and *1962* (Washington: Government Printing Office, 1961, 1962, 1963, and 1964); U.S. Department of Commerce, *1963 Census of Manufactures, Preliminary Report, Summary Series: General Statistics for Industry Groups and Industries,* Dec., 1964.

Finally, one might ask what difference subcontracting makes to the concentration of defense awards. Systematic and complete data on subcontracting are not presently available from the Department of Defense, although the department, the Census Bureau, and the Arms Control and Disarmament Agency are now engaged in a cooperative study of the names and locations of subcontractors. Peck and Scherer obtained figures for subcontracts given and received and for prime contracts received by fifty-eight major prime contractors. Concentration ratios for the prime contracts alone were compared with ratios for net defense business of the fifty-eight after adding subcontracts received and subtracting those given, and the degrees of concentration were found to be similar.[19] Most of the major prime contractors are also substantial subcontractors. One example is found in a recent $213 million award to Western Electric, a subsidiary of the American Telephone and Telegraph Company. In reporting this award, the *Wall Street Journal* stated:

The Army said subcontractors that share in the contract include: Avco Corp., Everett, Mass.; Cornell Aeronautical Laboratories, Buffalo, N.Y.; Douglas Aircraft Co., Santa Monica, Calif.; General Electric Co., Syracuse; Martin Marietta Corp., Orlando, Fla.; Raytheon Co., Wayland, Mass.; Sperry Rand Corp., Great Neck, N.Y.; and Sylvania Electric Products division of General Telephone & Electronics Corp.[20]

The prime contractor and all the subcontractors listed except Cornell Aeronautical Laboratories were among the 50 largest prime contractors on the last list issued by the Department of Defense before the Western Electric award. In the FY 1963 list of 100 largest prime contractors American Telephone and Telegraph ranked 7; Avco, 21; Douglas, 14; General Electric, 5; Martin Marietta, 6; Raytheon, 18; Sperry Rand, 10; and General Telephone and Electronics, 35.

Each week the magazine *Missiles and Rockets* lists current contracts and procurements. For the past few years one section of this list has shown subcontract awards, giving the name of the firm making the award and the recipient for each subcontract reported. A list was made of the total subcontract awards issued by industry, for which dollar amounts were reported, in *Missiles and Rockets* from

19. *The Weapons Acquisition Process: An Economic Analysis*, pp. 150–152.
20. *Wall Street Journal,* Oct. 2, 1963, p. 32.

July, 1962, through June, 1963. These awards were summed, and the reported subcontracts received by firms listed among the top 50 prime contractors in FY 1963 were separately identified. These largest contractors, who received 65.6 per cent of the dollar volume of prime contract awards in FY 1963, also received 41.6 per cent of the dollar volume of subcontracts reported by *Missiles and Rockets* over the same twelve-month period. The *Missiles and Rockets* list is far from complete and should be interpreted as merely suggestive, since it reported subcontracts by dollar value totaling only $576 million, and listed many other subcontracts only by names of awarding companies and recipients.

Thus there does not appear to be any reason for fearing that findings based on prime contract award data alone will be meaningless or will distort badly the resulting depiction of the structure of the final market in which defense agencies purchase from their prime contractors.

B. Multi-year Measures of Structure

The second major shortcoming of the conclusions expressed in Chapter II stems from the fact that they were arrived at on the basis of annual contract award data. A contract may be made for a project extending over a period longer than one year, but it is recorded only for the fiscal year in which it was awarded unless there are subsequent change orders or cancellations. If there is a cancellation, it is netted against the current year's contract awards and does not reduce the figure for the contract actually canceled unless the cancellation occurs in the fiscal year of the original award. Cancellations actually rarely take place in the same year as the award. In addition, payments on the contract are geared to progress or are not made until completed items are delivered to the using service, tested, and accepted by it. As a result, sales revenues lag behind contract awards and are more evenly distributed over time. Most of the very largest prime contractors have a number of contracts outstanding at any one time, covering several projects in various stages of completion, so that the distortions caused by using annual data are not normally serious. Still, annual data alone are thoroughly misleading in the case of Grumman, whose cancellations exceeded new awards in FY 1957. Equally misleading is the case of Merritt-Chapman and Scott, which went on and off the list almost rhythmically in time with the receipt of a few large ship construction contracts.

To correct these distortions, use was made of a Department of Defense list covering the two-and-a-half-year period from January, 1955, through June, 1957, or the last half of FY 1955 and all of FY 1956 and FY 1957. Three-year lists for subsequent periods were compiled by summing contract awards reported for individual companies in each of the three-year periods which occurred between FY 1957 and FY 1964, i.e., for FY 1957 through FY 1959, for FY 1958 through FY 1960, and so on. Many major weapon system programs run far longer than three years, but in these cases there are inevitably a number of separate contracts. There may be, for example, one or more research and exploratory awards, a development contract, a prototype production contract, and several separate awards for successive production runs and manufacture of spare parts if the weapon system is accepted for deployment. Two knowledgeable individuals, one presently and one formerly with the Department of Defense, and both familiar with contracting procedures and the details of numerous contracts, have advised me that individual contracts rarely if ever ran for more than three years during the period in question and that the method employed here is an appropriate one.

It is quite likely that many of the firms which were listed among the top 100 in only one or two years of a three-year period received some awards in the year or years in which they did not appear on the list. To make the bottom of the list in recent years, a firm has needed approximately $25 million in net new awards. Thus the total dollar value of awards going to a firm is in all likelihood understated if that firm is not reported in every year included in one of the three-year periods; the three-year rankings may therefore be incorrect, especially near the bottom of the list. However, since contract awards for the 100 largest contractors in individual years were summed and attention is confined to the 50 largest in any one of the three-year periods, the distortions can safely be assumed to be negligible if any still exist. To appear among the top 50 contractors from FY 1957 through FY 1964, a company needed awards of $53.0 million, $57.6 million, $70.4 million, $61.9 million, $65.8 million, $83.8 million, $72.7 million, and $68.4 million successively.

Table III-4 shows the percentage of total prime contract awards going to the 50 largest recipients for multi-year periods. The table confirms the extent of and increase in over-all concentration shown in Table II-1. The similarity between the absolute sizes of the last six percentages shown on Table III-4 and those for the corresponding individual years in Table II-1 reflect year-to-year stability of the group. If many firms had been on the list in one year and had fallen far below the top 50 in the next, or vice versa, concentration of total awards among those appearing in the top 50 by virtue of summing their large and small contracts for three years would have been substantially lower than the concentration in any one year. The annual concentration figures would reflect only those awards large enough to put their recipients into the top 50 in a single year.

Table III-5 presents turnover in the top 50 during the three successive multi-year periods for which Department of Defense data are available. By using a two-and-a-half-year period and the two succeeding three-year periods, all cases of exit and re-entry are eliminated. That is, of the seven firms which disappeared from the top 50 between January, 1955–June, 1957 and FY 1958–60, not one subsequently reappeared on the FY 1961–63 list of 50 largest. Only one joint venture, Brown-Raymond-Walsh, and one university, Massachusetts Institute of Technology, appear among the top 50 in any of the three multi-year periods.

Table III-4: Percentage of total U.S. military prime contract awards received by the 50 largest prime contractors

Period	Percentage	Period	Percentage
June 1940–Sept. 1944	57.6	FY 1959–61	64.7
FY 1950–53	56.3	FY 1960–62	64.1
Jan. 1955–June 1957	59.5	FY 1961–63	64.4
FY 1957–59	63.4	FY 1962–64	64.4
FY 1958–60	64.9		

Table III-5: Disappearances from multi-year lists of the 50 largest prime contractors

From	To	Unadjusted	Adjusted for mergers, etc.
Jan. 1955–June 1957	FY 1958–60	7	6
FY 1958–60	FY 1961–63	7	4

Tables III-6 through III-9 indicate what happened to the firms which disappeared and the origins of their replacements.

Table III-6: Disappearances—firms on the list of 50 largest prime contractors from January, 1955, through June, 1957, but not on FY 1958–60 list

1955–57 rank	Name of firm	Status after disappearance
28	Brown-Raymond-Walsh	A joint venture. FY 1958–60 rank: 58. Not among top 100 after FY 1959.
38	Fairchild Engine & Airplane	FY 1958–60 rank: 53. FY 1961–63 rank: 86.
42	Cities Service	FY 1958–60 rank: 57. FY 1961–63 rank: 98.
44	Bath Iron Works	FY 1958–60 rank: 62. FY 1961–63 rank: 63.
47	Olin Mathieson	FY 1958–60 rank: 54. FY 1961–63 rank: 57.
48	Hayes Aircraft	FY 1958–60 rank: 60. FY 1961–63 rank: 72.
49	Tidewater Oil	FY 1958–60 rank: 65. Not on FY 1961–63 list.

Table III-7: Disappearances—firms on the list of 50 largest prime contractors in FY 1958–60, but not in FY 1961–63

1955–57 rank	FY 1958–60 rank	Name of firm	Status after disappearance
17	25	Chance Vought Aircraft	Merged
34	36	Philco	Merged. On basis of FY 1961 awards alone, FY 1961–63 rank: 71.
30	40	Goodyear Tire & Rubber	FY 1961–63 rank: 51.
36	44	Socony Mobil Oil	FY 1961–63 rank: 55.
32	45	Bell Aircraft	Merged.
50	49	Garrett	FY 1961–63 rank: 61.
27	50	Merritt-Chapman & Scott	FY 1961–63 rank: 58.

Table III-8: Entrants—firms on the list of 50 largest prime contractors in FY 1958–60, but not on list from January, 1955, through June, 1957

FY 1958–60 rank	FY 1961–63 rank	Name of firm	Comments
17	16	Grumman Aircraft Engineering	Not among top 100 in 1955–57.
28	23	Newport News Shipbuilding & Dry Dock	1955–57 rank: 89.
32	25	Thiokol Chemical	1955–57 rank: 93.
39	33	Pan American World Airways	1955–57 rank: 73.
33	43	Thompson Ramo Wooldridge	Not among top 100 in 1955–57.
48	48	Massachusetts Institute of Technology	1955–57 rank: 51.
46	49	Royal Dutch Petroleum	1955–57 rank: 57.

Tables III-6 and III-7 suggest that the turnover during these three multi-year periods resulted in only a mild displacement of most of the 14 firms leaving the lists. Of the 11 firms which vanished for reasons other than merger, 7 were among the top 60 in the ensuing three-year period and the other 4 were among the top 65. Indeed, the only disappearing firm suffering a serious decline over the last six years covered in the tables, other than two petroleum refiners, was Fairchild.

The lists of firms entering the top 50, in Tables III-8 and III-9, suggest somewhat more volatility in turnover than do the lists of those vanishing. Two electronics firms, Litton and General Telephone and Electronics, enjoyed rapid rise to prominence in the defense market after entering through merger. Several of the other entrants have benefited greatly from the growth of missile programs; the rise of Thiokol and Hercules is associated with the increased demand for propellant fuels for ballistic missiles. Pan American acts as manager of the Atlantic Missile Range, used by all three services and the National Aeronautics and Space Administration. Missile program contracts are also predominant in the awards going to American Machine and Foundry, which manufactures ground support equipment for missile sites as well as weapon systems and components.

An interesting issue in procurement policy lies behind the entry of Thompson Ramo Wooldridge to the FY 1958–60 list. The entering firm grew out of a complete merger in 1958 between Thompson Products, Incorporated, and its then partially-owned subsidiary, Ramo-Wooldridge Corporation. Ramo-Wooldridge, with financial backing from Thompson Products, rose to prominence among de-

Table III-9: Entrants—firms on the list of 50 largest prime contractors in FY 1961–63, but not in FY 1958–60

FY 1961–63 rank	Name of firm	Comments
30	Hercules Powder	FY 1958–60 rank: 52. 1955–57 rank: 95.
31	FMC	FY 1958–60 rank: 56. 1955–57 rank: 65.
32	Ling-Temco-Vought	Entry through merger.
36	American Machine & Foundry	FY 1958–60 rank: 89. 1955–57 rank: 88.
38	General Telephone & Electronics	Entry through merger.
39	Textron	Entry through merger.
43	Litton Industries	Entry through merger.

fense contractors in the fifties as the major SETD contractor for Air Force ballistic missile development projects. By 1959 Ramo-Wooldridge and its subsidiary, Space Technology Laboratories, Incorporated, had acted as technical directors on the Atlas, Thor, Titan, and Minuteman programs. However, the Ballistic Missile Division of the Air Force, recognizing that the SETD would be in a favored position to bid on program work, stipulated in the original contract that Ramo-Wooldridge would be barred from development and production contracts in the ballistic missile field. Thompson Products was a manufacturer of military products; and in October, 1958, Thompson Products and Ramo-Wooldridge merged completely and established Space Technology Laboratories as a wholly-owned subsidiary with careful safeguards to assure its complete managerial independence from Thompson Ramo Wooldridge. But the Air Force, instead of making Thompson Ramo Wooldridge eligible to bid for development and production contracts as the firm had hoped, applied the prohibition against the entire corporation. According to testimony, the Air Force hoped to induce Thompson Ramo Wooldridge to spin off Space Technology Laboratories entirely. As a result of this situation and of congressional criticism of the whole relationship between the Air Force and the company, most of the organization's SETD contracts were terminated in 1960, and Space Technology Laboratories was reorganized as a normal commercial laboratory and military producer. Shortly thereafter, in 1961, the Air Force established a non-profit organization, Aerospace Corporation, as an SETD contractor for its Space Systems Division. Aerospace was in more than one respect a successor to Space Technology Laboratories, although the latter survived, since within six months after Aerospace had been created, 250 technical staff members and over one thousand administrative and support employees transferred from Space Technology Laboratories to Aerospace.[21]

21. Extensive hearings were held in 1959 on the relationship between Ramo-Wooldridge and the Air Force, and on the propriety of having profit-making organizations perform the SETD function. The hearings were followed by a recommendation that, if the SETD function could not be performed internally, it should be contracted to non-profit organizations. U.S. Congress, House Committee on Government Operations, Military Operations Subcommittee, *Hearings: Organization and Management of Missile Programs* (Washington: Government Printing Office, 1959). Also, U.S. Congress, House Committee on Government Operations, *Organization and Management of Missile Programs, Eleventh Report by the Committee on Government Operations* (Washington: Government Printing Office, 1959). For another, briefer account, see U.S. Congress, House Committee on Appropriations, Subcommittee on De-

Tables III-10 and III-11 present rank and product-moment correlations similar to those of Tables II-6 and II-7, but for the multi-year periods. There was no perceptible pattern to the correlation coefficients, interpreted as indexes of stability, when the correlations were of contract awards, by firms, between two consecutive years. The most that can be concluded from Tables II-6 and II-7 is that there is no evidence of decreasing stability. Tables III-10 and III-11 yield a somewhat clearer impression of increasing stability.

Two points should be noted regarding the observation that the multi-year correlations appear to indicate a more distinct movement than did those for pairs of individual years. First, the multi-year data include an additional year and a half, from January, 1955, through

partment of Defense Appropriations, *Hearings: Department of Defense Appropriations for 1960, Part 5, Procurement,* pp. 692–704. Figures on transfers from Space Technology Laboratories to Aerospace taken from U.S. Congress, House Committee on Armed Services, Subcommittee for Special Investigations, *The Aerospace Corporation: A Study of Fiscal and Management Policy and Control* (Washington: Government Printing Office, 1965) , p. 7.

Table III-10: Rank and product-moment correlations of prime contract awards between pairs of successive multi-year periods, for firms among the 50 largest recipients in both periods

	Jan. 1955–June 1957 to FY 1958–60	FY 1957–59 to FY 1960–62	FY 1958–60 to FY 1961–63	FY 1959–61 to FY 1962–64
r_s	.815	.866	.918	.883
r	.932	.950	.968	.958
n	43	44	45	44

Table III-11: Product-moment correlations of the logarithms of prime contract awards between pairs of successive multi-year periods, for firms among the 50 largest recipients in either period

		Jan. 1955–June 1957 to FY 1958–60	FY 1957–59 to FY 1960–62	FY 1958–60 to FY 1961–63	FY 1959–61 to FY 1962–64
A.	r	.940	.949	.966	.957
	n	50	49	50	49
B.	r	.923	.917	.941	.936
	n	48	50	50	49

A. Eliminating only those of the 50 largest in the earlier period for which contract data of the later period were not available (i.e., including as many as possible of those *disappearing*) .

B. Eliminating only those of the 50 largest in the later period for which contract data of the earlier period were not available (i.e., including as many as possible of those *entering*) .

June, 1956. Second, both the rank and product-moment correlations between FY 1960 and FY 1961, as shown in Tables II-6 and II-7, were remarkably high; as a result, high coefficients are to some extent built into the correlations between the multi-year periods FY 1958–60 and FY 1961–63. Nevertheless, it seems highly probable that shifts in rank and percentage changes in dollar volume of contract awards have both undergone a meaningful decrease. The comparatively very high degree of stability between FY 1960 and FY 1961 could not have offset changes which carried over from the FY 1958–59 period into the early sixties. Although the highest correlations are found between FY 1958–60 and FY 1961–63, the general movement throughout the period was toward higher coefficients and the coefficients for FY 1959–61 to FY 1962–64 are all higher than their counterparts for 1955–57 to FY 1958–60 and for FY 1957–59 to FY 1960–62. While the word "trend" still seems inappropriate, it can be said that stability within the group of the 50 largest prime contractors appears to have increased somewhat between 1955 and FY 1964. However, tests for the statistical significance of the differences between successive correlation coefficients indicate that none in either Table III-10 or Table III-11 is significant at the .05 level of probability.

Increasing stability has not meant, however, that each firm among the top 50 has had a reasonably steady growth of contract awards and sales since FY 1958. Several individual firms experienced particularly sharp increases or decreases in multi-year contract awards. Some of the shifts which appear to be outstanding in their severity are shown in Table III-12.

In the absence of valid comparisons with other markets, no at-

Table III-12: Some dramatic shifts in contract awards between FY 1958–60 and FY 1961–63

| Company | Contract awards ($ millions) | | FY 1958–60 rank | FY 1961–63 rank |
	FY 1958–60	FY 1961–63		
Lockheed	$2724.4	$4111.7	3	1
Boeing	4306.2	3408.9	1	3
Hughes	1315.7	878.3	10	17
General Motors	710.3	1174.8	21	10
Avco	427.1	828.0	26	20
Thiokol	289.7	626.9	32	25

tempt is made here to describe the defense market as stable or unstable. Yet even if we cannot say that the degree of stability would justify a label of "stagnant" or one of "volatile," we can conclude that the market became more stable during the cold war years, at least in respect to the positions of the largest prime contractors.

Table III-13 merely corroborates the decrease in inequality of award distribution among the top 50 prime contractors already shown in Table II-8. There are slight differences of emphasis when the three-year periods are used. The great but temporary increase in awards going to Boeing and General Dynamics in FY 1958 does not have so marked an effect on the Gini coefficient for FY 1958–60 as it does on the coefficient for FY 1958 alone; therefore the increasing equality of awards within the top 50 in recent years is more evident. The increase in the Gini coefficient between FY 1963 and FY 1964 does not appear, and the final three-year period in Table III-13 shows the lowest degree of internal concentration.

Table III-14 compares changes in the distribution of contract awards by size class, with firms classified by size of contract awards in the initial period. This table shows in part how the changes in equality of award distribution, which are indicated by the Gini coefficients, affected firms of various ranks within the top 50 prime contractors.

The firms which ranked from 41 to 50 in 1955–57 received, on the average, a greater percentage increase in contract awards between 1955–57 and FY 1958–60 than any other size class. However, the degree of inequality, as measured by the Gini coefficient, was virtually undisturbed during this period, primarily because the average percentage increase among the top 10 was so substantially above the percentage increase in total procurement from United

Table III-13: Gini coefficients of inequality for multi-year awards to the 50 largest prime contractors

Period	G	Period	G
June 1940–Sept. 1944	.46	FY 1959–61	.50
FY 1950–53	.49	FY 1960–62	.48
Jan. 1955–June 1957	.50	FY 1961–63	.46
FY 1957–59	.51	FY 1962–64	.45
FY 1958–60	.51		

States firms. In each of the three subsequent periods shown, during which inequality within the group was decreasing, the percentage increase of the top 10 was less than that for total procurement. With the exception of the period FY 1958–60 to FY 1961–63, the greatest percentage growth in awards each period was achieved by firms which had initially had the smallest dollar volume of awards. But firms nearer the middle of the lists also enjoyed high rates of increase; and when the FY 1958–60 to FY 1961–63 period is taken into account, it appears that equalization took place because those near the middle of the group as well as those near the bottom received far greater percentage increases in contract awards than did those closer to the top.

In summary, there were fairly evident changes in the structure of the defense market from January, 1955, through FY 1964, which can be described from information contained in the periodic lists of dollar value of contract awards granted to the 100 largest prime contractors. Use of annual figures is in some respects misleading, and it seems preferable for several reasons to confine attention to the top 50. Yet when two-and-a-half- and three-year periods are used, and the number of firms is reduced, the following conclusions can be drawn:

Table III-14: Average percentage increase in prime contract awards, by rank class in earlier multi-year period

1955–57 rank	Percentage increase to FY 1958–60	FY 1958–60 rank	Percentage increase to FY 1961–63
1–10	57.5	1–10	3.8
11–20	48.2	11–20	5.5
21–30	58.9	21–30	35.7
31–40	45.6	31–40*	41.4
41–50	78.9	41–50	16.5
Total procurement from U.S. companies	45.9	Total procurement from U.S. companies	13.4

FY 1957–59 rank	Percentage increase to FY 1960–62	FY 1959–61 rank	Percentage increase to FY 1962–64
1–10	7.7	1–10	1.5
11–20	1.3	11–20	19.3
21–30	31.2	21–30	20.3
31–40	6.5	31–40*	35.4
41–50	36.8	41–50	36.1
Total procurement from U.S. companies	9.4	Total procurement from U.S. companies	15.5

* Omitting Philco Corp. but including Ford Motor Co. without adjustment.

(*a*) The over-all level of concentration, expressed in terms of the percentage of total prime contract dollars going to the 50 largest prime contractors, increased. (*b*) While no attempt is made in this study to characterize the defense market as either stable or unstable, it is not nearly so unstable as would appear from uncritical use of annual turnover as the sole indicator. (*c*) The defense market became more stable, at least in respect to apparent shifts in rank and percentage change in dollar volume of contract awards among the 50 largest prime contractors. (*d*) Awards were spread somewhat more evenly among the 50 largest prime contractors, so that the degree of inequality within the group diminished.

IV. MARKET STRUCTURE: PRIMARY PRODUCT GROUPINGS AND SPECIALIZATION IN MILITARY PRODUCTS

A. Problems of Disaggregation and Classification

Any meaningful description of the structure of the defense market and of shifts in this structure should contain some sort of breakdown and classification of the major defense contractors. However, several factors typical of these firms and of the defense market make it difficult to define appropriate types and degrees of subdivision. The first part of this chapter discusses both the need for disaggregation and the conceptual problems that must be faced. The second and third parts present structural data broken down by two criteria which seem reasonable and feasible, although not ideal.

In the first place, both "market" and "industry" are imprecise words when used in connection with the structure being described, and either could be misleading. The semantic problem is well illustrated in *Planning and Forecasting in the Defense Industries*, a collection of papers presented during a two-day seminar at the University of California, Los Angeles, in May, 1960.[1] The volume's title uses the word "industries" rather than "industry"; and the editor, J. A. Stockfisch, refers in the Preface to the "defense sector" and notes such distinct industries within the sector as airframe, propulsion, electronics, ground equipment, ordnance, vehicles, shipbuilding, and construction.[2] The first paper, "The Scope and Nature of the Defense Sector of the U.S. Economy," by N. H. Jacoby and Stockfisch, discusses the problems of defining this sector. The authors argue convincingly that the defense sector cannot be defined in terms of firms, products, or industries. Even if viewed in terms of resources devoted to the defense of the nation, the concept is an ambiguous one. Jacoby and Stockfisch suggest that at a limited extreme the defense sector might be confined to the activities of both

---

1. J. A. Stockfisch (ed.), *Planning and Forecasting in the Defense Industries* (Belmont, Calif.: Wadsworth, 1962).
2. *Ibid.*, pp. vi–viii.

government employees and non-governmental organizations which are financed by the budget of the Department of Defense. However, they continue, since the threat to the nation's survival is not purely military, national defense could be regarded as encompassing all forms of activity connected with meeting the over-all threat of communism. In such a broad view, not only the space, atomic energy, strategic stockpile, and foreign aid programs would be included, but also distinctly non-military programs such as public health, housing, and education.

The concept of the "defense market," as it is being used here, is even narrower than the most limited definition of the defense sector proposed by Jacoby and Stockfisch. The market in which the Department of Defense operates is limited by that part of its budget, somewhat over one half, which is devoted to the outside procurement of the goods and services needed to support its activities. Thus, although it would be impossible or extraordinarily difficult to define the defense or military market in terms of the goods and services

Table IV-1: Changes in procurement programs, FY 1957–63 and FY 1963–64

Program	Amount ($ millions)			FY 1963 as percentage of FY 1957	FY 1964 as percentage of FY 1963
	FY 1957	FY 1963	FY 1964		
Missile systems	$1,864	$6,689	$5,579	358.9	83.4
Aircraft	5,019	5,479	6,067	109.2	110.7
Electronics & communications equip.	1,889	3,061	2,918	162.0	95.3
Ships	927	1,683	1,485	181.6	88.2
Services	2,771	1,504	1,800	54.3	119.7
Misc. hard goods	883	1,133	1,054	128.3	93.0
Construction	1,633	1,132	1,360	69.3	120.1
Tank-automotive	364	1,032	745	283.5	72.2
Ammunition	434	886	661	204.1	74.6
Fuels & lubricants	952	877	788	92.1	89.9
Subsistence	510	586	579	114.9	98.8
Textiles, clothing & equipage	331	259	262	78.2	101.2
Weapons	274	214	211	78.1	98.6
All actions of less than $10,000	1,281	2,610	2,710	203.7	103.8
Total (All business firms for work in U.S.) *	$19,133	$27,144	$26,221	141.9	96.6

* Does not add because of rounding.
Source: OSD, *Military Prime Contract Awards and Subcontract Payments, July 1962–June 1963,* p. 22, and *July 1963–June 1964,* p. 22.

produced and acquired, as we might define the wheat market, the definition can be made perfectly clear in terms of the customer, as would be the case when reference was made to the export market. The selling side of the market whose structure is under investigation here is composed of business firms and other non-governmental organizations producing goods and services for ultimate sale to one customer, the Department of Defense.

Even after restricting its scope to non-governmental suppliers of the Department of Defense, we are left with an extremely large and complex market. The Department of Defense distinguishes thirteen "procurement programs," which, as indicated in Table IV-1, have grown or shrunk at very different rates from FY 1957 to the peak year of FY 1963.

Table IV-1 also indicates how unevenly the slight decline from FY 1963 to FY 1964 was distributed among procurement programs. A detailed classification of companies which was quite fitting for one year might be rendered completely obsolete by the following year's contract awards, a few mergers and acquisitions, or a technological breakthrough in any procurement program by either a contractor's research organization or a government laboratory.

In light of the great variation in the composition of defense spending shown in Table IV-1, one of the most remarkable features of the structure of the market is the relative stability of the composition and ranking of its membership. In large part, this stability may be attributed to the ability of most of the major aircraft manufacturers to shift into missile production with ease and to the fact that the largest contractors are diversified into several procurement programs. Both the extent to which aircraft firms have moved into missile work and the various procurement programs under which the largest firms hold prime contracts are suggested by the following statement submitted by the Department of Defense for the record during congressional hearings on appropriations for FY 1963.

General Dynamics leads the 1961 list with 8.5 percent and has been first in 4 of the past 5 years. This company is a producer of all major types of military hardware; its Electric Boat Division builds nuclear submarines; Astronautics Division produces the ATLAS intercontinental ballistic missile and space booster, and is involved in other classified missile and space programs; Fort Worth Division makes the supersonic

B-58 jet bomber, and does research on nuclear-powered aircraft; Pomona Division is producing TERRIER and TARTAR guided missiles, the REDEYE man-carried missile and MAULER battlefield defense system; and the Stromberg-Carlson Division is engaged in electronics work.

North American Aviation, Inc., second in 1961 with 5.2 percent of the total, was fifth in 1960. Los Angeles and Columbus Divisions conduct aircraft development and manufacture, including production of the A3J-1 Vigilante attack plane and T2J-1 Buckeye trainer for the Navy, and T-39 Sabreliner for the Air Force. Development projects include the Air Force B-70 strategic weapon system and X-15 rocket-powered experimental aircraft. The basic project of the Space and Information Systems Division is the HOUND DOG air-to-surface missile. Astronautics Division has contracts for guidance control of the MINUTE-MAN missile and for the navigation system of the POLARIS submarine.

Lockheed Aircraft Corp., with 5.2 percent of the total, is in third place but is only $22 million below the second-place company. Lockheed has greatly expanded and diversified its military production in the past 2 years through acquisition and merger. Shipbuilding and heavy construction were added by acquisition of Puget Sound Bridge & Dry Dock Co. in April 1959, electronics through acquisition of Stavid Engineering in October 1959 and solid-propellant rocket engines through acquisition of Grand Central Rocket Co. in February 1960. Principal military contracts are in aircraft, missile, and satellite systems. Examples are C-130 Hercules turboprop jet transport, C-140 jet transport, F-104 fighter jet, P2V-7 Neptune piston-engine patrol bomber, and the P3V-1 Electra advance jet version. It is the prime contractor for Navy's POLARIS fleet ballistic missile, and for three leading satellite systems: DISCOVERER, MIDAS, and SAMOS.

In fourth place, with 4.1 percent, is Boeing Co., down from third place in the previous year. Current military projects include the B-52 global bomber, KC-135 jet tanker-transport, and C-135 jet cargo transport. It is prime contractor for the BOMARC missile project and an associate contractor for the MINUTEMAN missile program. The company added helicopter production by the purchase of Vertol Aircraft Corp. in March 1960.[3]

Not only are major contractors likely to hold contracts in more than one procurement program at a time, but the mix among new programs, as indicated by annual contract awards, frequently changes sharply from one year to the next. A staff member of the Office of the Secretary of Defense very kindly made available to me

3. U.S. Congress, House Committee on Appropriations, Subcommittee on Department of Defense Appropriations, *Hearings: Department of Defense Appropriations for 1963, Part 4, Procurement*, pp. 528–529.

an unpublished analysis showing the procurement program in which each of the firms appearing on the list of 100 largest prime contractors had received its largest dollar volume of awards for each of the fiscal years 1960 through 1963. Since the tabulation indicated only the single largest procurement program for each firm, a firm might not have had the majority of its awards in the program shown if it had awards in more than two programs. Of the 63 firms listed for all four years, 47 remained in the same procurement program category throughout, including 7 petroleum refiners in the fuels and lubricants program and 4 firms in the tank-automotive program. There were 13 contractors listed under two procurement programs during these four years, and 3 firms—Westinghouse Electric, Goodyear Tire and Rubber, and Ryan Aeronautical—received the largest single dollar value of awards in three different procurement programs during four consecutive years. Some of the shifts may be more apparent than real, because of the necessarily arbitrary assignment of contracts to a procurement program. For example, Westinghouse was classed as a ships contractor when it was manufacturing steam turbines and nuclear reactors for ship propulsion. Had Westinghouse been producing electronic components for use on ships, it would have been classified in the electronics and communications equipment program, as in fact it was in other years. On the other hand, very real shifts, such as from helicopters to supersonic jet bombers, could be obscured within a single procurement program. It would therefore be inappropriate to attempt to disaggregate the defense market by procurement programs, to treat each procurement program as analogous to an industry, and to assign each of the major prime contractors to a particular procurement program.

Yet the fact remains that it is very difficult to make meaningful judgments about the structure of the defense market, taken as a whole, in the absence of valid comparisons. For example, the Arthur D. Little study, *How Sick is the Defense Industry?*, after presenting a table showing the percentages of total Department of Defense prime contract awards received by the 100 largest prime contractors from FY 1957 through FY 1962, continues:

> To put these figures into the context of all American industry, the first 100 companies listed in *Fortune's* "500" for 1961 had sales totaling about $133.4 billion, or only 35% of the sales of all manufacturing companies.

The awards and sales ratios are not directly comparable, because awards do not represent sales by contractors in any one accounting period, but the two ratios are sufficiently different to point out the extreme concentration of the defense industry and the extent to which our national security depends upon the health of relatively few organizations.[4]

It is, in my opinion, erroneous to conclude that concentration in the defense market is "extreme" because the 100 largest prime contractors received 74.2 per cent of total Department of Defense prime contracts in FY 1961 whereas the 100 largest manufacturers made only 35 per cent of manufacturing sales in 1961. Direct comparisons between contract awards and manufacturing sales are, as the Arthur D. Little report noted, possibly misleading because of the time lag. It is much more important to note that they are difficult to interpret if not utterly meaningless when made between prime defense contracts, which totaled $25 billion in FY 1961, and a "market" more than ten times as large. Sales of all United States manufacturers, some of which were made to other manufacturers, totaled $380 billion in the same year. The differences in size are too great for meaningful comparisons. Moreover, if all sales in the defense market, both to the Department of Defense and to other defense firms, were included in a base, and all defense sales of the largest 100 prime contractors were computed as a percentage of this base, the resulting measure of "concentration" would undoubtedly be quite a bit less than 74 per cent.

Another comparison can be made which makes the defense market look rather unconcentrated. So-called concentration ratios, showing the percentages of an industry's total sales or assets accounted for by the largest four or eight firms, have been published from time to time for the standard industrial classifications of the Bureau of the Census. Two prominent students of industrial organization, Carl Kaysen and Donald F. Turner, consider a "structurally oligopolistic market" to be one in which the eight largest firms account for one-third or more of total market sales. They admit that the dividing point is "somewhat arbitrary," but they continue by noting that below this point "the majority of markets with which we are familiar" do not function in an oligopolistic fashion. They further subdivide structural oligopoly into two types. Type one, in

4. *How Sick Is the Defense Industry?*, p. 15.

which "recognition of interdependence by the leading firms is extremely high," requires the first eight firms to have at least 50 per cent of total market shares and the first twenty to have at least 75 per cent. Their type two oligopoly requires only that the leading eight firms make one-third of total sales. Type two is considered "partial oligopoly."[5] Kaysen and Turner found that their type one oligopoly accounts for a little over 25 per cent of all manufacturing in national markets.[6] By these standards, and treating the entire defense market as an "industry," concentration of defense contracts is quite low, as shown in Table IV-2.

In terms of relative magnitude, it makes more sense to compare concentration ratios in the defense market with those for census industries than it does to compare concentration of defense contracts with the over-all concentration of sales for all manufacturing.

5. Carl Kaysen and Donald F. Turner, *Antitrust Policy: An Economic and Legal Analysis* (Cambridge: Harvard University Press, 1959), p. 27.
6. *Ibid.*, p. 31.

Table IV-2: Concentration ratios for Department of Defense prime contracts

Fiscal Year	Percentage of net value of military prime contract awards, accounted for by the largest:			
	Firm	4 Firms	8 Firms	20 Firms
1957	5.4	18.5	29.2	45.2
1958	9.8	23.3	34.7	52.7
1959	7.2	21.0	32.7	50.6
1960	6.0	20.5	32.3	49.0
1961	6.5	21.0	33.1	49.8
1962	5.6	18.7	30.0	46.5
1963	5.9	19.2	30.5	47.3
1964	5.8	19.9	32.3	48.0

Table IV-3: Defense procurement and sales of the three largest U.S. industrial concerns, 1961–63 ($ billions)

	1961	1962	1963	1964
Total Department of Defense procurement awards, except governmental, by fiscal year	$24.7	$28.1	$29.0	$28.2
Sales, by calendar year:				
General Motors	11.4	14.6	16.5	17.0
Standard Oil (New Jersey)	8.4	9.5	10.3	10.8
Ford	6.7	8.1	8.7	9.7
Total	$26.5	$32.2	$35.5	$37.5

Sources: Table I-1 and *Fortune, Directory of the 500 Largest Industrial Corporations,* July, 1962, 1963, 1964, and 1965.

While $25–30 billion is certainly a very large amount of money by any standard, one should not think of the defense market as being so huge as to defy comparison. Indeed, as Table IV-3 shows, total defense procurement in recent years was of lower dollar amount than the combined sales of the nation's three largest industrial concerns.

If the operating revenue of the largest public utility, American Telephone and Telegraph, is substituted for the sales of Ford, the third largest industrial firm, the comparison becomes even more striking. American Telephone and Telegraph's operating revenues were $8.4 billion in 1961, $9.0 billion in 1962, $9.6 billion in 1963, and $10.3 billion in 1964.

The difficulty in treating the defense market as an industry lies not in its size but in its complexity and the diversity of its products. Certainly it offends common sense to include in one so-called industry both a major oil refiner with a very small percentage of its total sales made to the government and an aerospace firm which is almost entirely dependent on continued Department of Defense orders. There are other, only slightly less glaring, difficulties with the concept of one defense industry. An electronics firm is far more likely to complement producers of missiles, aircraft, and ships as a subcontractor or an associate contractor than it is to compete with them. Firms within a single procurement program may manufacture products which are quite dissimilar and are in no way substitutes for each other. Only a few of the firms in the missile systems and ships procurement programs are capable of acting as system managers under prime contracts for such products as a new intercontinental ballistic missile system or a nuclear submarine.

Thus there are good reasons for attempting to classify the major defense contractors, but it seems inappropriate to set up rigorously defined and carefully distinguished subgroups. The classifications used below do not represent a solution to the problem of disaggregation of the defense market. They are, rather, a compromise between the reluctant conclusion that it would be impossible to establish a reasonable and stable set of groupings based on products manufactured for the Department of Defense and the assumption that some sort of breakdown would yield additional insights into the structure of the market. The firms appearing among the top 50 prime contractors in any one of the multi-year periods used in

Chapter III were grouped, first, by primary product classifications and, second, by the percentages of total sales made for military purposes.

The primary product classifications are based on Standard Industrial Classification (SIC) three-digit industries. Firms are assigned to SIC classes on the basis of their primary products, or the single most important set of products of the firm. For almost all the firms among the top 50, a three-digit classification was found in the 1963 and earlier editions of the *Directory of Companies Filing Annual Reports with the Securities and Exchange Commission*.[7] In a few cases, firms were assigned to an industry group as the result of information taken from annual reports or financial manuals. Hughes Aircraft, which is privately owned and therefore not required to file information with the Securities and Exchange Commission or to publish annual reports, is generally recognized as an electronics rather than an aircraft firm and is so listed. General Tire and Rubber is listed in the Securities and Exchange Commission's *Directory* under SIC 301, tires and inner tubes; but Aerojet-General, of which 84 per cent is owned by General Tire and Rubber, is separately classified under SIC 372, aircraft and parts. Since well over one-half of General Tire and Rubber's consolidated sales, including those of Aerojet-General, are for military purposes, General Tire and Rubber is classified as an aircraft firm in this study. The primary product classification scheme employed here is shown below:

I. *Aircraft and Propulsion*, SIC 372

Bell Aircraft Corp.
Boeing Co.
Curtiss-Wright Corp.
Douglas Aircraft Co.
Fairchild Engine & Airplane Co.
Garrett Corp.
General Dynamics Corp.
General Tire & Rubber Co.
Grumman Aircraft Engineering Corp.
Hayes International Corp.
Ling-Temco-Vought, Inc. (Chance Vought Aircraft, Inc.)
Lockheed Aircraft Corp.
Martin Marietta Corp.
McDonnell Aircraft Corp.

I. (*cont.*)

North American Aviation, Inc.
Northrop Corp.
Republic Aviation Corp.
Textron, Inc.
Thiokol Chemical Corp.
Thompson Ramo Wooldridge, Inc.
United Aircraft Corp.

II. *Electronics*, SIC 357, 361, 365, 366, 381, 481

American Bosch Arma Corp.
American Telephone & Telegraph Co.
Avco Corp.
Bendix Corp.
Burroughs Corp.
Collins Radio Co.

7. U.S. Securities and Exchange Commission, Division of Trading and Exchanges, *Directory of Companies Filing Annual Reports with the Securities and Exchange Commission* (Washington: Government Printing Office, various dates).

II. (*cont.*)

General Electric Co.
General Precision Equipment Corp.
General Telephone & Electronics Corp.
Hughes Aircraft Co.
International Business Machines Corp.
International Telephone & Telegraph Corp.
Litton Industries, Inc.
Minneapolis-Honeywell Regulator Co.
Philco Corp.
Radio Corp. of America
Raytheon Co.
Sperry Rand Corp.
Westinghouse Electric Corp.

III. *Other, except Petroleum Refining*

American Machine & Foundry Co.
Bath Iron Works Corp.
Bethlehem Steel Corp.
Brown-Raymond-Walsh

III. (*cont.*)

Chrysler Corp.
Continental Motors Corp.
FMC Corp.
Ford Motor Co.
General Motors Corp.
Goodyear Tire & Rubber Co.
Hercules Powder Co.
Kaiser Industries Corp.
Massachusetts Institute of Technology
Merritt-Chapman & Scott Corp.
Newport News Shipbuilding & Dry Dock Co.
Olin Mathieson Chemical Corp.
Pan American World Airways, Inc.

IV. *Petroleum Refining*, SIC 291

Cities Service Co.
Royal Dutch Petroleum Co.
Socony Mobil Oil Co.
Standard Oil Co. (California)
Standard Oil Co. (New Jersey)
Texaco, Inc.
Tidewater Oil Co.

The grouping of firms by primary products has one advantage, other than ease of classification, over distinguishing firms by Department of Defense procurement programs. The primary product designation covers products which are predominant for the entire firm, including its civilian as well as military sales. It therefore reflects the firm's fundamental capabilities and general industrial orientation better than do the year-to-year awards broken down by procurement programs. Westinghouse Electric, for example, is assigned by the Securities and Exchange Commission to SIC 361, an electrical equipment designation, and is therefore listed here as an electronics firm. Presumably, Westinghouse's most important attribute as a defense contractor is its ability to handle large and complex contracts related to electrical technology and construction. Yet Westinghouse had its single largest dollar volume of contract awards in the ships procurement program in FY 1962, when it received its turbine and nuclear reactor awards, and in missile systems in FY 1963. Most of the electronics firms, in fact, have the majority of their awards in procurement programs other than electronics and communications equipment. The Securities and Exchange commission did not classify any of the companies under SIC 19, ordnance; therefore, producers of missiles, missile subsystems, ground control equipment, and propellants are found in all the primary product classes listed except Group IV, petroleum refining.

The groupings are admittedly crude, but it is believed that any finer categories would have been unwise. Further refinement would have required quite arbitrary classification decisions in respect to a number of diversified contractors and would have resulted in year-to-year shifts in the composition of the classes which would in all likelihood have shed more confusion than light on inter-period comparisons.

B. Classification by Primary Products

Table IV-4 breaks down the concentration of total prime contract awards by primary product groups for firms among the 50 largest prime contractors.

It does not appear possible to make the most obvious and perhaps most interesting disaggregated measurement of concentration in the defense market. One would like to see the percentage of total aircraft procurement accounted for by the aircraft company receiving the largest amount of contract awards, by the top four and top eight aircraft companies, and similar percentages for electronics, shipbuilding, and so forth. But, as has been argued above, defense submarkets simply do not coincide with primary product groupings.

Nevertheless, Table IV-4 does indicate some additional features of over-all concentration in defense contracting. The increase in concentration between 1955–57 and FY 1958–60 resulted from an increase in the share of awards going to major electronics firms as well as to the large aircraft contractors and was in part offset by a rather sharp decline in the percentage accounted for by the diverse firms in Group III. Once again, it seems clear that factors other than the FY 1958 increase in awards to Boeing and General Dynamics were at work. The constancy in both average rank and number of firms among the top 50 in Group I, aircraft, suggests the ability of the aircraft industry as a whole to adjust to the missile age without a severe structural shake-up. Although the percentage of total contract awards going to aircraft firms among the 50 largest prime contractors fell from FY 1958–60 to FY 1960–62, it was still a substantially higher percentage of the total in FY 1962–64 than it had been in 1955–57. But the demand for missile systems with

Table IV-4: Percentage of total U.S. military prime contracts accounted for by the 50 largest prime contractors, by primary product groups

Period	Primary product group	Number of firms	Average rank	Percentage of total U.S. awards
Jan. 1955–June 1957	I	17	19	31.6
	II	17	25	18.0
	III	10	31	7.1
	IV	6	36	2.8
	Total	50		59.5*
FY 1957–59	I	18	19	35.6
	II	16	29	19.8
	III	11	36	5.5
	IV	5	36	2.4
	Total	50		63.4*
FY 1958–60	I	18	19	37.1
	II	17	23	20.3
	III	10	36	5.2
	IV	5	37	2.3
	Total	50		64.9*
FY 1959–61	I	17	19	35.6
	II	17	21	21.0
	III	11	36	5.9
	IV	5	39	2.3
	Total	50		64.7*
FY 1960–62	I	17	18	35.0
	II	18	25	20.5
	III	12	34	7.0
	IV	3	34	1.6
	Total	50		64.1*
FY 1961–63	I	17	18	35.1
	II	18	25	20.1
	III	11	33	7.3
	IV	4	39	1.9
	Total	50		64.4*
FY 1962–64	I	17	18	35.3
	II	17	24	19.4
	III	12	34	7.8
	IV	4	38	1.9
	Total	50		64.4*

* Totals may not add because of rounding.

technologically advanced guidance systems, ground control devices, and telemetry was also of real benefit to electronics firms. The firms of Group II, like those of Group I, had a higher percentage of total awards in FY 1962–64 than they had had in 1955–57.

From FY 1958–60 to FY 1962–64, the share of prime contracts going to the firms in Group III rose dramatically. Much of this increase must be attributed to the emphasis put on increasing the nation's capabilities for conventional and limited warfare. Despite the fact that strengthening non-nuclear forces involved an increased demand for airlift, tactical aircraft for the Army, and Air Force and Navy aircraft capable of giving close support to ground operations, the percentage of total procurement accounted for by the aircraft companies among the top 50 declined from FY 1958–60 through FY 1962–64. Many people hoped that the increased spending for the Army's general purpose forces would raise the share of prime contract awards made to small business, and indeed the initial increase achieved under Operation Booster in FY 1962 did coincide with the first year of the Army build-up. But while procurement for general purpose forces continued to grow at a rapid rate through FY 1963 and FY 1964,[8] we have seen that the percentage of prime awards going to small business slipped in FY 1963 and only recovered lost ground in FY 1964. The principal beneficiaries of the renewed emphasis on limited and conventional warfare, at least before accelerated procurement to meet the nation's increased commitments in Vietnam, were evidently not small firms but Group III companies among the 50 largest prime contractors.

A second important factor in the Group III firms' increased share from FY 1958–60 was the rise in shipwork expenditures and the larger percentage of this work performed in private shipyards, as shown in Table IV-5.

---

8. The following exchange is found in U.S. Congress, Senate Subcommittee of the Committee on Appropriations, *Hearings: Department of Defense Appropriations for 1964* (Washington: Government Printing Office, 1963), p. 138.

Senator RUSSELL. . . . last year and the year before that, I think, we almost doubled the appropriations for 1961 to equip the Army. I wonder how long this is going on before we get the Army equipped?

Secretary McNAMARA. I think General Wheeler and I might differ a little bit on this but I personally believe we are at a high point in fiscal 1964.

Senator RUSSELL. It looks to me we are at the point where we should start tapering off.

Secretary McNAMARA. I think that is true.

Four of the firms in Group III—Newport News, Bethlehem Steel, Merritt-Chapman and Scott, and Bath Iron Works—are shipbuilders. In the last few years there has been considerable controversy over the relative roles of private and naval shipyards. The appropriation bills from FY 1962 through FY 1964 each included a requirement that at least 35 per cent of all repair, alteration, and conversion work be assigned to private shipyards. Further, under the Vinson-Trammel Act of 1934, the Navy is required to alternate construction of new vessels so as to achieve an approximately equal distribution between naval and private yards.

The second aspect of market structure to be reconsidered in light of the primary product classifications is stability. Table IV-6 indicates turnover among the 50 largest prime contractors by primary product groups.

Despite the fairly large number of exits and entries in Group I, aircraft, the turnover in this group was really quite mild, especially in the most recent period shown. Two of the three aircraft firms dropping out of the 50 largest prime contractors between FY 1958–60 and FY 1961–63, Bell and Chance Vought, vanished through merger; their purchasers, Textron and Ling-Temco-Vought, are the two entrants for the same period. The third aircraft firm which disappeared, Garrett Aircraft, ranked only 49 in FY 1958–60 and 61 in FY 1961–63.

Table IV-5: Allocation of shipwork between naval and private shipyards, FY 1958–63

Fiscal year	Total repairs, alterations, conversions, and new construction ($000)			
	Naval shipyards	Private shipyards	Total	Percentage to private shipyards
1958	$ 825,856	$1,349,000	$2,174,856	62.0
1959	1,086,040	1,472,998	2,559,038	57.6
1960	531,478	504,984	1,036,462	48.7
Total	$2,443,374	$3,326,982	$5,770,356	57.7
1961	$ 972,352	$1,568,635	$2,540,987	61.7
1962	1,372,615	1,786,624	3,159,239	56.6
1963	859,216	2,213,915	3,073,131	72.0
Total	$3,204,183	$5,569,174	$8,773,357	63.5

Source: U.S. Congress, House Committee on Appropriations, Subcommittee on Department of Defense Appropriations, Hearings: Department of Defense Appropriations for 1964, Part 6, Research, Development, Test and Evaluation; Appropriation Language; Testimony of Members of Congress, Organizations, and Interested Individuals (Washington: Government Printing Office, 1963), p. 693.

The single disappearance from Group II, electronics, was Philco, acquired by Ford to bolster the latter's sagging defense business. The two entrants were Litton and General Telephone and Electronics.

The type of instability indicated by turnover data was somewhat harsher among the mixed group, Group III, than for the aircraft and electronics groups. The number of exits and entries is comparable to that for the aircraft group, even though the number of firms in this group is much smaller. None of the disappearances from Group III can be accounted for by merger. Yet even within this group, instability does not appear to have been particularly severe.

Increased missile spending had a pronounced effect on Group III. Two of the three FY 1958–60 entrants, Pan American and Massachusetts Institute of Technology, are associated with missile programs, and two of the three Group III entrants to the FY 1961–63 list, Hercules Powder and American Machine and Foundry, are primarily missile contractors.

Table IV-7 shows product-moment correlations of the logarithms of prime contract awards for firms remaining among the top 50 for two consecutive multi-year periods, by primary product groups.

The breakdown by primary products makes it possible to compare stability in the various groups as well as changes in stability over time. The over-all rise in stability for the 50 largest prime contractors, as suggested in Table III-10, now appears to have resulted from relatively high and constant degrees of stability among both aircraft and electronics concerns, coupled with a most dramatic increase among the varied firms of Group III. Since the number of petroleum refiners in each pair of periods compared is so small, the high

Table IV-6: Number of firms entering and leaving successive multi-year lists of 50 largest prime contractors, by primary product groups*

Primary product group	1955–57 to FY 1958–60		FY 1958–60 to FY 1961–63	
	Exits	Entries	Exits	Entries
I	2	3	3	2
II	0	0	1	2
III	3	3	2	3
IV	2	1	1	0
Total	7	7	7	7

* These firms have already been identified by name in Chapter III.

correlation coefficients are not of much significance, and the decline in the coefficient for Group IV had only a very slight effect on stability within the aggregated group.

Despite the far greater stability achieved by Group III firms by FY 1958–60 to FY 1961–63, this group continued to have by far the lowest correlation coefficients in the final two pairs of periods.[9] Thus, whether indicated by turnover of membership in the 50 largest prime contractors or by variations in contract awards from period to period for firms neither entering nor leaving the list, the firms of Group III appear to have experienced substantially greater instability than either the aircraft or electronics firms.

Table IV-8 presents correlation coefficients for all firms for which data are available in each product group, including, first, those leaving the lists and, second, those entering.

The correlation coefficients taking account of the disappearing firms show much the same pattern as those of Table IV-7. In almost every case, the coefficient including entrants is lower than the corresponding coefficient taking account of disappearing firms, a difference which may most probably be attributed to the fact that

9. For each of the pairs of time periods shown in Table IV-7, the difference between the correlation coefficient for Group I and that for Group III is significant at the .01 level of probability, provided the former is treated as the sample. All but one of the comparable differences between the coefficients for Group II and Group III are also significant at the .01 level; the remaining difference, between the FY 1958–60 to FY 1961–63 coefficients, is significant at the .05 level. As noted previously, the test of significance used becomes less reliable as the number of observations in the assumed sample decreases. See chap. ii, n. 25, *supra*.

Table IV-7: Product-moment correlations of the logarithms of prime contract awards between pairs of successive multi-year periods, for firms among the 50 largest recipients in both periods, by primary product groups

		Jan. 1955–June 1957 to FY 1958–60	FY 1957–59 to FY 1960–62	FY 1958–60 to FY 1961–63	FY 1959–61 to FY 1962–64
Group I:	r	.952	.944	.971	.961
	n	15	17	17	16
Group II:	r	.964	.962	.964	.960
	n	17	16	16	15
Group III:	r	.335	.790	.882	.831
	n	7	8	8	9
Group IV:	r	.992	.991	.974	.978
	n	4	3	4	4

Table IV-8: Product-moment correlations of logarithms of prime contract awards between pairs of successive multi-year periods, for firms among the 50 largest recipients in either period, by primary product groups

A. Including as many as possible of those disappearing

		Jan. 1955–June 1957 to FY 1958-60	FY 1957-59 to FY 1960-62	FY 1958-60 to FY 1961-63	FY 1959-61 to FY 1962-64
Group I:	r	.965	.946	.974	.963
	n	17	18	18	17
Group II:	r	.964	.962	.949	.952
	n	17	16	17	16
Group III:	r	.599	.813	.894	.844
	n	9	10	10	11
Group IV:	r	.978	.979	.959	.975
	n	6	5	5	5

B. Including as many as possible of those entering

		Jan. 1955–June 1957 to FY 1958-60	FY 1957-59 to FY 1960-62	FY 1958-60 to FY 1961-63	FY 1959-61 to FY 1962-64
Group I:	r	.940	.944	.971	.959
	n	16	17	17	17
Group II:	r	.964	.965	.934	.892
	n	17	18	18	17
Group III:	r	.420	.570	.742	.818
	n	10	12	11	11
Group IV:	r	.959	.991	.974	.978
	n	5	3	4	4

most of the disappearing firms did not drop very far below the fiftieth rank while their replacements generally rose from positions farther down the list. The divergence is far greater in Group III than in Groups I and II, and the fact that entrants to Group III rose in general from lower ranks than the firms entering Groups I and II suggests that barriers to entry into the defense market are lower for Group III than for firms in the aircraft and electronics groups.

Inequality in award distribution within the ranks of the 50 largest prime contractors is again measured by Gini coefficients (G) in Table IV-9, this time for each of the four primary product groups.[10] The table also shows the Herfindahl index of concentration (H) within each group.

Care must be exercised in interpreting the Gini coefficients, since the coefficient is designed as a measure of inequality and takes no account of numbers. An increase (decrease) in the Gini coefficient for any one group would indicate that awards were being less (more) evenly distributed among the firms in that group, but

10. All the Gini coefficients in this study, being based on 50 or fewer observations, were computed from discontinuous Lorenz curves. This method of computation leads to a slight overestimation of the area under a continuous Lorenz curve and hence to a slight underestimation of the Gini coefficient. The underestimation is greater the greater the degree of inequality (with no underestimation where there is a perfectly equal distribution) and also is greater the fewer the observations. Thus the Gini coefficients for the various primary product groups are not directly comparable with those for the groups of 50 presented in Chapters II and III. Further, intergroup comparisons may be misleading where the numbers of firms in the groups being compared are substantially different. However, the possible distortions caused by changes in the numbers of firms in particular groups are extremely small (well under .01 in every instance except for Group IV); therefore valid comparisons may be made for one group in different time periods. Also, since the numbers are fairly large and close together, valid comparisons may be made between Group I and Group II.

Table IV-9: Inequality and concentration within primary product groups for the 50 largest prime contractors

| | Primary product group | | | | | | | |
| | I | | II | | III | | IV | |
Period	G	H	G	H	G	H	G	H
Jan. 1955–June 1957	.46	.101	.46	.116	.34	.152	.22	.199
FY 1957–59	.49	.106	.41	.103	.28	.124	.22	.237
FY 1958–60	.49	.106	.40	.096	.28	.136	.21	.235
FY 1959–61	.48	.106	.37	.091	.27	.118	.21	.232
FY 1960–62	.46	.103	.39	.090	.26	.106	.15	.360
FY 1961–63	.44	.100	.37	.087	.26	.115	.16	.271
FY 1962–64	.43	.097	.33	.088	.28	.107	.13	.265

it would not reflect change in the number of firms in the group between the periods being compared.

An alternative measure which does take account of numbers and hence can be used as a measure of concentration is the Herfindahl index, which is expressed as $\dfrac{\Sigma (c^2)}{(\Sigma c)^2}$ where c equals contract awards expressed in dollars. As an example of the differences between the Gini coefficient as a measure of inequality and the Herfindahl index as a measure of concentration, if ten firms each received one-tenth of total awards in one period, and in the next period the number of firms fell to three, each of which received one-third of that period's total, the Gini coefficient as computed from a continuous Lorenz curve would remain unchanged, while the Herfindahl index would rise substantially. On the other hand, an increase in the percentage of awards going to the largest firms coupled with the entry of additional firms might leave the Herfindahl index unchanged even though it would raise the Gini coefficient.

Inspection of Table IV-9 shows that both inequality of award distribution and concentration of awards within the top 50 moved in the same direction and declined for all of the primary product groups except IV, petroleum refining. In Group IV, awards were spread more equally among firms within the 50 largest prime contractors, but concentration as measured by the Herfindahl index nevertheless increased as the number of firms in this group declined from six in 1955–57 to four in FY 1962–64, reaching a minimum of three (and hence the highest Herfindahl index) in FY 1960–62. Table IV-9 indicates that the virtual stability of the Gini coefficient for the entire 50 between 1955–57 and FY 1959–61 (Table III-13 showed a rise from .50 to .51 and a subsequent fall to .50) resulted from an increase for the aircraft firms offset by decreases for each of the other three groups. Thus it would appear that the great increase in awards going to Boeing and General Dynamics in FY 1958 ran counter for one year to a general movement toward greater equality of award receipts within the top 50 during the entire period from 1955 through FY 1964. Finally, it can be seen that while both the Gini coefficient and the Herfindahl index for Group I fell after FY 1959–61, the declines in inequality and concentration were substantially greater over the whole period for Groups II and III than they were for the aircraft group.

Table IV-10 shows the percentage increase in contract awards, by primary product group, between two successive pairs of multi-year periods. The table indicates that while firms in the electronics group experienced a far greater percentage increase in contract awards between 1955–57 and FY 1958–60 than did the aircraft firms, the situation with respect to inroads by electronics firms was afterward more than stabilized, so that contract awards to Group II grew by a smaller percentage than those to Group I between FY 1958–60 and FY 1961–63. Between these last two periods the "other" firms of Group III experienced the greatest percentage growth in contract awards, presumably as a result of the increased emphasis on build-up of limited and conventional war capabilities in FY 1961–63.

To summarize, the previous description of the structure of the defense market may be supplemented in the following ways by the breakdown of the major contractors into four primary product groups:

1. Major contractors in every primary product group but Group IV, petroleum refiners, contributed to the increase in over-all concentration of the defense market. The percentage of total awards going to firms in Group I, aircraft, rose substantially as a result of the very large awards to Boeing and General Dynamics in FY 1958 and declined slightly thereafter, although it never again dropped to its former level. However, the small decline in the share of Group I firms after FY 1958–60 was offset by increasing shares of the total awarded to firms in Group II, electronics, throughout the entire period, and to Group III, others except petroleum refiners, after

Table IV-10: Percentage increase in contract awards, by product groups, for firms among the 50 largest prime contractors in the earlier period

Group	Average percentage increase in contract awards	
	1955–57 to FY 1958–60	FY 1958–60 to FY 1961–63
I	54.9	17.2
II	83.0	15.0
III	49.1	34.0
IV	34.6	5.9

FY 1958–60. In FY 1962–64, Groups I, II, and III each had a higher percentage of total prime contract awards than had been the case in 1955–57.

2. The immediate beneficiaries of the emphasis on strengthening of limited-war capabilities were major contractors in Group III rather than small business firms.

3. The slight apparent increase in stability among the major contractors, viewed both as turnover and stability among firms remaining within the 50 largest prime contractors, was primarily the result of a great increase in stability for Group III. Nevertheless, by FY 1962–64, Group III still remained much less stable than either Group I or Group II. Turnover for Groups I and II was particularly mild between FY 1958–60 and FY 1961–63.

4. Inequality of award distribution within the primary product group declined fairly steadily throughout the entire period for Groups II and III, as did internal concentration. The early stability of the Gini coefficient for the entire list of the 50 largest prime contractors was the result of a rise in inequality among Group I firms, resulting from the FY 1958 awards to Boeing and General Dynamics, offset by a decline in Groups II and III. After FY 1958–60, awards became more equally distributed within Group I as well as within Groups II and III. But during the entire period from 1955 through FY 1964, inequality of awards and internal concentration both showed greater decreases for Groups II and III than for Group I.

C. Classification by Degrees of Specialization in Military Sales

The second method of classifying the major defense contractors is by the percentage of total sales made for military purposes. Many of the 71 firms (omitting non-profit organizations and joint ventures) which appeared among the top 50 prime contractors in the 1955–57 list or in any of the subsequent annual lists through FY 1963 publish the percentage of total revenue derived from "government," "military," "defense," or "defense and space" sales. Letters were written to the others, asking them for "the percentage of total sales made for purposes of national defense" in 1957 and 1962. The information was obtained on 58 out of the 71 from either published sources or replies to my letter. I requested firms classifying sales on some such basis as "government" or "defense and space" to supply me with these percentages if figures for purely defense sales were unavailable.

The year 1957 was selected because it is generally regarded as signaling the end of the post-Korean War period and as the beginning of the missile and space age for defense contractors.[11] 1962 was chosen as the terminal year in order to come as close to FY 1964 as possible without having the impact of the National Aeronautics and Space Administration's civilian space program render comparisons misleading between firms reporting "military" sales and those reporting "space and defense" or "government" in a single category. The calendar year 1962 covers one-half of FY 1962 and one-half of FY 1963, but since sales receipts lag behind contract awards it may be safely assumed that most of the sales made to the National Aeronautics and Space Administration in 1962 grew out of FY 1962 and earlier contracts, with few if any significant FY 1963 awards being reflected.

The impact of the National Aeronautics and Space Administration's procurement program and the apparent desirability of not going beyond 1962 may be seen in recent procurement award figures. In FY 1961 the National Aeronautics and Space Administration's contract awards to business firms totaled $755 million. The comparable figure for FY 1962 was $1,053 million. For FY 1963 it rose to $3,231 million and in FY 1964 reached $4,594 million.[12] Many of the major defense contractors are also important suppliers to the National Aeronautics and Space Administration. The budget of the National Aeronautics and Space Administration is separate from that of the Department of Defense, and care is taken to assure that the costs of civilian projects are thoroughly segregated from those of military ones. Nevertheless, it is impossible to predict in advance

11. See, for example, Stanford Research Institute, *The Industry-Government Aerospace Relationship,* which notes three "periods of major change" for the aerospace industry since the end of World War II. The first period, 1947–51, is distinguished by "low volume of business in the initial postwar period." The second period, 1952–56, covers "the Korean fighting and the accompanying deterioration in the international situation." The final period, 1957–61, is "characterized by relative stability in total sales and by the transition from long production runs to research, development, test, and evaluation contracts for missiles and space systems" (I, 42).

12. *Aviation Week and Space Technology,* LXXVIII (Jan. 21, 1963), 34; LXXX (March 30, 1964), 58; and LXXXII (March 1, 1965), 70.

the extent to which the results of so-called peaceful space exploration programs will turn out to have military implications; the real objectives of programs described as "civilian" are inevitably suspect. Therefore, not only may contractors' figures after 1962 contain large non-military awards, but with the rise of the National Aeronautics and Space Administration it becomes very difficult to separate, even conceptually, civilian from military procurement in the space programs. In describing the Gemini program, under which the National Aeronautics and Space Administration had let the contracts, an Air Force official explained that an interagency committee had been formed "to insure that the requirements or objectives of both NASA and the Department of Defense are recognized in the conduct of the program," and to make recommendation or program change proposals "to be sure that both military and civilian programs are getting the most out of the program." [13]

In the aggregate, from 1957 to 1962 there was very little if any change in the degree of specialization in military sales for the fifty-five firms for which total sales and the percentage of total sales made to the Department of Defense or the government were available for both years. The "typical" major defense contractor, as indicated by simple unweighted averages, increased its military or government sales from 49.1 per cent to 51.3 per cent of total sales. But when the averages were weighted by total sales, the figure remained constant at 22.7 per cent. These aggregates, however, disguise rather substantial shifts for individual firms, as indicated in Table IV–11.

As shown in Table IV–12, there was a slight compression in the range between 1957 and 1962, with fewer major contractors reporting 90 per cent or more of their total sales being made for defense purposes or to the government in the latter year; at the other end of the distribution, fewer reported 10 per cent or less in 1962.

There does not appear to be any consistent or notable relationship between numerical rank on the Department of Defense lists of largest prime contractors and the percentages of sales made for military purposes among contractors below the top ten.

---

13. U.S. Congress, House Committee on Appropriations, Subcommittee on Department of Defense Appropriations, *Department of Defense Appropriations for 1964, Part 6, Research, Development, Test and Evaluation; Appropriation Language; Testimony of Members of Congress, Organizations, and Interested Individuals* (Washington: Government Printing Office, 1963), p. 577.

Table IV–13 indicates that on a weighted average basis the reporting firms among the ten largest prime contractors were a good deal more specialized in defense sales than others among the 50 largest in both 1957 and 1962, despite shifts in membership in the top ten between 1955–FY 1957 and FY 1960–62. On an unweighted

Table IV-11: Changes in percentage of total sales made to the Department of Defense or government from calendar year 1957 to calendar year 1962, for 56 reporting firms *

Change in percentage of total sales to DOD or government**	Number of companies
Increase of 10% or more	11
Increase of 5% through 9%	8
Increase of 1% through 4%	10
No change	4
Decrease of 1% through 4%	11
Decrease of 5% through 9%	6
Decrease of 10% or more	6
	56

* The number is one higher than the number for which both sales and percentage of sales data are available for 1957 and 1962 since Hughes Aircraft Co., which is privately owned and does not publish financial data, furnished the requested percentage figures.
** Percentages reported by firms have been rounded to the nearest full percentage. The greatest increase reported was from 50 per cent to 88 per cent, and the sharpest decline was from 99 per cent to 67 per cent.

Table IV-12: Distribution of firms by percentage of total sales made to the Department of Defense or government in calendar years 1957 and 1962, for 58 reporting firms

Percentage of sales to DOD or government	Number of companies	
	1957	1962
90–100	13	10
80–89	5	6
70–79	5	10
60–69	5	3
50–59	1	2
40–49	3	2
30–39	2	6
20–29	5	5
10–19	4	3
0–9	14	10
	57*	57*

* Bell Aircraft Corp. is included for 1957. It does not appear among the 1962 group since Bell sold all its defense assets to Textron in 1960. Since Textron reported a substantial share of its total sales made for defense purposes in 1957 it is included for that year, although Textron did not appear on the lists of the largest prime contractors until after its acquisition of Bell's assets. Litton Industries is included in 1962, but the 1957 figure is not available.

or "typical firm" basis, the firms ranking 1 through 10 in 1955–FY 1957 stand out in their average degree of specialization in 1957; but those among the ten largest prime contractors for FY 1960–62 do not appear to be significantly different in the division of their 1962 sales from any class other than those ranking from 31 to 40. When only the prime contractors ranking below the top ten are considered, there is no evident or systematic relationship between contract rank and specialization in defense sales. Perhaps the most interesting aspect of Table IV–13 is the decline in specialization shown in both the weighted and unweighted averages within the highest ten and the increase in both these averages for those in the lowest ten.

Table IV–14 cross-classifies the major defense contractors by primary products and degree of specialization in defense sales. The relationships shown in the table throw an interesting light on the results of analysis of market structure in terms of primary products alone.

Whether a simple average indicative of the "typical" firm is used, or a weighted average more indicative of the sales experience of the primary product group as a whole, the degree of primary product group specialization in defense or government sales is positively correlated with the size of both total and average contract awards going to each group. The aircraft firms among the top 50, which accounted for by far the highest percentage of total procurement awards and had the highest average rank, are also the most highly

Table IV-13: Specialization in military sales for the calendar years 1957 and 1962, as related to size of contract awards

Rank by size of contract awards		Average percentage of total sales to Department of Defense or government	
		Unweighted	Weighted by total sales
1955–57:	1–10	73.9	45.1
	11–20	58.3	14.9
	21–30	29.7	10.5
	31–40	60.0	10.5
	41–50	35.7	11.2
FY 1960–62:	1–10	59.4	40.3
	11–20	61.3	17.6
	21–30	55.2	10.5
	31–40	33.8	22.1
	41–50	58.8	35.2

specialized in defense sales. The electronics firms come second on all three measures; Group III is third; and the petroleum refiners are lowest on all counts.

Turnover, as noted above, was substantially higher for Group III firms, and stability of awards within this group was much lower than in either the aircraft or electronics groups. The percentage of total sales going to the Department of Defense was also substantially lower for Group III firms in the aggregate, which tends to bear out part of an observation made by F. T. Moore: "It [rapid entry and exit] is due to the fact, of course, that only a few of the firms consider defense business as their sole or major line of activity; most, if not all, of them have private commercial business, but the percentage division between defense and non-defense business can vary greatly from one year to the next." [14]

In some respects the petroleum refiners appear to have suffered most from the vagaries of defense procurement. Their turnover was far more rapid than that of any other primary product group, relative to the number of firms involved. The number of petroleum refiners appearing among the top 50 shrank from six to four. The share of total procurement awards accounted for by petroleum firms among the top 50 declined from 2.8 per cent to 1.9 per cent at a time when the percentage accounted for by the top 50 as a group was increasing. Total awards for procurement of petroleum products, as indicated by awards in the fuels and lubricants procurement program, declined from $952 million in FY 1957 to $788 million in FY 1964.[15] Yet the petroleum firms faced their declining

14. *Military Procurement and Contracting*, p. 109.
15. OSD, *Military Prime Contract Awards and Subcontract Payments, July 1962–June 1963*, p. 22, and *July 1963–June 1964*, p. 22.

Table IV-14: Specialization in military and government sales for the calendar years 1957 and 1962, by primary product groups

Primary product group	Average percentage of total sales for military or government purposes			
	Unweighted		Weighted by total sales	
	1957	1962	1957	1962
I	83.8	80.1	84.3	77.6
II	46.0	51.9	22.1	24.4
III	21.1	30.9	7.3	6.8
IV	3.6	2.6	2.0	1.6

role in the defense market with outward equanimity and there were no anguished expressions of concern for their fate from Congress, unions, trade associations, or newspapers, nor were there dire warnings of the risks being taken with the nation's security through reduction in the procurement of fuels and lubricants. The refiners' attitude may be attributed to the relative unimportance of sales to the Department of Defense and to the fact that production of refined petroleum products can easily be shifted from types required by the military to those sold on civilian markets. The aircraft firms are, of course, in an almost opposite position, with a very high percentage of total sales being made to the Department of Defense and an extremely small percentage of their defense-oriented plant, equipment, and know-how readily convertible to civilian production. Thus, despite the fact that the turnover and stability experiences of Group I were the most favorable in the defense market during the cold war years, the aircraft firms have good reason for an intense concern with almost any actual or predicted change in the Department of Defense's procurement policies or shifts in the structure of the defense market. The stake of Group II firms in the defense market is second highest and that of firms in Group III is quite a bit lower.

V. CHARACTERISTICS OF DEMAND IN THE DEFENSE MARKET

A. Subsurface Features of Market Structure

Concentration, turnover, and the stability or instability of size-distribution of firms in a market are, in a sense, only the highly visible manifestations of the environment within which the market functions. Underlying immediately obvious and easily quantifiable structural factors such as those reviewed in the preceding chapters are a complex of less directly observable aspects of structure. These subsurface characteristics of the market environment are important, although not amenable to precise depiction, since they are major determinants of such readily visible features as measured concentration and turnover, since they exert a great influence on the economic performance of the market whatever the size-distribution of firms might be, and since they thus have inescapable relevance to any analysis of the likely effects of public policies designed to re-structure the market. As was noted in the Introduction, the phrase "market structure" is understood to encompass all aspects of the environment which restrict or give latitude to business decisions; therefore it is neither possible nor sensible to describe market structure in full. Rather, one must be selective and focus attention on those parts of the environment which are believed to play important explanatory roles, either independently or in interaction with one another. In the defense market there seem to be three most crucial factors: the nature of the Department of Defense's demand for military goods and services, the technological base of the market, and conditions affecting firms' entry into and exit from the market.

In one respect it is simple to discuss demand in the defense market, since it is by definition a single-customer market. Indeed, contractors and the trade press often refer to the Department of Defense simply as the "customer." Yet at the same time a meaningful description of defense demand is exceptionally difficult since the "customer" is undoubtedly one of the most complicated buyers that a private firm could conceivably face in a market, both in terms of the variety and complexity of products and services purchased and in terms of the diversity of motives underlying its demand pattern.

B. Elasticity of Demand

Both the level and composition of military spending in wartime have been viewed by previous writers as restrained primarily by limited real resources and as highly insensitive to monetary costs. T. B. Worsley, for example, noted that in time of war the government is normally prepared to exercise its powers to appropriate existing money and create new money to whatever extent it considers necessary to meet mobilization objectives. In such circumstances, he continued, over-all demand is of zero elasticity or simply not a function of price.[1] J. P. Miller, discussing procurement of individual items, observed that "the procurement officer comes to the market committed to a fairly specific bill of goods, and there is little likelihood that he will be deterred by considerations of price or related matters from proceeding to place contracts."[2] Attitudes did not change substantially with the transition from active conflict to the circumstances of the cold war, although peacetime budgets set a much sharper constraint on the over-all level of the military's effective demand. A 1955 report of the Second Hoover Commission stated:

> *Because survival is at stake, cost cannot be the primary factor.* In the words of a prominent flag officer, "our military people are not hired primarily to see how little they can get along with; they are hired primarily to seek to get enough material to meet their responsibilities."
> An Assistant Secretary of Defense said along the same line, ". . . it is not unreasonable to expect responsible military personnel to desire sufficient manpower and material at any place and at any time to minimize potential military risks. Cost, even though given active and sympathetic recognition, tends to assume a secondary role."[3]

1. *Wartime Economic Stabilization and the Efficiency of Government Procurement* (Washington: Government Printing Office, 1949). See especially the discussion of the shortcomings of the price system in wartime, pp. 4–8.

2. "Military Procurement Policies: World War II and Today," Papers and Proceedings of the Sixty-fourth Annual Meeting of the American Economic Association, *American Economic Review*, XLII (May, 1952), 455. Miller makes a similar point in "Military Procurement in Peacetime," *Harvard Business Review*, XXV (Summer, 1947), 445–446.

3. U.S. Commission on Organization of the Executive Branch of the Government (1953–1955), *Business Organization of the Department of Defense* (Washington: Government Printing Office, 1955), p. 4. Italics in original.

Secretary McNamara has frequently indicated that the continuing urgency of adequate national defense requires a continuation of the willingness to spend whatever may be required. He has customarily opened his congressional testimony on appropriations for the Department of Defense by repeating the basic instructions given him by President Kennedy when he was appointed to his present office and reiterated by President Johnson: "(1) develop the force structure necessary to meet our military requirements without regard to arbitrary budget ceilings; and (2) procure and operate this force at the lowest possible cost." [4]

The aggregate demand of the Department of Defense is, of course, the sum of the demands for a vast number of individual goods and services. An over-all demand of extremely low elasticity is perfectly consistent with very high elasticities of demand for specific items. If there are several products capable of performing closely similar functions, relative prices may be important determinants of the quantity of each purchased, even though the buyer is willing to pay almost any price to have that general class of functions performed in one way or another. Nevertheless, there are plausible reasons for assuming that the military market is a market characterized by low price elasticities of demand for the great majority of the numerous items purchased.

Essentially, a basic decision must be made to develop a level and composition of defense forces appropriate to an assumed set of threats and national objectives. Taking the threats and objectives as given, defense planners presumably seek an optimum mix of military capabilities such as firepower, megatonnage, and mobility which in turn is translated into such organizational units as Army divisions, Air Force wings, and Navy fleets of various types. The determination of quantities of specific weapons, items of support equipment, and provisioning of personnel therefore involves a host of interrelated decisions among goods which are to be used in conjunction with one another and which are sought not in their own right but as various means to a predetermined and overriding set of ends. The demand for a given good or service in the defense market is, then, very likely to be a demand for an essential good, a good

4. U.S. Congress, House Committee on Armed Services, *Hearings on Military Posture and H.R. 2440* (Washington: Government Printing Office, 1963), p. 287.

complementary to many others, and a good for which the demand derives from the fundamental and vastly larger demand for an adequate level of defense. All three of these features tend to reduce elasticity of demand for the individual good or service.

The demand curve facing any one supplier is identical with the market demand curve only if the supplier is a monopolist. The greater the number of potential suppliers, other things being equal, the less vulnerable is a buyer to excessively high price offers based on his inelastic demand. Thus, a competitive market structure alleviates the problems associated with inelastic demand. A second conceivable solution to these problems, increasing the elasticity of the buyer's demand for a specific good, may be reached through the discovery or establishment of substitute products. Both competition and substitution have long been recognized as highly desirable for efficient military procurement, and Secretary McNamara has reemphasized their crucial importance in the procurement policies and procedures established by the Department of Defense since his appointment.

Secretary McNamara is certainly not the originator of the idea that competitive procurement should be encouraged. Legislation since the time of the Civil War has made procurement by sealed competitive bids mandatory unless negotiation or sole-source procurement can be justified under some specific exemption. Courtney Johnson, Assistant Secretary of the Army for Logistics during the Eisenhower Administration, testified:

As you know, the objective in military procurement is to acquire the supplies and services required for defense purposes, where and when they are needed, at the lowest cost to the Government, price, quality, and other factors considered. It is our aim in accomplishing this objective to obtain maximum competition among prospective suppliers to the maximum extent practicable and to assure the reasonableness of the prices paid.[5]

5. U.S. Congress, Senate Committee on Armed Services, Procurement Subcommittee, *Hearings: Procurement Study* (Washington: Government Printing Office, 1960), p. 128. The phrase about acquiring required supplies and services, when and where needed, at the lowest cost to the Government—price, quality, and other factors considered—was taken almost directly from the *Armed Services Procurement Regulation*, paragraph 1–302.2 in the 1963 edition. Secretary McNamara has also paraphrased this provision in congressional testimony, as being the "Defense Department's policy now, as in the past" (U.S. Congress, House Committee on Armed Services, *Hearings on Military Posture and H.R. 2440*, p. 305).

Assistant Secretary Johnson went on to describe the Army's use of subcontracting requirements and breakout as parts of a policy to expand sources of supply.

Under Secretary McNamara the Department of Defense has made determined efforts to promote competitive procurement. In his frequent explanations to congressional committees of the "Five-year Cost Reduction Program" initiated shortly after his arrival at the Pentagon, Secretary McNamara has emphasized efforts to shift from non-competitive to competitive procurement. In testimony on Department of Defense appropriations for FY 1964, he stated, "Failure to use competition more extensively in Defense procurement in the past has not only resulted in higher prices, but has also deprived us of a broader industrial base among suppliers, both large and small." Percentage goals had been set by commodity categories, McNamara continued, for the competitive procurement volumes of each military department and for the Defense Supply Agency. "In fiscal year 1961 the overall percentage was 32.9 percent and, in fiscal year 1962, 35.6 percent. Our goal by fiscal year 1965 is to reach 39.9 percent, which will require the shifting of about $1.9 billion from sole source to competitive procurement." Savings appear substantial. "Based on our experience to date," McNamara concluded, "and the studies of the General Accounting Office, we anticipate initial price reductions on the order of 25 percent upon transferring items to competitive procurement." [6]

In the same testimony, however, the Secretary of Defense did warn that the potential of competitive procurement is limited. With the exception of off-the-shelf commercial products, the Department of Defense must take specific and sometimes costly action in order to establish competitive conditions. McNamara cited two promising lines of effort to promote competitive procurement other than simply setting departmental competitive goals: first, breakout of high-value and high-use items for separate competitive procurement; and sec-

6. U.S. Congress, House Committee on Appropriations, Subcommittee on Department of Defense Appropriations, *Hearings: Department of Defense Appropriations for 1964, Part 1, Secretary of Defense* (Washington: Government Printing Office, 1963), pp. 199–200. "Competitive procurement," as used in Secretary McNamara's figures, includes competitively negotiated procurement as well as procurement by formal advertising. The actual figure rose to 37.1 per cent in FY 1963 and to 39.1 per cent in FY 1964. U.S. Congress, Joint Economic Committee, Subcommittee on Federal Procurement and Regulation, *Hearings: Economic Impact of Federal Procurement* (Washington: Government Printing Office, 1965), p. 13.

ond, attempts to obtain competitive bids on early production runs rather than virtually automatic reliance on the developer as a sole-source supplier for at least the first volume order and quite probably for the next.

In later testimony on the FY 1964 appropriation the Chief of the Bureau of Naval Weapons, Rear Admiral K. S. Masterson, commented that the increase in competitive procurement had raised both costs and problems for the Navy. The need for compatibility among items and systems increases the Navy's problems of co-ordination as the number of contractors increases; similarly, the number of documents, drawings, and specifications which the Navy must handle increases with the number of contractors, as do the burdens of inspection and engineering support. "The thought I would like to leave you with," Admiral Masterson concluded, "is that the Government is assuming an increased burden of procurement responsibility because of the greater breakout for competition. This was formerly discharged by prime contractors in handling subcontracts. It can only be handled by a compensating increase in supporting budgets. That is, some of what you save in the procurement area has to be used in supervising this breakout." [7] Although it should be noted that prime contractors did not, presumably, perform these functions at no charge to the government, Admiral Masterson's statement does point up the problems of competitive procurement of non-standard and complex items. And the proportion of such procurement has increased.

Murray L. Weidenbaum has noted that in 1951, at the height of the Korean War, about one-fourth of military expenditures were devoted to "capital outlays" and three-fourths to "operating expenses." In 1953 the two types of expenditure were of approximately equal size, and the ratio remained almost constant at 50/50 during the following decade of the cold war. The shift is significant, Weidenbaum observes, because most procurement under operating expense categories is for standard commercial items or close substitutes for civilian-type goods and services, while procurement of the capital-outlay sort is characterized by complex weapon systems, research,

---

7. U.S. Congress, House Committee on Appropriations, Subcommittee on Department of Defense Appropriations, *Hearings: Department of Defense Appropriations for 1964, Part 5, Procurement*, p. 749.

development, and advanced technology.[8] Further, production in quantity of capital-outlay types of goods became less important with completion of the missile build-up; and more emphasis was placed on research and development. In a 1962 address to the American Rocket Society, Simon Ramo described the shift as follows:

The output is characterized by a small quantity of more expensive, "big-step-forward" apparatus, obsoleted often before it can be made in reasonable quantity, its design depending on the latest discoveries in science, even before that scientific background is well understood, and all of this in an environment in which the strategy for the utilization of technology to achieve practical goals, and the goals themselves, fluctuate rapidly.[9]

In the procurement of complex, technically advanced weapon systems with the emphasis on research and development rather than production, the Department of Defense has necessarily focused its efforts on widening its initial range of choice rather than on the promotion of competition in the purchase of delivered systems. But although increased alternatives among weapon systems may add to the efficiency of the nation's defense, the greater latitude given the Department of Defense is almost entirely confined to the earliest and cheapest phases of the procurement cycle and does little to increase the elasticity of demand over the later and more costly stages of the lifetime of a weapon system.

The essential element in the Department of Defense's present effort to increase substitutability is five-year program planning. Under this type of program planning not only are alternative feasible weapon systems evaluated in terms of cost and effectiveness, but alternative components within each conceivable system are similarly examined. Five-year program planning should not be confused with the five-year cost reduction program. "What weapons to acquire and what force levels to support are program decisions and are not

8. "The Impact of Military Procurement on American Industry," in J. A. Stockfisch (ed.), *Planning and Forecasting in the Defense Industries*, pp. 135–174.

9. *Aviation Week and Space Technology*, LXXVI (Jan. 8, 1962), 99. See also Stanford Research Institute, *The Industry-Government Aerospace Relationship*, which notes, among significant trends affecting the relationship, a "decreasing requirement for volume production of system hardware and an increasing attention to R&D" (I, 1).

included in this cost reduction program," Secretary McNamara testified.[10]

In the early days of the McNamara regime, the procedure was referred to as "program packaging." The Department of Defense budget is now broken down into nine major program packages, such as strategic retaliatory forces, continental air and missile defense forces, general purpose forces, and civil defense. For internal planning purposes, budgets are established for program packages, cutting across service lines where necessary. For example, both the Air Force's Minuteman missile and the Navy's Polaris submarine-missile system are included among the strategic retaliatory forces.[11] The planning budgets, revised periodically, consider all costs for a projected five-year period, and include personnel, training, maintenance, and support equipment as well as the major weapon systems themselves. As the concept of the program package became generally understood and accepted by defense planners and congressmen,[12] emphasis has shifted to development of five-year plans for specific program components such as individual major weapon systems. Secretary McNamara described the criteria by which program proposals submitted by the individual services are now reviewed by the Department of Defense:

> First. The mission to be accomplished.
> Second. The cost-effectiveness relationships among the various alternative means of performing the mission, and
> Third. The latest intelligence data on the capabilities of the Soviet Union and its satellites.[13]

10. U.S. Congress, House Committee on Appropriations, Subcommittee on Department of Defense Appropriations, *Hearings: Department of Defense Appropriations for 1964, Part 1, Secretary of Defense*, p. 198.

11. *Missiles and Rockets*, XII (March 25, 1963). The entire issue is devoted to the reorganization of the Department of Defense under Secretary McNamara. For an excellent and more recent discussion, see Charles J. Hitch, *Decision-Making for Defense* (Berkeley: University of California Press, 1965), esp. chap. ii, "Planning—Programming—Budgeting," pp. 21–42.

12. The advantages of such a budgetary procedure were explained and convincingly argued in Charles J. Hitch and Roland N. McKean, *The Economics of Defense in the Nuclear Age* (Cambridge: Harvard University Press, 1960). This book, reportedly, became popular reading among those concerned with procurement problems when Hitch became comptroller at the Department of Defense. See also Hitch, *Decision-Making for Defense*.

13. U.S. Congress, House Committee on Armed Services, *Hearings on Military Posture and H.R. 9751* (Washington: Government Printing Office, 1962), p. 3162.

But once the program planning or packaging stage is past, it is difficult if not impossible to retain flexible options. A decision at the Department of Defense level to go ahead on a specific major project, based on both program planning and a technical evaluation, will lead to a request for proposals issued to potential contractors by the sponsoring service. An editorial in *Aviation Week and Space Technology* noted that most of the competition in the procurement of technically complex weapon systems occurs at this point, where it "can easily degenerate into a high-powered lying contest distinguished by the most glittering technical double-talk, or a triumph of brochuremanship, where the best artwork and most elaborate charts turn the tide." [14] Secretary McNamara's concern about this problem and the Department of Defense's response to it were described as follows:

Poor planning, unrealistic schedules, unnecessary design changes, and enormous cost increases over original estimates have continuously disrupted the efficient operation of our research and development program. Most of these difficulties have resulted from inadequate prior planning and unwarranted haste in undertaking large-scale development, and even production, before we have clearly defined what is wanted and before we have clearly determined that a suitable technological basis has been developed on which to build the system. We have often paid too little attention to how a proposed weapons system would be used and what it would cost and, finally, whether the contribution the development could make to our forces would be worth the cost.

Accordingly, we are now following the practice of inaugurating large system development projects only after the completion of what we call a "program definition" phase. To the greatest extent possible, we want to do our thinking and planning before we start "bending metal." Pencils and paper, and even the feasibility testing of "pacing" components, are a lot cheaper than the termination of programs. By a more thorough and complete study and assessment of the facets of each new development—prior to major commitments—we can reduce the number of expensive projects which might otherwise later have to be reoriented, stretched out, or terminated.[15]

By the time the program definition phase is reached, however, a potential contractor or contractors must have been selected, for the

14. LXXV (Oct. 9, 1961), 17.
15. U.S. Congress, House Committee on Armed Services, *Hearings on Military Posture and H.R. 2440*, pp. 462–463.

developer must work closely with the prospective procuring agency in program definition. Harold Brown, Director of Defense Research and Engineering, described the program definition phase in the following words:

Program definition is simply the process whereby, with reasonable precision, a proposed weapon system is defined as regards its performance, schedule, and cost. . . .

Perhaps the most important feature of the program definition phase procedure is that contractors who will do the full-scale development job if it is done are funded to work with the buying agency that is one of the military departments and with one another to define critical interfaces and to settle upon the most promising approaches to the solution of mutual problems. From the resultant understanding of the real job to be done emerge greatly improved schedule and cost estimates.[16]

In a simple and orderly procurement cycle, development should culminate in the production of a prototype which could be tested and "debugged." Then orders could be placed for certain quantities of "hardware" and at this point development would end, to be followed by one or more production runs. In the real defense procurement world, stages of the procurement cycle are frequently not so readily distinguishable. As Secretary McNamara noted, in cases in which a weapon system is complex, the initial technology uncertain, questions answered only by testing, and the state of the art advanced as the system progresses, it is difficult to determine where development ends and production begins.[17] As a result, the procuring agencies often find themselves wed to a specific contractor for the life of a project. Not only is the appropriate timing of breakout for competitive procurement often difficult to ascertain, but the developer's experience in solving problems, possession of specialized plant and equipment, recruitment and specialized training of technical personnel as teams, knowledge of production techniques and costs, and history of successful production of at least a working prototype may all serve to make sole-source procurement advisable if not absolutely necessary for several production runs. Even if competitive sources are actively sought for later production runs, the original developer is very frequently in an extremely strong position

16. *Ibid.*, p. 600.

17. U.S. Congress, House Committee on Armed Services, *Hearings on Military Posture and H.R. 9751*, p. 3325.

to make not only the lowest, but also the most responsible and well-informed bid. Furthermore, the activation of a new major weapon system program establishes a host of inelastic derived demands. On this point, Secretary McNamara observed, "Each new weapon or major piece of equipment entering the operational inventory brings with it thousands of new and different items of spares and supporting equipment." [18]

It appears most reasonable to assume that the customer's demand in the defense market is quite inelastic in the vast majority of procurement actions. In addition, it seems that, in its purchases of complicated and technically advanced capital-outlay items, the Department of Defense cannot materially reduce its exposure to the possibility of excessively high prices from its suppliers either through creation of more competition on the supply side of the market or through increasing the elasticity of demand for any given item by developing substitutes. And the firms which have appeared among the 50 largest prime contractors in recent years, with the obvious exception of the petroleum refiners, are predominantly producers of such capital-outlay items. Apparently the Department of Defense's most important source of protection from excessively high pricing, apart from the patriotic motivation of its suppliers, lies in the fact that many of the larger defense firms are utterly dependent on continuation of defense business and hence on the continuing good will of the customer.

Price inelasticity is only one of the significant characteristics of demand in the defense market. Other important features which influence demand patterns are the heavy weight the customer gives to delivery time and performance, the stability of demand over time, the efficiency or lack thereof of defense agencies as purchasers, political influences on military procurement decisions, and distortions in rational procurement procedures created by congressional or business reaction to the existence of government-owned defense facilities.

C. Time and Performance as Determinants of Demand

Cost is only one factor taken into account—frequently far from the

18. U.S. Congress, Senate Subcommittee of the Committee on Appropriations, *Hearings: Department of Defense Appropriations for 1964*, p. 19.

most important one—in procurement decisions involving selection of major weapon systems. As F. M. Scherer has noted, "When additional reliability or technical performance can make the difference between success or failure on a combat mission, or when the race may go to the swiftest in terms of development lead time, military decision makers are not inclined to pinch pennies." [19] Scherer's observation is based not only on an intuitively convincing appeal to the overriding importance of quality and time advantage, but also on empirical studies made by the Weapons Acquisition Research Project of the Harvard Business School and reported in the earlier study by Peck and Scherer. An analysis of sixteen specific weapon programs led the Harvard researchers to conclude that "maximizing quality (state of the art exploitation) was slightly more important in weapons programs, than minimizing development time, which in turn was much more important than minimizing development cost." [20] The statement is perhaps misleading if read literally. The problem certainly does not involve maximizing quality, minimizing time, or minimizing cost regardless of the effect on one or both of the other two criteria, but rather involves trade-offs among the three. Still, the meaning is clear: in the decision-makers' preference functions, according to the findings of the Harvard group, quality was typically weighted somewhat more heavily than time and much more heavily than cost; i.e., a very high price would often be paid for a relatively minor improvement in performance or a slight reduction in development time.

Peck and Scherer have developed at some length the formal properties of optimization of time-quality-cost preference functions, under the assumption that trade-offs are in general capable of improving one dimension of the function only at the cost of accepting sacrifices in one or both of the others. That is, in most cases an improvement in performance characteristics requires an increase in development time, greater expenditures, or both; a "crash" program

---

19. *The Weapons Acquisition Process: Economic Incentives*, p. 32.

20. Peck and Scherer, *The Weapons Acquisition Process: An Economic Analysis*, p. 293. For a rigorous discussion of cost functions involving total planned volume of output, rate of production, the time at which the first unit is to be completed, and the length of time for which the product is to be available, see Armen Alchian, "Cost and Outputs," in Moses Abramovitz (ed.), *The Allocation of Economic Resources: Essays in Honor of Bernard Francis Haley* (Stanford: Stanford University Press, 1959), pp. 23–40.

designed to make a weapon system operational at the earliest possible moment typically involves both higher cost and the necessity of foregoing conceivable refinements and improvements. Cost may be de-emphasized, however, not just because of its relative unimportance but also because of its great uncertainty at the time trade-off decisions must be made. Peck and Scherer note a "hierarchy in the prediction errors" among the weapons developments studied by the Harvard Business School research group. The error in cost estimates was indicated by an average actual cost 3.2 times as large as estimated cost, while the average time factor, similarly expressed, was 1.36 and actual performance, although extremely difficult to measure, was more often judged to be above than below original expectations.[21]

The Harvard case studies were made on projects which were completed before the Kennedy Administration took office. It might be argued that the findings just summarized have been rendered obsolete by the great emphasis the Department of Defense has placed on cost consciousness under Secretary McNamara's intense prodding. Indeed, Peck and Scherer specifically warn the reader of this problem, and in his later volume Scherer speculates, somewhat skeptically, on the prospects for success of some of the cost-saving programs announced by mid-1963 but not yet in effect long enough for observation and evaluation. There are good reasons for skepticism or limited optimism, quite well recognized by Secretary McNamara and his colleagues.

Cost consciousness involves two conceptually separate elements, sometimes confused with each other. First, there is control and reduction of actual costs, sought through efforts of both the customer and the contractor, ranging from such things as restrictions on allowable entertainment expenses, application of value engineering techniques and elimination of "gold-plating," through attempts to achieve a more intense degree of competition in the military procure-

21. *The Weapons Acquisition Process: An Economic Analysis*, pp. 23–24. Peck and Scherer note that the sample was not representative but was biased toward larger, higher priority weapons (p. 294). However, they do state, "It is reasonable to conclude from this evidence that, on the average, the organizations charged with conducting U.S. weapons development programs have been fairly successful in meeting quality predictions, but not in meeting cost and time predictions. This conclusion is no more than common knowledge among government personnel and weapons industry members" (p. 430).

ment process. Second, and far more relevant to the role of cost in basic procurement decisions, there is the problem of estimating future cost, so that when procurement officials are exhorted to be more conscious of cost in making their decisions they can base their consideration on reasonably reliable projected figures. The program definition phase and increased use of incentive contracts, under which profit is reduced as a predetermined cost target is exceeded, are major devices for achieving this second objective. The two goals are in large part complementary, as tighter controls may eliminate uncertainties, but there is an inevitable element of conflict between the two in that there are real and unavoidable costs involved in obtaining the information necessary for better estimates, and the controls themselves are not costless.

In 1955 the Procurement Task Force of the Second Hoover Commission recorded that "shortly after its organization, the Task Force became convinced that the processes by which strategic objectives are set and strategic and logistic plans are developed are perhaps even more significant to defense procurement activities than are the processes by which supplies are actually procured by the Army, Navy, and Air Force." [22] Most of the Commission's criticisms and recommendations for change in methods of developing strategic and logistic plans were concerned with budget preparation and internal organization of the Department of Defense, but the Task Force was critical of procurement officials' preoccupation with negotiation of "fair" profit levels and the relative disregard shown for over-all costs. Yet it does not seem unreasonable or surprising to find that in bargaining sessions during the early stages of major procurement decisions both parties tended to focus attention on the contractor's fee, which could be set with precision, and that there was relatively little hard negotiation on such a nebulous figure as final total cost. Uncertainty is one factor which dulls cost consciousness; urgency has already been noted as a second. For example, in 1959 testimony on the ballistic missile program, James H. Douglas, then Secretary of the Air Force, said:

Now our concern in the Air Force is that we accomplish the development of a missile that can be produced at a relatively early date.

22. U.S. Commission on Organization of the Executive Branch of the Government (1953–1955), Task Force on Procurement, *Five Staff Papers Prepared for the Task Force on Procurement*, 3 vols. (mimeographed, dated June, 1955), p. A–1.

We would like to do it as economically as is possible under any circumstances, but I am entirely ready to express the view that in this kind of a program you have to subordinate the expenditure involved in getting these tools you need to the urgency of looking to the end result.

I think on hindsight we have nothing to apologize for with respect to how the organization was set up, with respect to its overall costs, and with respect to the relationship between, let's say, the technical direction systems engineering costs which were new in this enterprise in relation to the overall program costs.[23]

Secretary McNamara has indicated his understanding of the limitations which uncertainty and urgency place on cost consciousness. In testifying on the program definition phase in 1963 he emphasized the Department of Defense's intention of applying that procedure only to programs which would "add only marginally to our combat strength." A basic new weapon, such as the atomic or hydrogen bomb or the intercontinental ballistic missile, would be handled in a different fashion. "When the potential payoff is extremely great," he continued, "correspondingly great costs and risks are justified. But developments which meet this test are rare." [24] The Director of Defense Research and Engineering, Harold Brown, made it clear at the same hearings that the program definition phase was designed to give both the contractor and the buying agency a better idea of ultimate cost, performance, and delivery dates than had normally been the case in the past, but that truly accurate estimates were unattainable because of technological uncertainties and the likelihood of requirements changes during the development period. And in Senate hearings on the 1964 Department of Defense appropriation, Major General H. F. Bigelow stated that the need to compress development and production often necessitates placement of the first "hardware" order with the developer at the sacrifice of possible savings through competitive procurement. One major trouble with competitive procurement, General Bigelow noted, was that the buying service often could not describe precisely what it wanted during the development stage.[25]

23. U.S. Congress, House Committee on Government Operations, Military Operations Subcommittee, *Hearings: Organization and Management of Missile Programs*, p. 78.

24. U.S. Congress, House Committee on Armed Services, *Hearings on Military Posture and H.R. 2440*, p. 471.

25. U.S. Congress, Senate Subcommittee of the Committee on Appropriations, *Hearings: Department of Defense Appropriations for 1964*, pp. 783–784.

Comments from observers outside the current Department of Defense leadership confirm the impression that cost must frequently be given a lower priority than time and quality, no matter how deeply cost consciousness becomes imbedded in procurement attitudes. D. A. Kimball, chairman of the board of Aerojet-General, and former Secretary of the Navy, was quoted by the magazine *Armed Forces Management* as thoroughly in favor of Secretary McNamara's efforts at cost reduction. But, added Kimball, "If a new critical situation were to be encountered such as that found by the von Neumann committee in 1953 and 1954 when they urged the development of ICBMs on the highest priority, I should think we would have to proceed as we did in that situation and define the program as we go along." [26] In a similar interview an executive of General Electric reflected what appears to be a fairly common attitude among contractors:

From a policy standpoint, I believe the defense customer does put as much emphasis on performance as on price but in practice this literally breaks down. There is a tendency to lean more on price than is warranted. And, on the matter of price alone, I am reminded of the astronaut undergoing six Gs pressure on his way to an orbit attempt, who, when asked what he thought of, answered, "All I can think of is that every single part of this system was awarded to the lowest bidder." [27]

While other findings and observations suggest that the statement just quoted unfairly exaggerates the importance of price to the Department of Defense, and while the testimony of business executives may not be entirely free of the influence of self-interest, the two statements are illustrative of reactions rather widely stimulated among interested groups outside the Department of Defense by Secretary McNamara's efforts to bring cost under more effective control.[28]

26. "The Risks Lie in Substituting Method for Wisdom," X (Oct., 1963), 43.

27. Robert Brown, "How Much Control Do We Need?" *Armed Forces Management*, IX (May, 1963), 35–36.

28. Angry reactions to Secretary McNamara's emphasis on cost control were not confined to the business community. See New York *Times*, Sept. 5, 1963, pp. 1, 19, for an account of a speech by Admiral George W. Anderson. Admiral Anderson had just been sworn in as ambassador to Portugal after his appointment as Chief of Naval Operations had not been extended for a second term, contrary to customary practice. The New York *Times* reported that Admiral Anderson had fallen into disfavor because of "outspoken criticism of the Pentagon decision on the TFX fighter plane contract and partly because of what was regarded as his uncooperative attitude toward the civilian staff of the Secretary of Defense." In his speech, before the National

It seems eminently reasonable to conclude that the Department of Defense's demand not only has been but will remain far more responsive to the attractions of shorter development time and better performance than to lower price.

D. Stability of Demand over Time

Another characteristic of demand which is likely to be an important determinant of observed structure is the stability or instability over time of quantities demanded as a function of price or of some non-price variables. In earlier chapters it was noted that, despite radical shifts in amounts of funds devoted to the various procurement programs such as missile systems, aircraft, weapons, and tank-automotive, the size-distribution and composition of the 50 largest prime contractors had been quite stable. Established defense contractors evidently adjusted to the major procurement shift, from manned aircraft to missiles, without severe dislocations. There are two features of the defense market which may in large part explain the absence of a sharp structural shake-up. First, large defense contractors typical of those found in the lists of the largest 50 are not, basically, specialized manufacturers of given product lines such as aircraft but are, rather, organized in whole or at least in their defense divisions to meet the shifting needs of the one customer. Their fundamental products are not hardware of some particular types, but comprise research and development personnel and facilities, familiarity with new and exotic aspects of science and engineering, and skills in the co-ordination and management of the development of complex weapons. Second, since the end of the Korean War total military procurement expenditures have grown at a fairly steady pace.

If a year such as 1939 is taken as a base, defense and wartime military spending naturally appear to be incredibly unstable during two wars and an intervening period of demobilization. But, as indicated in Table I-1, in the decade following the cutback at the end of the Korean War there was a fairly steady rise in procurement awards from FY 1954 through FY 1963, interrupted by only one dip

---

Press Club, Admiral Anderson emphasized the "decisiveness of narrow edge in superior performance" for both safety and success in combat, and observed that Congress is a "sometimes forgotten partner in civilian control."

in FY 1960. The rate of increase in procurement awards exceeded that of the gross national product for the period as a whole; and over the ten years the defense market contrasted quite favorably with some major civilian markets in stability. For example, revenue from sales of automobiles and equipment for 14 major producers fell in three of the ten years (1956, 1958, and 1961), and 101 corporations in the durable goods industries with sales of over $150 million each in 1957 experienced sales declines twice, in 1958 and 1961. In neither civilian-market case was the over-all sales trend as strongly upward as it was in military sales.[29]

Department of Defense procurement awards fell rather sharply in FY 1964, by 13 per cent. By comparison, automobile and related equipment producers, with sales volume of levels similar to those for military procurement, suffered revenue declines of 14 per cent in 1956 and 21 per cent in 1958. And it is undoubtedly rare in civilian markets to have such an elaborate early warning system as that which exists in the defense market. Each year extended hearings are held in both houses of Congress on the Department of Defense appropriation for the coming fiscal year, and the record of these hearings is published quite promptly. In recent years procurement alone has merited a separate volume of some five hundred or more pages in the *Hearings* of the House Subcommittee on Department of Defense Appropriations, with amounts requested for quite finely subdivided categories published in full, subject to occasional security deletions. Procurement ultimately takes place under authorizations contained in the federal budget. Defense officials are continuously engaged in efforts to publicize their latest estimates on procurement levels and composition for future years in voluminous testimony before various congressional committees, press conferences, speeches, interviews for the numerous trade magazines, both public and private conferences with representatives of contractors, and occasional lavish meetings with leaders of the defense industry in such resort areas as Williamsburg, Virginia, or Monterey, California. Thus, with the end of the missile build-up, an expected leveling off and 5 per cent decline in aerospace procurement through 1970 was widely reported in 1963 and 1964; the expansion of the Army

29. U.S. Department of Commerce, Bureau of the Census, *Statistical Abstract of the United States* (Washington: Government Printing Office, various dates).

ground forces, emphasis on limited non-nuclear war and the subsequent increase in demand for tactical weapons were publicized from the beginning of the Kennedy Administration; and at the time of this writing, defense officials are predicting stepped-up procurement in response to the growing needs of the Vietnamese conflict but are warning that the increase will in all probability be moderate. The *Wall Street Journal* of November 3, 1965, contained an article on the Army's most recent five-year program package, as revised to respond to the intensified conflict in Vietnam, including a "shopping list" broken down by major items, and estimated procurement spending for each item.[30] Finally, five-year program planning and use of the program definition phase will, in the future, reduce still further the uncertainties faced by major weapon systems contractors.

It would seem more appropriate to the basic technical and managerial nature of the major contractors to consider stability of demand in the defense market from the viewpoint of over-all procurement, rather than by individual products. On this basis, demand during the cold war would more aptly be described as stable than unstable; and such stability on the part of the customer surely contributed to structural stability on the supply side of the market. It should be emphasized, however, that an ex post showing of stability is irrelevant as an indication of the amount of risk faced by contractors who certainly could not discount, ex ante, either a general disarmament agreement or the outbreak of a full-fledged war at any time during the period. But expectations of a sudden and unpredictable increase in demand must have outweighed expectations of a similarly sudden collapse of the market for most contractors during most of the decade.

E. Factors Impeding Rational Choice

A final set of characteristics to be considered is the extent to which demand in the military market is influenced by factors that impede rational choice, with "rational" understood in the customary economic sense as relating to the logic of means employed to a given end without any judgment as to the wisdom of the end itself. Three such factors which have been of concern are the inefficiency of de-

30. Pp. 1, 12.

fense agencies as purchasers, the role of political considerations in procurement decisions, and the criteria for choice between use of facilities and equipment owned by the government and those owned by contractors. All three areas are subject to controversy, and a strong caveat is a necessary prelude to any discussion of them: there may be substantial differences between published criticisms and justifications on the one hand and, on the other, the facts of specific cases which are known only to those directly engaged and even then are often seen from an imperfect perspective.

Rear Admiral M. L. Ring, at the time Acting Vice Chairman for Supply Management of the Munitions Board, described vividly the problems which various procurement policies posed for the individual procurement officer in 1952 testimony:

Congress has enunciated a small business policy. Mr. Wilson has issued a directive which is known as ODM directive No. 4, which says, "Let's give special attention to distressed areas." We have a big program of off-shore procurement. We have a statute called the Buy-American Act. We have today, I will recite them if you want me to, at least 14 major policies under which your purchasing officer today is working, and I don't care how good a catalogue he has and how good a specification, there are factors which are going to affect every single procurement that is made. Yes, you have price control. Yes, you have people who would say, "Negotiate all your contracts so that you can direct your contracts to small business or to a distressed area." You have also got a committee of this House, a committee of the Senate, select committees on small business, which say, "Formal advertising and competitive buying is the best way for a small-business man to get in." If you would ask me today, if I were a purchasing agent, which one of these directives I would follow, I would tell your [sic], sir, that I would follow the one on which the pressure was greatest right now, and then duck.[31]

Yet defense procurement policies cannot entirely escape inconsistencies and will inevitably give an impression of inefficiency. A basic problem is the lack of specific objectives which can yield observable standards of efficiency, such as profit provides for a business firm. When one is expected to manage an existing establishment economically and at the same time be prepared for smooth expansion in the event of mobilization, when it is not clear whether present

31. U.S. Congress, House Committee on Armed Services, *Hearings Before the Special Subcommittee on Procurement: Waste in Defense Department Procurement Including Testimony on H.R. 1033, Cataloguing and Standardization and H.R. 7405* (Washington: Government Printing Office, 1952), p. 3215.

efficiency is measured by the current level of performance of procurement officers or by the intensiveness and extensiveness of training being received by personnel exposed to a number of responsibilities through rotation, and when objectives of procurement may include maintenance of a mobilization base and geographical dispersion of defense facilities as well as low cost of current equipment, it is neither surprising nor of much concern that diligent investigators can unearth twenty-year supplies of shoelaces, shortages of certain spare parts, or hand tools acquired at prices considerably above those found for similar items in retail hardware stores. Such findings should not obscure the more important fact that a great deal of progress has been made between the 1949 formation of the Department of Defense and the period of the McNamara reforms. The task of developing and administering appropriate procurement policies has, furthermore, been accomplished in the face of previously unknown conditions of protracted cold war, the subsequent rise of what is now known as the "military-industrial complex," and the difficulties in recruiting and maintaining able procurement and negotiating personnel during peacetime.[32]

Efforts to increase efficiency and to establish Department of Defense procurement practices geared to the needs of the cold war did

32. Military officers find it difficult to build up adequate experience because they are frequently faced with rotation, and it has been said that career officers generally believe that a procurement post is less likely to lead to promotion than most other military assignments. Under Civil Service pay scales and regulations, it is difficult for the Department of Defense to compete with industry for the best civilians. Yet both within and outside of the Department of Defense one finds spirited defense of the caliber of procurement personnel. For example, the U.S. Commission on Organization of the Executive Branch of the Government (1953–1955) , Task Force on Procurement, *Report on Military Procurement* (Washington: Government Printing Office, 1955) , p. 101, observed, on the basis of a questionnaire returned by 226 contractors, "The great majority of Government employees are competent, industrious and dedicated to the interests of the United States. The personal and professional shortcomings in the performance of government contracting personnel lie more in the personnel system than in the individual employee" (p. 101). In specific reference to the abilities of procurement officials and negotiators, Secretary McNamara has stated that "the quality of the defense business operation is quite as good as that of any private business in the country" (*Armed Forces Management*, VII [June, 1961], 38). Assistant Secretary of the Air Force (Materiel) Joseph S. Imirie testified in 1963 that he had received complaints from industry that "their high-level people were not treated with sufficient deference by the Air Force personnel with whom they have to negotiate." If the procurement personnel were not good, Imirie pointed out, the services would not be plagued with the problem of having them hired away by industry. "In comparing them to outsiders I have known," Imirie concluded, "I would pretty well rather have the Air Force people" (U.S. Congress, House Committee on Appropriations, Subcommittee on Department of Defense Appropriations, *Hearings: Department of Defense Appropriations for 1964, Part 5, Procurement*, pp. 481–482) .

not begin with Secretary McNamara, as he has repeatedly acknowledged. "Many of the actions we have taken during the last two years," he stated, "to improve the management of our procurement and logistics operations were recommended by this and other committees of the Congress and by various non-governmental committees and commissions, 10 and even 15 years ago." [33] As an example, Secretary McNamara noted that establishment of the Army Technical Services had been recommended by Secretary of Defense Robert Lovett in 1952. There are numerous other examples that could have been cited, including efforts within the Department of Defense under a Republican administration. The weapon system approach to major development and production programs evolved during the fifties. During the Eisenhower Administration both General Maxwell Taylor and Bureau of the Budget Director Maurice Stans advocated something quite similar to program package planning. The Air Force, over rather harsh criticism from the Renegotiation Board and influential congressmen, began making extensive use of incentive contracts in the fifties. McNamara's predecessor, Secretary of Defense Thomas Gates, unleashed the first vigorous offensive in the campaign Secretary McNamara inherited and carried on to re-establish civilian control at the Pentagon. The Defense Reorganization Act of 1958 authorized consolidation of supply activities common to more than one service, following the establishment of several single supply managers within individual services under the regime of Charles E. Wilson. Substantial progress was made in developing a uniform Federal Supply Catalogue to meet the problem of duplication in procurement and inventory holdings. And Charles J. Hitch, in describing the changes he had put into effect in the Office of the Comptroller, stated, "First I want to make clear that we are not starting this task from scratch. No one who has studied the budgetary process as it existed in the War and Navy Departments at the end of World War II can help but be impressed by the tremendous progress achieved since that time." [34]

Secretary McNamara's greatest contribution to the Department of Defense, apparently, was not as an innovator but as a highly effective administrator. It in no way downgrades his role to point out that he

33. *Aviation Week and Space Technology*, LXXVIII (April 8, 1963), 33.
34. *Armed Forces Management*, VIII (Nov., 1961), 95.

recognized and seized upon promising proposals, most of which had been in circulation for some time, and overcame formidable obstacles in either putting them into effect for the first time or in revitalizing those which had already been instituted. The need for a person of McNamara's particular abilities had been highlighted when, in 1956, Secretary of Defense Charles E. Wilson referred sarcastically to the Second Hoover Commission as "so much benefit of free service," and told a congressional committee, "I really do not need advice as much as I need some doers." [35]

Progress both before and during the McNamara regime was fairly evaluated in an article by the former Army Chief of Staff, General G. H. Decker. After praising the Chairman of the House Subcommittee on Department of Defense Appropriations, Representative George H. Mahon, for his role in urging new budgetary procedures similar to the Five-year Force Structure Program in 1959 and 1960, General Decker continued:

Within the Department of the Army, the period 1950–1962 probably witnessed more changes in management procedures than perhaps were instituted throughout the previous history of the Army. Many of the techniques have been of great value, while others, like ill-fated missiles, never really got off the launching pad. . . .

Certainly the most noteworthy of recent actions taken in pursuit of improved management has been the initiation by Secretary McNamara and his assistants, principally Assistant Secretary Charles Hitch, of a new defense management system. . . .

As head of the Defense Department he [McNamara] was in the position to light the fuse to long circulating ideas.[36]

Military demand is also influenced by political pressures. As noted by a perceptive editorial in the magazine *Missiles and Rockets,* the word "political" can have many meanings:

It can take the purely partisan form of an effort to buy votes. It can refer to an attempt to spread government procurement into depressed areas. It can express the need to give a program, such as the national space program, the broad base across the nation which will assure its fullest support in Congress. Or it can include the international effects of domestic procurement decisions. . . .

35. U.S. Congress, House Committee on Appropriations, Subcommittee on Department of Defense Appropriations, *Hearings: Department of Defense Appropriations for 1957, Procurement Policies and Practices of the Department of Defense,* pp. 189–190.

36. "Costing Strategy," *Armed Forces Management,* IX (Sept., 1963), 36–37.

It also is true that many weapon systems have become so costly that the decision to procure or not procure can alter the entire national budget picture. The impact of such procurement decisions must be weighed from a national standpoint. Only the White House can do this, not the Dept. of Defense.

It is therefore plain—for reasons both valid and invalid—that politics play a major role today in procurement decisions.[37]

The over-all level of defense procurement may be affected by political rather than military considerations. Certainly, indications that this might occur abound in the record of the 1960 elections, in which the putative "missile gap" figured so prominently. The 1960 volumes of *Missiles and Rockets* repeatedly emphasized the editors' convictions that the coming election would have a great impact on the aerospace industry. As a somewhat extreme example, the magazine ran the following note in April of 1960:

Moneyman for Symington . . . presidential campaign will be Oklahoman Hal Stewart, who was an assistant AF secretary when Symington was boss of the Air Force. Lots of big oil and defense industry tie-in here. Ed Hogan, former Air Force Association publicist now with GE's Evandale group, has been offered an important spot in the Symington publicity setup.[38]

It is utterly impossible to assess the effect of this sort of political influence on the total amount spent for procurement. The issue is far beyond the scope of the present study. In the absence of access to classified information and with a painful sense of bewilderment in the face of concepts such as credibility, overkill, and megatonnage, I would consider it presumptuous on my part to attempt any evaluation of deficiencies or excesses in the over-all state of the nation's defenses,[39] or to express any opinion of the correctness or sincerity of political judgments on the defense budget. There is, I believe, a present consensus and certainly a national tradition that defense policy should not be determined solely or even predominantly by military authorities; and once the issue is drawn into political debate it is not surprising that business interests support men of sympathetic views.

37. "Politics and Procurement," XII (March 4, 1963) , 58.
38. VI (April 4, 1960) , 9.
39. For an impassioned but carefully developed argument that the level of military spending in the United States has been and is grossly excessive, see Seymour Melman, *Our Depleted Society* (New York: Holt, Rinehart and Winston, 1965) .

Given the size of the budget and a set of national objectives, determined wisely or unwisely through some sort of interplay of strategic and political considerations, the Department of Defense has the responsibility of ascertaining the composition of forces and weapons which will most effectively serve these objectives. At this administrative level, the influence of politics is less defensible. Charges have been made that military bases are located and contracts placed in certain states in order to win the favor of influential congressmen, that contractors and politicians are able to reverse or delay decisions to cut back or cancel programs, that contracts are awarded to reward supporters of the political party in power and to punish its opponents, that "insiders" are in a position to get awards for their clients through "influence peddling," that procurement is unduly influenced by a host of retired military officers who are either on the payrolls of major contractors or lobbying for industry as Washington representatives of various trade and industry associations, and that a more insidious pressure is put on active procurement officials by tempting them with lush positions in private industry after retirement. One example, particularly damning because of the source, came out of the extensive TFX hearings of 1963, when a 1960 memorandum written by Deputy Secretary of Defense Roswell L. Gilpatric was publicized. Gilpatric, then a private lawyer, had noted that "political considerations" might play a role in the TFX source selection and added, "Nixon for California v. Johnson for Texas." [40] And we must note the now famous warning in President Eisenhower's farewell address: "In the councils of Government, we must guard against the acquisition of unwarranted influence, whether sought or unsought, by the military-industrial complex. The potential for the disastrous rise of misplaced power exists and will persist." [41]

The extent of political influence on procurement decisions is, however, debatable. The TFX hearings eventually focused on and emphasized the subject of controversy between military source selection boards and civilian defense authorities and, indeed, gave the impression that internal disagreements on selection criteria were far

40. New York *Times,* Nov. 20, 1963, p. 18.
41. "Liberty Is at Stake: Farewell Address by Dwight D. Eisenhower, President of the United States," *Vital Speeches of the Day,* XXVII (Feb. 1, 1961), 229.

more important than any alleged political favoritism. Fred J. Cook, in his harshly critical study, *The Warfare State,* refers to "inevitable suspicions of influence peddling." But in the next sentence Cook concedes, with some evident frustration, that "so far, proof is lacking, though the grounds for suspicion seem more than ample." [42] Charges of political influence have been vehemently denied. In response to an editorial in *Missiles and Rockets* charging that "it is no secret" that "the White House" was increasingly interfering in contract awards, Secretary McNamara replied, "I cannot speak for NASA contracts, but there is absolutely no truth in it from a Defense Department point of view. I think it is well nigh libelous for a magazine to print it. I would like to see one shred of evidence that supports it. . . . We will not tolerate any interference whatsoever with the contracting procedure in the Defense Department. To the best of my knowledge, we have none." [43] Both Secretary McNamara and President Kennedy indicated that the influence of the military-industrial complex had been exaggerated. "The potential dangers have been overstated," according to Secretary McNamara.[44] In a 1963 television interview with three newsmen, President Kennedy was asked about the threat posed by the complex. He replied that there were, of course, pressures because of the number of jobs affected by any cancellation and then added, "But I must say as of today I don't feel that the pressure on us is excessive." [45]

Official denials are hardly surprising. But not all the trade journals support the position of *Missiles and Rockets* on the importance of political factors. An editorial in *Aerospace Management,* criticizing the congressional campaigns of 1962, commented that "claims were made by both parties as though they, the politicians, were the sole marketing and technical arm of the aerospace industry. Unfortunately, the companies made no claim to the contrary to set the record straight." The editorial went on to state that in reality contracts are based on firms' capabilities and that the problem has no basis in fact, but is actually one of public impression.[46] One piece

42. *The Warfare State* (New York: Macmillan, 1962), p. 22.
43. U.S. Congress, House Committee on Appropriations, Subcommittee on Department of Defense Appropriations, *Hearings: Department of Defense Appropriations for 1964, Part 1, Secretary of Defense,* pp. 502–503.
44. *Aviation Week and Space Technology,* LXXVIII (April 29, 1963), 21.
45. *Ibid.* (Jan. 7, 1963), p. 91.
46. "Politics, Progress, and Profits," *Aerospace Management,* V (Dec., 1962), 5.

of objective evidence suggesting the lack of power of the military-industrial complex and industry's lobbyists is the failure, despite persistent effort, to eliminate provisions for renegotiation of "excessive" profits on defense contracts.

Large sums of money and vital regional interests are involved in defense procurement. It would be absurd to deny that powerful interests seek to influence the Department of Defense. It is, indeed, only reasonable to assume that there is some actual dishonesty in a market of such size. But while the record of charges and denials is certainly not conducive to complacency, I have found no evidence that is inconsistent with President Kennedy's assessment that the pressures are not excessive. The political environment does not appear to be incompatible with efficient management of procurement by the Department of Defense, nor with the assumption that the fortunes of the major defense contractors are overwhelmingly the result of their relative efficiencies and of objective procurement decisions by the customer rather than political favoritism.

Another group of "political" influences comprises the restraints placed on procurement decisions by law or by the *Armed Services Procurement Regulation* for purposes of using military procurement to help achieve non-military political objectives. The most important of these restraints are the following: preference must be given to small business and labor surplus areas; contractors must agree not to practice racial or religious discrimination in their hiring and promotion policies; preference must be given to American suppliers by the Department of Defense and to American shipping by contractors and the Department of Defense alike; and contractors must pay "prevailing" wage rates as determined by the Secretary of Labor on work done under contract. Prime contractors must in turn impose similar restrictions on their subcontractors. These provisions undoubtedly influence selection of contractors, and doubtless affect decisions by firms on whether or not to enter the defense market. But they probably have only a very slight effect on decisions as to what to buy and on prices paid. Every appropriation approved by the Congress in recent years has included a prohibition against payment of premium prices to small businesses or to firms in distressed areas. The *Armed Services Procurement Regulation,* accordingly, contains provisions dealing with small-business and labor-surplus-area set-asides which forbid payment of a set-aside price above the highest price paid on the non-set-aside portion of a procurement. Only partial set-asides are permitted for labor-surplus areas and distressed industries, but an entire procurement action may be set aside for small business.[47] As Assistant Secretary of Defense T. D. Morris pointed out, it is possible that higher prices are paid under total set-asides for small business than would be the case if larger firms were permitted to compete, but total set-asides are permitted by the regulations only in cases in which it is certified that fair and reasonable prices can be anticipated because of competition.[48] The restrictions on price differentials contained in annual appropriations have been welcomed by the Department of Defense. Secretary McNamara has spoken in favor of the prohibition,[49] and a defense official interviewed in connection with this study stated that the ban on price premiums is regarded within the Department of Defense as making it quite possible to reconcile efficient procurement with the non-defense objectives sought by Congress.

Controversies surrounding the use of government-owned plant and equipment have also influenced procurement. Table V-1 indicates the number and value of government-owned plants in mid-1963, after disposal of fifty-five plants during the first two years of the Kennedy Administration.[50] The disposal program has evidently slowed down a good deal, for in April of 1965 a Department of Defense statement referred to the sixty-three plants disposed of "during the past 4 years." [51]

The great majority of government-owned facilities were constructed to meet emergency needs and to draw firms into military work during World War II and the Korean War. In 1960 A. J. Racusin, of the Office of the Assistant Secretary of the Air Force for Materiel, testified that the Air Force had invested in plant and equipment because experience had shown that when there was a

47. *Armed Services Procurement Regulation*, 1963 edition, paragraphs 1–700 to 1–708, and 1–800 to 1–806.
48. U.S. Congress, House Committee on Appropriations, Subcommittee on Department of Defense Appropriations, *Hearings: Department of Defense Appropriations for 1964, Part 5, Procurement*, p. 136.
49. *Ibid., Part 1, Secretary of Defense*, p. 107.
50. *Ibid., Part 5, Procurement*, p. 161.
51. U.S. Congress, Joint Economic Committee, Subcommittee on Federal Procurement and Regulation, *Hearings: Economic Impact of Federal Procurement*, p. 46.

high degree of risk involved potential contractors were not interested in investing in facilities. The same firms, Racusin continued, were very interested in bidding on contracts which called for the government to furnish facilities.[52] It is an elementary principle of economics and sound business practice that previously incurred and irrevocable costs are irrelevant to current operating decisions. The government-owned facilities do exist, whether or not they should have been acquired in the first place and regardless of the past public investment in them; if the objective is economic rationality, only prospective costs and returns should be taken into account in determining whether to hold the facilities, sell them to private firms, or scrap them. Similarly, one should ignore sunk or irretrievable costs which are not affected by production in making an economic decision whether a particular job should be done in a government-owned plant or one owned by a contractor. The General Accounting Office has recognized the applicability of this principle in respect to government-owned, government-operated (GOGO) facilities. In computing costs of production in GOGO plants, the

52. U.S. Congress, House Committee on Armed Services, Special Subcommittee on Procurement Practices of the Department of Defense, *Hearings Pursuant to Section 4, Public Law 86–89* (Washington: Government Printing Office, 1960), p. 379.

Table V-1: Government-owned industrial plants, both government and contractor operated, as of March 26, 1963

Major commodity area	Number of plants	Government investment ($ millions) *
Aircraft and engine production and maintenance	29	$881.6
Munitions (ammunition and explosives) production and maintenance	50	2,465.3
Weapons (guns, tanks, etc.) production and maintenance	18	694.5
Missile production and maintenance	19	647.2
Ship construction, repair and maintenance	21	1,622.0
Electronic manufacture	10	79.4
Other miscellaneous commodity areas	43	1,050.3
Total	190	$7,440.3

* Includes both the plants and installed production tools and equipment therein.
Source: U.S. Congress, House Committee on Appropriations, Subcommittee on Department of Defense Appropriations, *Hearings: Department of Defense Appropriations for 1964, Part 5, Procurement* (Washington: Government Printing Office, 1963), p. 117.

General Accounting Office forbids inclusion of interest on government capital, hypothetical taxes, and depreciation unless the Secretary of Defense is considering disposing of the facility in the event it is not used. Quite rightly, only the costs added because of production are to be compared with prices to be paid for similar work which might be done in privately-owned facilities.[53]

Yet the use of government-owned plant and equipment is not determined by economic considerations alone. Government competition with private enterprise raises issues of ideology and equity which have been of concern to congressional committees since before World War II.[54] Specific restrictions have been imposed by law and regulation on the division of work between naval and private shipyards, and the uses of military air and sea transport services have been limited where contractual arrangements with commercial carriers are available as alternatives. The Bureau of the Budget has in effect a statement of policy, issued during Eisenhower's presidency but indorsed by the Kennedy Administration, which states, "It is the general policy of the administration that the Federal Government will not start or carry on any commercial-industrial activity to provide a service or product for its own uses if such product or service can be procured from private enterprise through ordinary business channels." An exception to this policy on the basis of comparative costs is to be made only when the cost of procurement from private sources is "relatively large and disproportionately higher." [55]

The Department of Defense, in reaction to pressures against its commercial activities, has sought for several years to control not only its holdings but also its acquisition of government-owned

53. U.S. Congress, House Committee on Appropriations, Subcommittee on Department of Defense Appropriations, *Hearings: Department of Defense Appropriations for 1962, Part 5, Procurement* (Washington: Government Printing Office, 1961), p. 53.

54. For a summary of previous hearings and investigations of both the House and Senate Committees on Government Operations and a discussion of the issues, see U.S. Congress, Senate Committee on Government Operations, *Government Competition with Free Enterprise* (Washington: Government Printing Office, 1963). For an account of congressional concern before World War II, especially the activities of the House Special Committee to Investigate Government Competition with Private Enterprise (the Shannon Committee), formed in 1932, see H. P. Yoshpe and M. V. Massen, *Procurement Policies and Procedures in the Quartermaster Corps during World War II,* Quartermaster Corps Historical Studies, No. 17 (Washington: Government Printing Office, 1947), pp. 12–18.

55. Bureau of the Budget Bulletin No. 60–2, dated Sept. 21, 1959, paragraphs 2 and 3B.

facilities.[56] In March of 1963 Deputy Secretary of Defense Gilpatric issued a directive to the effect that "no commercial or industrial activities within the United States will be started or continued in operation under military control" unless a "clear determination" was made that "compelling reason" existed.[57] In the name of "fairness" to contractors without government-owned plant and equipment, the *Armed Services Procurement Regulation* contains a section providing that, while government-owned facilities may be made available to a firm without charge if it is to the government's advantage to do so, no contractor or subcontractor is to be given a competitive advantage thereby. Any advantage in pricing must be eliminated by charging a rental fee based on "sound commercial principles," including prevailing rates, or by adding such an amount to the contractor's proposed price in evaluating bids.[58] The Department of Defense is thus hindered in making most effective use of government-owned, contractor-operated (GOCO) property, since a price differential on any contract greater than the rental the department could actually earn by leasing the property—in most cases, presumably, for less than prevailing rents—would provide a rational cost justification for award of the contract to the occupant of the government-owned property. These *Armed Services Procurement Regulation* provisions are in striking contrast to those of the General Accounting Office, noted above, which require incremental cost computations on the operations of GOCO facilities. However, the amount of GOCO plant and equipment is still being reduced. Critics should be aware that to the extent that procurement rules preclude purely economic decisions they operate in favor of private

56. While conceding that, in general, private enterprise should be used to the maximum possible extent, the Department of Defense has not been consistently successful in eliminating its ownership of productive facilities, as indicated by the following table ($ millions):

	FY 1960	FY 1961	FY 1962	FY 1963
Real property	$ 46.1	$ 61.7	$ 41.5	$ 28.5
Production equipment	81.2	123.9	223.7	215.4
Other	15.9	21.7	7.9	5.4
Total	$143.2	$207.3	$273.1	$249.3

(*Source:* U.S. Congress, House Committee on Appropriations, Subcommittee on Department of Defense Appropriations, *Hearings: Department of Defense Appropriations for 1963, Part 4, Procurement*, p. 578).

57. Department of Defense Directive No. 4100.15, dated March 5, 1963, Section IV.
58. *Armed Services Procurement Regulation*, 1963 edition, paragraph 13-407.

investment rather than to its detriment. At the same time, the government's reluctance to provide plant and equipment raises a barrier to entry into the defense market.

F. Summary

Demand in the defense market under cold war conditions is usually inelastic, frequently responsive to relatively small but very costly improvements in time and quality, and relatively stable in the most meaningful over-all sense. Defense demand does not reflect a set of optimal solutions to strategic and tactical problems; but the distorting effects of internal inefficiencies, improper political pressures, and government ownership of plant and equipment appear to be of only minor importance as determinants of the structure of the market.

VI. INFLUENCES OF ADVANCED TECHNOLOGY ON THE DEFENSE MARKET

A. The Pervasive Role of Advanced Technology

One of the most distinguishing characteristics of the defense market is the pervasive and crucial role of highly advanced and complex technology. There are civilian industries in which research and technological advance are vital to the fortunes of individual firms, and in which price competition is less significant to the industry's structure and performance than are competitive efforts to develop new products and more efficient methods of production. But it is highly unlikely that any sizeable civilian market could be found which is so marked by the impact of modern technology as is the defense market. In three respects, the technological base of the defense market seems to distinguish it from others.

First, the percentage of procurement money going to experimental, development, test, and research work (EDTR) is much higher than research and development (R & D) as a percentage of sales in civilian industries.[1] In FY 1960 EDTR contracts accounted for 25.6 per cent of all military procurement, by dollar volume, while in the calendar year 1960, for the entire economy, funds committed to R & D amounted to 4.3 per cent of net sales of those manufacturing concerns performing R & D. Company-financed R & D in that year averaged only 1.8 per cent of net sales; virtually all of the remainder, some 58 per cent of total R & D spending in the nation, was financed by the federal government. The highest percentage figures for company-financed R & D in 1960, by major industry groups, were 4.3 per cent of net sales for professional and scientific instruments, followed by 3.7 per cent for electrical equipment and communications, and 3.6 per cent for chemicals and allied products.

1. "R & D" has become a standard abbreviation for research and development. It will be so used throughout the text. However, to distinguish technological activities in civilian-oriented industries from those performed under contract in the defense market, the term "R & D" will be confined to the former. In reference to military contracts, "EDTR" will be used. This distinction should be of some help in avoiding confusion in the following discussion; it has, as well, the dubious advantage of conforming with current jargon.

To consider for comparison an industry which illustrates the role of the Department of Defense in R & D, the aircraft and missiles industry spent 22.5 per cent of net sales on R & D of which a little over one-tenth, or 2.6 per cent of net sales, was company-financed.[2]

Second, technological advance is clearly a means to an end in civilian markets. Commercial R & D pays off only after new products are sold or cheaper processes of production are installed. In the military market, by contrast, technological advance is frequently viewed as more of an end in itself. For example, EDTR work which supplied this nation with the demonstrated ability to create an effective defense against a fleet of nuclear-armed orbiting satellites (perhaps necessarily including production of one prototype to actually destroy one of our own satellites as a visible and convincing demonstration) might discourage potential enemies from attempting to develop such a satellite system and thus obviate the need on our part for further production of the defensive device. In such a case, capability rather than operating hardware is really the end product. Further, technical superiority in weapons is a far more overriding objective than superiority in civilian markets. A civilian-oriented business firm which has just developed a product will consider costs of production and marketing, the degree to which its potential product is superior to its competitors' goods, and the impact of the new product on sales of its older products; and on the basis of such considerations the firm will consider the various prices and rates of output and may or may not decide to put the product on the market. If the decision is to produce, it is often the case that the most profitable price, output, and timing of market penetration are such that competitors are still able to market less advanced products, although possibly in lower volume than before and at a reduced price. The Department of Defense cannot afford the luxury of decisions based on such cost-revenue calculations—despite Secretary McNamara's emphasis on cost-effectiveness analysis—when a small advantage must often be viewed as decisive. A new weapon system, though only slightly superior to its predecessor, may render similar systems of our own and of the "competitor," along with defensive

2. National Science Foundation, *Research and Development in Industry 1960: Final Report on a Survey of R & D Funds and R & D Scientists and Engineers* (Washington: Government Printing Office, 1963), pp. 11, 40, 41.

or offensive counter-weapons, completely obsolete almost overnight. Superiority cannot be evaluated by such relative measures as increased market share or rate of profit when the competitor is a potential enemy and the ultimate pay-off and penalty to be considered are the promise of absolute victory and the threat of utter defeat.

Third, not only does EDTR take an extremely high portion of the procurement budget, but the ensuing production of sophisticated weapons also demands a very high level of technical skill. Men on production lines must cope with minute tolerances, exotic and dangerous materials, and complexities of circuitry, assembly, and testing that are rarely if ever met in the manufacture of civilian goods. The demands for reliability are extraordinarily severe, since the life of an operator or the successful mission of a multi-million-dollar piece of equipment may hinge on the proper performance of every one of hundreds or thousands of small components.

The pervasive influence of complex technology appears to be relevant to the present study of the structure of the defense market in two major respects: technological considerations have had direct and in most cases probably unavoidable influences on important features of market structure and behavior; and the Department of Defense has reacted to these aspects of the market by establishing procurement policies which have further differentiated military and civilian purchasing and have raised a new set of problems. The performance of the market, in terms of both its own military functions and its impact on the rest of the economy, has thereby been profoundly affected by the imperatives of its advanced technology.

B. Effects of Advanced Technology on Structure and Behavior

Turning first to the direct influences on market structure and behavior, technological forces appear to have promoted concentration, both hindered and modified the competitive behavior of defense firms, and created a singular relationship between the customer and its suppliers.

R & D, whether civilian or military, has long been viewed as both a cause of and justification for very large firms and market concentration.[3] Some of the contentions relating to civilian industry are irrelevant to the military market. It has been argued, for example, that R & D expenditures are inherently fraught with risk and that the principles of probability therefore favor large firms capable of spreading the risk over a large number of projects. But EDTR contracts issued by the armed services are almost invariably of a cost-reimbursement type, whether with a fixed or an incentive fee; and the specific project, once contracted for, is therefore virtually riskless from the viewpoint of the firm. In civilian markets, a newly developed product must be sold, and another line of argument points out that a firm with a nationwide distribution system and a large budget for advertising and selling expenditures has an advantage over an individual or a small firm with an equally good product. Past monopolistic profits have been credited with providing funds for performance of R & D and insurance against failure, and the prospect of monopolistic earnings is sometimes considered an additional incentive to innovative activity. None of these considerations as customarily formulated apply to the defense market since the government, which is the only customer, normally specifies the desired results and its interest in the product in the original contract, and thus eliminates the need for the sort of marketing done in civilian markets. Furthermore, the government, which is in a position to assure adequate funding through progress payments, assumes the bulk of the risk of failure on an individual contract, negoti-

3. It is not appropriate to this study to enter into a protracted discussion of the merits of this view, nor to survey the relevant literature. My own opinions on the relationship between modern R & D and industrial concentration were expressed in *Antitrust and the Changing Corporation* (Durham, N.C.: Duke University Press, 1961), pp. 186–197.

The most influential work in this area is without question Joseph A. Schumpeter, *Capitalism, Socialism, and Democracy* (New York: Harper, 1942). Views similar to but not identical with Schumpeter's were expressed in John K. Galbraith, *American Capitalism: The Concept of Countervailing Power* (Boston: Houghton Mifflin, 1952), and A. A. Berle, *The 20th Century Capitalist Revolution* (New York: Harcourt, Brace, 1954). A somewhat more skeptical position is taken by John Jewkes, David Sawers, and Richard Stillerman, *The Sources of Invention* (London: Macmillan, 1958), esp. pp. 156–178.

In recent years data published by the National Science Foundation have made possible empirical studies of the association between R & D and industrial structure. These studies do not show as strong a relationship between size and concentration on the one hand and R & D effort on the other as the Schumpeterian view would predict. See, for example, J. S. Worley, "Industrial Research and the New Competition," *Journal of Political Economy*, LXIX (April, 1961), 183–186, and Daniel Hamberg, "Size of Firm, Oligopoly, and Research: The Evidence," *Canadian Journal of Economics and Political Science*, XXX (Feb., 1964), 62–75.

ates the fee, and in most contracts is prepared to renegotiate if unforeseen difficulties arise.

Other arguments relating advanced technology to size and concentration, however, seem to apply with even greater force to defense than to a civilian market. There are significant economies of scale in R & D. Teams of researchers from various disciplines, supported by costly specialized equipment and technically-trained assistants, are considered necessary for the efficient conduct of many research projects. Regardless of the extent to which the big industrial laboratory actually has or should have supplanted the individual researcher, it is beyond question that expensive and complex products and processes in which requirements for engineering and technical know-how replace the need for science must usually be developed by large organizations able to manage the necessary funds and supply the personnel. The extraordinary technology embodied in military products, the magnitude of many projects, and the unparalleled percentage of procurement spending devoted to EDTR all tend to make the effects of modern technology on firm sizes and market structure more intense and inescapable in the defense market than in other areas of the economy.

Table VI-1 compares the distribution of EDTR awards with the distribution of over-all military procurement awards in FY 1962. EDTR was clearly more concentrated than over-all procurement in that year. Greater concentration ratios for EDTR are also found in other recent years.

Table VI-1: Concentration of EDTR awards and of over-all DOD procurement, FY 1962

	Percentage of total awards accounted for by the largest:				
	Firm	4 Firms	8 Firms	20 Firms	50 Firms
EDTR	8.3	31.2	50.6	72.4	87.2
Over-all procurement	5.6	18.7	30.0	46.5	63.4

Source: "The 500 Contractors Listed According to Net Value of Military Prime Contract Awards for Experimental, Developmental, Test, and Research Work; Fiscal Year 1962" (U.S. Congress, House Committee on Appropriations, Subcommittee on Department of Defense Appropriations, Hearings: Department of Defense Appropriations for 1964, Part 6, Research, Development, Test and Evaluation, pp. 177–183). The EDTR list has been adjusted to show subsidiaries on the same basis as the OSD list of 100 Companies and Their Subsidiaries According to Net Value of Military Prime Contract Awards for FY 1962.

Table VI-2 is designed to indicate the direct effect of concentrated EDTR on over-all concentration in the defense market. This table shows the percentage of EDTR awards to firms among the top 50 on the over-all list, regardless of the firms' ranks on the EDTR list. The high concentration shown for EDTR on this basis, only slightly less than that shown in Table VI-1 and still well above that for over-all procurement, indicates that the bulk of EDTR contracts went to the largest contractors and served to increase over-all concentration.

The emphasis on technological considerations in the defense market has affected the nature of competitive behavior as well as the level of concentration. There is no evidence that concentration has led to a state of conscious parallelism in which a "live-and-let-live" atmosphere has enveloped the major contractors; nor has fewness of number led to any publicized cases of overt collusion other than a few violations by minor contractors in unimportant segments of the market.[4] Comments of Department of Defense officials, industry executives, the trade press, and knowledgeable critics indicate an overwhelming, perhaps unanimous, agreement that competition in

4. F. M. Scherer, in *The Weapons Acquisition Process: Economic Incentives*, states that "no cases of collusion in weapon system or subsystem bidding not explicitly approved by the government are known" (p. 46).
In recent years the Department of Justice has reported only three cases of collusion in the defense market, involving sales of self-locking nuts, glass fiber industrial fabrics, and stainless steel welding electrodes. U.S. Department of Justice, press releases dated Aug. 29, 1963, Oct. 9, 1964, and May 11, 1965.
In April, 1961, an executive order was issued, requiring all agencies of the federal government to report submission of identical bids on advertised procurements to the Attorney General. In the first two years of this program, the Department of Defense reported a very small portion, even of advertised procurements, affected by identical bidding. U.S. Department of Justice, *Identical Bidding in Public Procurement: Report of the Attorney General under Executive Order 10936* (Washington, Government Printing Office, 1962), and *Second Report*, 1964. For a somewhat more suspicious view, see questions of Senator Paul H. Douglas, U.S. Congress, Joint Economic Committee, Subcommittee on Defense Procurement, *Hearing: Progress Made by the Department of Defense in Reducing the Impact of Military Procurement on the Economy* (Washington: Government Printing Office, 1961), pp. 26–27.

Table VI-2: Concentration of EDTR awards, by rank of firms in over-all procurement list, FY 1962

Percentage of total EDTR awards accounted for by the largest:				
Firm	4 Firms	8 Firms	20 Firms	50 Firms
8.2	31.2	48.1	65.7	80.5

Source: Same as for Table VI-1.

the sense of interfirm rivalry is intense in the defense market. The major contractors are generally assumed to be thoroughly independent of each other in their decisions to seek awards in particular programs and in their subsequent approaches to and negotiations with procurement officials. It would be surprising if anything other than independent competitive behavior typified the market relationship among defense firms. William Fellner, in one of the most significant postwar contributions to the theory of oligopoly, pointed out two reasons effective co-operation among firms, either tacit or explicit, is difficult in markets dominated by technological advance.[5] First, either agreement or unspoken understanding that aggressive competition among firms may hurt all and benefit none requires an assessment by each firm of its own and its rivals' present and prospective power in the market. In Fellner's words, "the present value of this future flow of inventiveness cannot be calculated with sufficient accuracy to include it in the present appraisal of relative strength. Therefore, in many cases competition remains less restricted, or possibly even unhampered with respect to these variables, especially if the oligopolistic group is not quite small." [6] Second, vigorous competition in development of new products or processes of production is less dangerous than price competition. "There are no limits to effective retaliation, even in the very short run," Fellner commented in discussing price competition.[7] When competitive efforts are directed toward technological superiority, however, effective retaliation may be impossible and is almost always less immediate and far more unpredictable.

But the competition which is so pervasive and intense throughout the technically advanced portions of the defense market is not price competition; and competitive behavior in the non-price realm, when not supplemented by price competition, brings problems as well as the obvious benefit of stimulus to technological development. There can rarely if ever be meaningful price competition in the intitial stages of programs to develop major weapon systems. National security may preclude any public announcement of the type of weapon desired by the Department of Defense. At best several firms

5. *Competition Among the Few: Oligopoly and Similar Market Structures* (New York: Knopf, 1949).
6. *Ibid.*, p. 185.
7. *Ibid.*

considered "responsible" may be sent highly classified requests for proposals. In order to take full advantage of the state of technology, it may be necessary to use patented items or proprietary information from private firms. Specifications must be flexible at the start or the Department of Defense must simply state a general "requirement," thus making award to the lowest responsible bidder as contemplated in formal competitive bidding a meaningless concept. Considering the greater importance attached to performance and time requirements than to cost, the purchasing agency may quite reasonably give primary consideration to technical features of bidders' proposals, firms' records of past performance, and their estimated present technical capabilities, rather than to projected prices. The Air Force quite frankly refers to the early stages of contractor selection as "design and technical competitions." [8] And finally, as noted in the preceding chapter, ultimate price may be equally unknown to buyer and seller, thus forcing bargaining on monetary matters to center on the relatively minor issue of the contractor's fee.[9]

Price competition is also infeasible in most of the early contracts for production-run quantities of newly developed weapon systems. Not only does the successful execution of EDTR contracts give the original developer an advantage in promising advanced delivery dates and in assuring performance, but his prior experience can often make open price competition more costly to the Department of Defense than sole-source procurement. This apparent paradox results from the fact that a developer's know-how and equipment may reduce his subsequent production costs to such an extent that he could quote a price well below that possible for any potential competitor but still much higher than the price he would accept after determined and informed negotiation with procurement officials. Thus a common pattern in weapon system programs is design and technical competition, followed by sole-source negotiated pro-

8. See testimony of Assistant Secretary of the Air Force for Materiel J. S. Imirie, U.S. Congress, Senate Subcommittee of the Committee on Appropriations, *Hearings: Department of Defense Appropriations for 1963* (Washington: Government Printing Office, 1962), p. 882.

9. J. P. Miller recognized and carefully analyzed difficulties with competitive bidding shortly after the end of World War II. Writers during the protracted cold war period and the missile age have added little to his treatment of the problems posed by advanced technology. See especially "Military Procurement in Peacetime," *Harvard Business Review*, XXV, 444–462.

curement of advanced development and initial hardware purchases, if any, from the winner or winners of the EDTR contracts. In 1963 testimony, Assistant Secretary of Defense T. D. Morris estimated that approximately 44 per cent of all military procurement falls into such a pattern and therefore offers very little potential for increased price competition.[10]

In company-financed R & D leading to new products in civilian-oriented markets, the sole and ultimate test of the success of a project is sales revenue. In this respect price and output expectations and concern over potential market competition exert important pressures on technological competition. Particularly when the product must be sold in competitive markets, a firm will not undertake a project unless it believes that there are reasonable prospects of success and customer acceptance of the product, and unless it is also likely that the R & D cost can be held low enough to justify the expenditure as an investment. Defense contractors are largely free from such market discipline in formulating EDTR proposals, and as a result representations to the Department of Defense tend to contain inflated estimates of performance and inadequate estimates of cost. In the defense market—with its great technical uncertainties and honest optimism, its financial risk borne almost entirely by the customer, and its freedom from the impersonal sanctions of a civilian market—open rivalry and intense competition for contracts simply heighten the dangers of misleading brochuremanship.

The high probability that the winner of a design competition will be awarded any production contract which follows has two offsetting effects. It should dampen contractors' propensities for making excessive performance claims in EDTR proposals, or at least it should encourage contractors to compete most vigorously for initial research and study awards in programs they consider most likely to carry through to development and production. A meaningful element of realism is thereby injected into the process of design and technical competition. On the other hand the prospect of follow-on production contracts, which are generally viewed as much more profitable than EDTR work, may encourage firms not only to under-

---

10. U.S. Congress, House Committee on Appropriations, Subcommittee on Department of Defense Appropriations, *Hearings: Department of Defense Appropriations for 1964, Part 5, Procurement,* pp. 10–12.

estimate cost but to accept promising EDTR contracts at very low profit or actual loss. The prevalence of this sort of "buying in" is difficult to assess. Some informed observers think it is a commonplace occurrence, while others consider it rare.[11] Still, I have found no instance in which any knowledgeable person denied that it happened. Buying into a program in this way may have two unfortunate effects. It may misallocate resources by encouraging the Department of Defense to support too much marginal research work and, incidentally, cause the reported figures on EDTR spending to understate slightly the relative proportion of the defense effort actually devoted to this purpose. The second possible untoward effect was noted by Congressman Gerald R. Ford in the following observation, made after he had expressed concern that contractors who bought in are frequently "let off the hook" by liberal repricing on change orders:

You are familiar with the problem, I am sure, Mr. Secretary. You have the Department make a decision that X Corporation has the lowest responsible bid. The Department may have been challenged in the process that this company was not responsible, that they could not deliver for the price, that they could not deliver on schedule. Then the contract is awarded. The people who made the decision are going to be very sure that on the record their decision stands up, so they are going to extend the time, increase the price, etc. There is the possibility of an unholy alliance between the people in the particular service and the contractor, so everybody comes out whole. The reputation of the service is protected, and the fiscal integrity of the company is protected. There are many possibilities for abuse in this area, and I am delighted that the Department is doing something.[12]

11. "There are many companies within our industry who, for example, practice deliberate low bidding on an initial design or development program with the intention of regaining losses during subsequent production contracts" (Clarence O. Nelson, *Missile and Aircraft Procurement Management* [New York: Vantage Press, 1961], pp. 125–126).

"Indeed, the propensity to 'buy into' attractive new programs with optimistic quality, time, and/or cost estimates is perhaps as much an industry practice in advanced weapons acquisition as list price cutting is in automobile retailing, or as the advertising of loss leaders is in department store operations" (Peck and Scherer, *The Weapons Acquisition Process: An Economic Analysis*, p. 412).

However, when the question was put to Thomas Coggeshall, Chairman of the Renegotiation Board, in 1960 hearings, he replied, "I have heard that ever since renegotiation has been in existence, and I have yet to see a case where it could be established as true" (U.S. Congress, House Committee on Armed Services, Special Subcommittee on Procurement Practices of the Department of Defense, *Hearings Pursuant to Section 4, Public Law 86–89*, p. 327). Later, on p. 328, there is a statement by Coggeshall conceding that the practice does exist in contracting for research.

12. U.S. Congress, House Committee on Appropriations, Subcommittee on Department of Defense Appropriations, *Hearings: Department of Defense Appropriations for 1964, Part 5, Procurement*, p. 122.

Representative Ford's comment also suggests one reason why there are differences of stated opinion on the frequency of buying in.

There is still another problem associated with advanced technology which is quite serious in its own right and which vitiates the favorable effect of anticipated production contracts on EDTR brochuremanship. It is frequently difficult to cancel a program even after it becomes clear that it should never have been started. Money already invested in a program is irrelevant to a rational termination decision. All that should be taken into account are current estimates of *total* military value of the completed program in comparison with the estimated *additional* costs of completion. The more advanced the technology involved, the more difficult it becomes to estimate final military value and total costs before committing substantial funds. Peck and Scherer have noted two other ways in which sunk costs, even if regretted, make termination difficult. First, alternative proposals which come along later for more effective weapons or less costly development are at a disadvantage, since total costs of a new program must be weighed against incremental costs of existing programs. Second, early EDTR expenditures will undoubtedly generate technical and cost data that reduce the element of uncertainty associated with continuing a program already under way.[13] In addition, there are factors beyond rational calculation working against cancellation. Military and contractor personnel become emotionally involved in programs to which they have devoted much time and intense effort, the future of identifiable communities and jobs are at stake, and the publicity surrounding an announcement of cancellation is generally unfavorable. As summed up by Deputy Director of Defense Research and Engineering J. H. Rubel, "Nobody down the line wants to make the decisions. Almost invariably, there is pain associated with stopping a project whereas it is usually pleasant deciding to start one." [14] Yet major projects with large sunk costs have been terminated or delayed, sometimes in the face of great political or economic pressure. The following list of canceled or drastically cut back major programs was compiled unsystematically in the course of this study and is far from all-inclusive; but it does in my opinion indicate a commendably tough-minded attitude in the Department of Defense under both Republican and Democratic ad-

---

13. *The Weapons Acquisition Process: An Economic Analysis*, p. 320.
14. *Armed Forces Management,* IX (Dec., 1962) , 17.

ministrations: Navaho and Snark guided missiles, nuclear-powered aircraft, nuclear-powered aircraft carrier, B-70 bomber, Nike-Zeus and Bomarc anti-missile missiles, Dynasoar atmosphere re-entry vehicle, Skybolt and Eagle-Missileer airborne missile weapon systems, Saint inspection satellite, Seamaster jet seaplane, and the Navy's Sparrow I and Regulus II missiles.

Above, sharp contrasts were drawn between EDTR contracts and commercial R & D. The market relationship between major defense contractors and the Department of Defense is, in fact, far more similar to that between a contract research organization and a business client than it is to the more impersonal relationship between a research-oriented manufacturer and the buyers of his finished products, despite the fact that defense contractors also manufacture and sell hardware. Indeed, the trade jargon which refers to the Department of Defense as the "customer" rather than the "client" seems singularly inappropriate. But even the "client" concept, although more apt than "customer," is a poor analogy to the close and continuing relationship between buyer and sellers in the defense market. The phrases "administration (or government) by contract," the "new arsenal system," the "government-industry partnership," and the "Relationship" with a capital R, as well as the value-loaded and better-known term "military-industrial complex," have been used to emphasize the unique system which has evolved in the defense market.

This Relationship has been perceptively and thoroughly analyzed elsewhere,[15] and all that seem necessary in the context of this study are a brief summary of the crucial effects of high-level technology on the Relationship and note of its importance to market structure. Don K. Price has written that

scientists, under the pressure of the Second World War, worked out a new type of contractual relationship that has brought private scientific institutions into a connection with the federal government as intimate and active as that of any land-grant college. And the extension of this

15. See the following:
Don K. Price, *Government and Science* (New York: New York University Press, 1954).
Albert C. Lazure and Andrew P. Murphy, Jr. (eds.), *Research and Development Procurement Law* (Washington: Federal Bar Journal, 1957).
Victor K. Heyman, "Government by Contract," *Public Administration Review,* XXI (Spring, 1961), 59–64.

system to industrial corporations may now be bringing about a new relationship between government and business following the quarrels of the Depression era, much as the grant-in-aid system transformed federal-state relations after the Civil War.[16]

Clarence H. Danhof observed:

What is new is not government's reliance on nongovernmental sources of research and development; such reliance has been traditional in all defense areas and only somewhat less obvious in the areas assigned to the arsenals. It is the government's recognition of the magnitude of that reliance, the government's aggressive pursuit of ideas, knowledge and advice, and the governmentally-determined concentration on specific objectives which are conspicuous in the present situation.[17]

Thus, Price and Danhof regard the government's recognized need to draw heavily on private sources of research, development, and technical competence as the greatest stimulus to growth of the administrative contract. But the Relationship encompasses non-technical aspects, as pointedly noted by Stanford Research Institute:

The simple phrase, "They administer the programs through contracts," is the key to the effectiveness of the relationship between government and industry. The single, binding legal tie between the two parties is the contract. It embodies all the requirements, limitations, and subsidiary tasks that go along with doing business with the government. Upon accepting the contract, industry exposes itself to the impact of statutes, regulations, and policies; their intent; their conflicting, duplicating, and sometimes obsolescent purposes; and the burdens of a social-economic nature they impose in addition to those related to the direct purpose of the contract—R & D or hardware.[18]

Two aspects of the Relationship seem most pertinent to market structure. First, since it is based on continuing interdependence, it is closer and more permanent than the usual market relationships. The Department of Defense's dependence on its contractors was expressed by Secretary McNamara: "We must rely heavily on our

---

"Where Industry Suppliers Think Defense Buyers Should Shape Up," *Armed Forces Management*, VIII (Feb., 1962), 14–18. Despite its title, this article is a brief but highly perceptive review of and commentary on the main issues in the relationship.

A. S. Miller (ed.), "Administration by Contract: An Examination of Governmental Contracting-Out," *George Washington Law Review*, XXXI (April, 1963).

Stanford Research Institute, *The Industry-Government Aerospace Relationship*.

16. "The Scientific Establishment," in "Administration by Contract," *George Washington Law Review*, XXXI (April, 1963), 723.

17. "From Improvisation to Policy," *ibid.*, p. 740.

18. *The Industry-Government Aerospace Relationship*, I, 31.

contractors. You spend . . . for us, and, for all practical purposes, act as our agents." [19] And defense-oriented firms, ignoring an old business axiom, have deliberately sought out and accepted complete or almost complete reliance on the continued business of a single customer. The second point is not, perhaps, quite so obvious. Several writers commenting in a 1957 symposium, *Research and Development Procurement Law,* emphasized the extent to which the Relationship is informal rather than genuinely contractual. James T. Ramey and John A. Erlewine described the term "adminstrative contract" as denoting an instrument designed for use by parties acting in good faith, in which both parties assume a "continuing cooperative relationship," and in which recourse to judicial processes is neither contemplated nor practicable.[20] Judicial enforcement would be difficult for two reasons. Ramey and Erlewine pointed out that the administrative contract must assume genuine agreement with a tacit understanding that details will be worked out as the job progresses, in order to obtain managerial flexibility and freedom from detailed requirements. Such flexibility and freedom, they observed, are essential to effective participation by private enterprise in technically advanced areas of interest to the government. James J. Kelly expressed concern about classified portions of a contract, normally contained in separate documents and included in the contract proper only by reference. What would happen, Kelly wondered, if a court were asked to adjudicate a dispute under classified portions of such a contract? In fact, he asked, should such an instrument be considered a contract at all? [21] Kimball Prince raised similar questions, but noted that no such dispute had ever come before the courts.[22] In this respect, even the term "government-industry partnership" seems weak, for the legal Relationship is even closer than the relationship between two business partners, who are quite likely to have a judiciable contractual agreement with each other.

19. "Where Industry Suppliers Think Defense Buyers Should Shape Up," *Armed Forces Management,* VIII, 15.

20. "Introduction to the Concept of the 'Administrative Contract' in Government Sponsored Research and Development," *Research and Development Procurement Law,* pp. 354–372.

21. "The Birth of a Missile—Legal and Contractual Aspects," *ibid.,* pp. 420–431.

22. "Sandia Corporation: A Science-Industry-Government Approach to Management of a Special Project," *ibid.,* pp. 432–443.

C. Contracting Procedures and Innovations

The Department of Defense has not passively accepted the market peculiarities brought about by the emphasis on technology. Rather, the problems of structure and behavior just reviewed have been recognized, and vigorous countermeasures have been taken. As the sole customer, the Department of Defense is undoubtedly in a strong position to influence the market in which it buys; but the widespread effects of technology are not easy to overcome when found undesirable, and the procurement policies and procedures put into effect to solve one set of problems have been only partially successful and have raised a new set of difficulties. The Department of Defense's responses have been of two major types—contractual and managerial.

The most widely publicized contractual innovation has been the greatly expanded use of incentive contracts in the face of objections and reservations by the General Accounting Office, the Renegotiation Board, and members of Congress. The 1963 edition of the *Armed Services Procurement Regulation* contains the following provision: "The introduction of incentives into development is of such compelling importance that, to the extent practical, firms not willing to negotiate appropriate incentive provisions may be excluded from consideration for the award of development contracts." [23] The incentive contract, whether cost-plus-incentive-fee or fixed-price incentive, normally provides that if actual costs are under originally estimated or target costs the savings will be divided between the government and the contractor according to some predetermined schedule. Cost overruns, on the other hand, will not be fully absorbed by the government. Time and performance incentives are also being written into incentive contracts today. As noted in 1960 by G. C. Bannerman, Department of Defense Director of Procurement Policy, the incentive contract lies between the extremes of a cost-plus-fixed-fee contract and a firm fixed-price contract:

On a cost-type contract you have what amounts to an incentive contract, with a 100 percent-zero sharing. In other words, all of the risk

23. Paragraph 3–403 (c).

and all of the rewards—risk for cost overrun and reward for cost underruns—are on the Government, in a cost-type contract. It is a 100-zero share.

On the other hand, at the other end of the spectrum, you have a firm fixed-price contract. In a fixed-price contract, 100 percent of the risk and 100 percent of the reward is on the contractor.

Now, an incentive contract is simply one that is in between these two— 80–20 usually, where 80 percent of the risk is on the Government and 20 percent on the contractor.[24]

Critics of incentive contracts fear that final profits may be raised by excessively high cost targets and unduly pessimistic initial estimates of time and performance. Their concern is certainly supported by evidence on comparative costs. In contrast to the average cost overrun of some 300 per cent in the programs studied by Peck and Scherer, a study of 290 incentive contracts by F. T. Moore showed underruns in approximately 75 per cent of the sample, with around one-fourth of the contracts ending up with underruns of over 10 per cent of initial target cost. Overruns exceeding 10 per cent, Moore found, were concentrated in the smaller contracts. Moore also studied 2,501 cost-plus-fixed-fee contracts, and his findings in general bear out those of Peck and Scherer on the preponderance of cost overruns in this type of contract.[25]

A major advantage claimed for the incentive contract is that it encourages the potential contractor to make the most accurate estimates possible in his initial proposals. Colonel W. W. Thybony, Chairman of the Armed Services Procurement Regulation Committee, described the pressures on contractors as follows:

Incentive contracts will, we believe, provide us with more realistic estimates and targets. The very nature of an incentive contract provides an inducement for sound estimating. For instance, prospective contractors submitting unduly conservative proposals, or targets which involve little or no risk, will endanger their competitive position and, hence, the likelihood of their getting the award. Conversely, if they are unduly optimistic in their promises they will be in danger of being awarded a contract at a very low profit or a loss.[26]

24. U.S. Congress, House Committee on Armed Services, Special Subcommittee on Procurement Practices of the Department of Defense, *Hearings Pursuant to Section 4, Public Law 86–89,* pp. 212–213.

25. *Military Procurement and Contracting,* chap. iii, "A Survey of Contract Results," pp. 20–51.

26. *Armed Forces Management,* VIII (May, 1962), 45.

Colonel Thybony's statement clearly illustrates the crucial role competition plays in the use of incentive contracts to discourage unduly pessimistic estimates. Yet in 1960 testimony Undersecretary of the Navy F. A. Bantz told congressional listeners that the incentive contract was generally used when there was little or no competition.[27] Undersecretary Bantz was, presumably, speaking of price competition. The influences of technological factors on the nature of competition in the defense market are such as to indicate that incentive contracts cannot ever be as useful in stimulating accuracy in cost estimates as they may be in encouraging realistic time and performance objectives. Because non-price competition for awards in new programs is intense, contractors' proposals in design and technical competitions must be as attractive as the firms' capabilities and existing commitments permit. Yet, following Colonel Thybony's reasoning, if a contractor knows that his proposal will be used to set time and performance targets in an incentive contract he will be careful not to make unrealistic claims which are likely to reduce his expected fee substantially. Thus, time and performance incentives may be most helpful to the Department of Defense in combating brochuremanship. But the conclusion is arrived at only on the assumption that competition protects the department against unwarranted pessimism among contractors. For good and sufficient reason price competition is not strong enough to serve a similar function at the EDTR level; therefore the mere fact that cost incentive contracts are being negotiated gives defense firms little if any additional incentive to estimate costs accurately. As suggested by Moore's study, the tendency will be rather for deliberate or subconscious overestimates to replace underestimates. The best that the Department of Defense can do, and is doing, in this situation is to attempt to become well enough informed to substitute its own evaluation of the accuracy of contractors' cost projections for judgments forced on suppliers by market forces. Efforts by the Department of Defense to strengthen its own internal technical competence will be reviewed below. These are supplemented by requirements that contractors use such devices as the PERT/COST system and instal value engineering staffs, use plant inspections, pre-audits and post-audits,

27. U.S. Congress, House Committee on Armed Services, Special Subcommittee on Procurement Practices of the Department of Defense, *Hearings Pursuant to Section 4, Public Law 86–89,* p. 291.

certificates of accuracy and completeness of cost data, and performance evaluation reports indicating a contractor's past ability to estimate costs, time, and performance. Inevitably, such attempts to gain cost information, and to force contractors to estimate costs precisely and then keep them under control, complicate the Relationship and arouse hostility among contractors. In the words of one company official, "Actually, the military, in effect, is taking over the management of companies. They insist on making our management decisions for which they have neither the background nor the training. They are reducing to postage stamp size the company's management prerogatives—and blaming us when things foul up." [28]

Another contractual device to provide the Department of Defense with adequate information on highly technical procurement and to increase competition is the "two-step procurement procedure." This scheme was pioneered by the Air Force in the late fifties and incorporated in the *Armed Services Procurement Regulation* during the McNamara regime. It was described as follows by Assistant Secretary of Defense T. D. Morris:

Under this procedure, bidders are first asked to submit proposals to meet specific performance criteria without providing a price quotation. These proposals are then examined by the Government engineers and buyers, and those which meet the desired performance characteristics are approved. In the second step, bidders whose products have been approved then submit sealed bids and the contract is awarded to the lowest responsible bidder under the formal advertising procedure.[29]

Contractors, quite understandably, have disapproved strongly of two-step procurement. They have objected that the best features of all original proposals may show up in the final set of specifications to be bid upon, with no compensation to the losers.[30] These fears are undoubtedly valid. Courtney Johnson, Assistant Secretary of the Army for Material, testified in 1960 that "a contractor did make such a proposal, and it was a very logical proposal, which would reduce

---

28. *Armed Forces Management,* VIII (Feb., 1962), 18. A rigorous demonstration of the Department of Defense's need to know the contractor's "production possibility function" in order to set optimal incentives is found in Neil S. Weiner, "Multiple Incentive Fee Maximization: An Economic Model," *Quarterly Journal of Economics,* LXXVII (Nov., 1963), 603–616.

29. U.S. Congress, House Committee on Appropriations, Subcommittee on Department of Defense Appropriations, *Hearings: Department of Defense Appropriations for 1964, Part 5, Procurement,* p. 13.

30. *Armed Forces Management,* VIII (June, 1962), 29.

the cost of the item. And there were other bidders. And we immediately stopped the negotiations at that point and gave everybody a chance to do the same thing." [31] While Secretary Johnson was not describing a two-step bidding procurement, the attitude he reflected is an ominous one from the contractor's point of view. The *Armed Services Procurement Regulation* offers no reassurance to contractors, but on the contrary provides that technically unacceptable first-step bids will not be rejected until after a conference with the government, if feasible.[32] The most that such a procedure would seem to accomplish is the injection of price competition into the technically advanced portions of the defense market at the sacrifice of vigorous and effective design and technical competition. Given the Department of Defense's emphasis on performance and time rather than cost, the bargain is a bad one.

The *Armed Services Procurement Regulation*, following a proposal by the Logistics Management Institute for "weighted guidelines" to contractors' fees, now contains a list of profit rate ranges considered "fair" on various types of cost. "Engineering labor," for example, is considered entitled to much higher rates of return than "purchased parts." Contractors are asked to negotiate on the basis of the guidelines. In such negotiations total estimated costs are broken down into the various listed categories, a partial fee within the suggested range is negotiated for each cost category, and the total fee is arrived at by summation of the partial fees.[33] If the profit ranges are chosen appropriately, the use of weighted guidelines could be quite effective in meeting the buying-in problem at its source, by making EDTR work attractive in its own right rather than considered as the cost of admission to production contracts.

The most heated controversy fanned by defense technology surrounds the issue of patent rights and rights to data. In the words of a report submitted by a committee of seven contractor representatives and two members of the staff of the Senate Small Business Committee, "The issues of proprietary rights in data have brought about a seriously disturbed climate which is not conducive to the collabo-

---

31. U.S. Congress, House Committee on Armed Services, Special Subcommittee on Procurement Practices of the Department of Defense, *Hearings Pursuant to Section 4, Public Law 86–89*, p. 299.

32. Paragraph 2–503.1 (b), (u).

33. Paragraphs 3–808.2 to 3–808.7.

ration and cooperation which must exist if the desirable Government-Industry partnership is to realize its full potential."[34]

Perhaps the sharpest and most effective stimulus to change in Department of Defense practices regarding acquisition of technical information from contractors came from investigations and three reports in the middle and late fifties by the Surveys and Investigation Staff of the House Subcommittee on Department of Defense Appropriations, strongly backed by George H. Mahon, chairman of the subcommittee. The single most important and repeated criticism in all three reports was that the services were not acquiring adequate technical data and engineering drawings for purposes of future competitive procurements. The committee staff noted two major failures: first, contracts frequently did not include a clause giving the government rights to data; and, second, often when data were obtained they were either accepted in inadequate condition or not filed and cross-filed in such a way as to be usable for procurement purposes.[35] The first shortcoming has been corrected, but it is easier to insert a mandatory clause in all appropriate contracts than it is to make effective use of the mass of data forthcoming. Senator Hubert H. Humphrey estimated in 1962 that $1 to $2 billion were lost annually because of inadequate facilities for exchange of technical information within the Department of Defense.[36] And in 1963, Senator Russell B. Long observed critically that the government still had no central agency to collect and disseminate information on patents and proprietary data.[37]

The 1963 edition of the *Armed Services Procurement Regulation* contains several provisions dealing with patents and rights to data. The Department of Defense requires, subject to specific exceptions, that the government be issued an "irrevocable, non-exclusive, non-

34. Military Procurement Advisory Committee, *How to Improve Federal Procedures for Buying National Defense Materials: Report to Senator George A. Smathers Prepared by His Military Procurement Advisory Committee*, Aug. 18, 1961, p. 15.

35. U.S. Congress, House Committee on Appropriations, Subcommittee on Department of Defense Appropriations, *Hearings: Department of Defense Appropriations for 1957, 1958, and 1959* (Washington: Government Printing Office, 1956, 1957, 1958).

For 1957 and 1958 *Hearings*, see volumes entitled *Procurement Policies and Practices of the Department of Defense*.

For 1959 *Hearings*, see volume entitled *Procurement, Supply, and Surplus Operations of the Department of Defense*.

36. *Missiles and Rockets*, XI (Oct. 22, 1962), 9.

37. U.S. Congress, Senate Select Committee on Small Business, Subcommittee on Monopoly, *Hearings: Economic Aspects of Government Patent Policies* (Washington: Government Printing Office, 1963), p. 87.

transferable" license under any patent obtained as the result of contracted work. This license must permit unrestricted, royalty-free use
of the patent by the government, any contractor or any subcontractor in connection with a government-sponsored project. The
government may require full title to an invention made under contract if there is no significant non-governmental prior experience
in the field, the prospective invention is likely to dominate its field,
the contractor's primary responsibility is direction or co-ordination
of others, or there is an "overriding public interest" relating to
health or safety. On the other hand, the government may waive its
claim to a royalty-free license if the invention is not reduced to practice during the contract, the developer has invested substantial sums
of his own in the project, the practicability was previously established, the invention covers developments which were not the primary purpose of the contract, or the invention is useful only for
military purposes and the contractor does not have facilities for
full-scale production. The contractor must agree to insert a clause
giving the government similar rights in all EDTR subcontracts of
over $3,000.[38]

In all EDTR contracts and subcontracts the contractor is required
to submit all data resulting from performance of the contract,
whether or not otherwise proprietary. In addition, the Department
of Defense demands all data necessary to reproduce or manufacture
the equipment or perform the process, except data on standard commercial items incorporated into the product or process, or data both
developed at substantial expense to the contractor and previously
offered for sale. When a military agency purchases standard commercial items or advertises the procurement, it may require information necessary for maintenance and cataloguing, but is not permitted
to include a request for proprietary data in the specifications. However, proprietary data can be purchased separately by negotiation,
and in such a case restrictions on use or disclosure by the Department of Defense may be written into the contract.[39]

The patent and proprietary data regulations just summarized
form the basis for what is referred to as the "procurement package."
Secretary McNamara has stated that early availability of procure-

38. Paragraphs 9–107.1 (a) to 9–107.2 (b).
39. Paragraph 9–202.

ment packages is essential to his objective of increasing competition through breakout for competitive procurement of certain components of weapon systems and greater use of competitive procurement on first or very early production-quantity orders.[40] Lieutenant General R. W. Colglazier, Army Deputy Chief of Staff for Logistics, defined procurement package as follows:

The term "procurement package" as I am using it here refers to the full set of manufacturing drawings and specifications and other descriptive data necessary for a prospective qualified producer to completely comprehend what is required, to prepare an intelligent, responsive bid or quotation on the job, and to produce the item to meet these stated specifications.[41]

General Colglazier emphasized the importance of analyzing, at the early research stages of a program, the procurement package to be required over the full development and procurement cycle. "Heretofore," he commented a little later, "there has been a tendency to delay the preparation of the procurement package until we had gone into production and had some experience." [42]

Another practice which supplements the procurement package as a device for obtaining technical information in order to increase competition is "reverse engineering." In the *Armed Services Procurement Regulation* proprietary data are defined as "the details of a Contractor's secrets of manufacture . . . to the extent that such information is not disclosed by inspection or analysis of the product itself." [43] All that is meant by reverse engineering is such inspection and analysis. Modern methods of analysis, it has been pointed out, are such that the Department of Defense's willingness to engage in reverse engineering makes a mockery of the concept of proprietary data. It has been argued, on the other hand, that reverse engineering is a common industrial practice. A firm with an unpatented product of interest to the Department of Defense is likely to benefit from proprietary data only if it is willing to sell the information for less than the cost of reverse engineering.

40. *Missiles and Rockets,* XII (March 25, 1963) , 33.
41. U.S. Congress, Senate Subcommittee of the Committee on Appropriations, *Hearings: Department of Defense Appropriations for 1963,* p. 737.
42. *Ibid.,* p. 750.
43. Paragraph 9–203.2.

The Department of Defense's privileges of providing contractors with royalty-free licenses under other firms' patents and disclosing proprietary information furnished under contract have been attacked by industry as unduly harsh, as discouraging firms from entering the defense market for fear their technical know-how will become public information after one contract, and as destructive of incentives to originality and innovation among existing contractors. Other critics, notably in Congress and academic circles, have maintained that the Department of Defense, by not demanding full title to patents arising from work done under contract, is unduly generous with its contractors, permitting private parties to profit unjustly from technological advances which should be in the public domain because they were made possible by public funds.

Once again, a crucial element in the issue seems to be the combination of full and free technological competition and minimal price competition that characterizes the advanced sectors of the defense market. In hearings before the Senate Small Business Committee's Subcommittee on Monopoly, two academic witnesses independently made the very interesting suggestion that contractors be permitted to offer two prices in bids on a project—one granting full rights to patents to the government and one retaining these rights.[44] The Department of Defense could then compare the difference between the two prices with its own estimate of the value of the anticipated patents and thus select the more advantageous contract. The suggestion might be expanded to cover proprietary data as well. Consider a hypothetical case in which the know-how generated in an EDTR contract, whether embodied in patents or proprietary information, would be of value only to ensuing production work in defense programs. Firms competing for the EDTR contract might submit very low bids, hoping to recoup through high profits on less competitive production contracts. The Department of Defense, on the other hand, would be interested in acquiring the know-how in order to increase competition for production awards and thus reduce the prospective high profits. Suppose further that firms are free to, or are required to, submit two bids on the EDTR contract—one yielding no rights to know-how and the other, at a higher price,

44. Testimony of Professors Robert F. Lanzillotti and Lee E. Preston, in U.S. Congress, Senate Select Committee on Small Business, Subcommittee on Monopoly, *Hearings: Economic Aspects of Government Patent Policies*, pp. 120, 244.

requiring submission of all know-how to the Department of Defense. In a purely competitive market the Department of Defense would ordinarily gain little or nothing from such an option, with any conceivable gain resulting from uncertainty. Each firm's estimate of the value of the expected know-how, and hence the price differential offered the Department of Defense in competition for the EDTR award, should be equal to the present value of the cost advantage that exclusive possession of the know-how would give in the anticipated competition for production contracts. Whatever the Department of Defense saved in the EDTR contract without know-how it would be likely to lose in the production contracts, or whatever it paid for know-how would most probably be returned in lower costs during procurement of production items.

In the real world of defense procurement, the Department of Defense would benefit from the alternatives proposed, because it could acquire the know-how at the most competitive stage of the procurement cycle and use the information to inject competition in a stage where it is now largely absent. It would seem that another significant merit in the suggestion is that it would force the contractor to estimate the total value of his defense-acquired know-how, including its value to him in civilian markets; and the Department of Defense could then, if it had the inclination and the capability, compare this private value with the total social benefits associated with the knowledge. Whenever social benefits exceeded total private value, the Department of Defense should buy the know-how in order to maximize public benefits obtained from public expenditures.

D. Changing Managerial Practices

Managerial as well as contractual innovations have been forced upon the military establishment by the size, permanence, and technical complexity of the armed forces since the end of World War II. The most obvious of these reforms was the creation of the Department of Defense itself. Procurement agencies have been reorganized, consolidated, and merged with technical agencies, in recognition of the fact that procurement cannot be administered separately from research because the former now depends so heavily upon the latter. The great bulk of research, development, procurement, and testing is now centralized in the Army Material Command, the Air Force Systems Command, the Bureau of Naval

Weapons, and, for common-use items, the Defense Supply Agency. Technological complexities of the defense market have forced the Department of Defense to develop internal technical competence. Such competence is utterly essential to intelligent selection decisions and efficient procurement. As a result, new agencies have been created, and despite centralization and administrative reform of procurement agencies, the organizational structure of the Department of Defense has become more intricate.

Near the top of the organizational pyramid is the Director of Defense Research and Engineering (DDR&E), a position established by the Reorganization Act of 1958. The DDR&E is designated as the chief adviser to the Secretary of Defense on scientific and technical matters and as director of research and engineering activities within the Department of Defense proper. He has no direct authority over programs carried out by agencies of the individual services, nor over contractor selection. Final decisions on major programs are made by the Secretary of Defense, and therefore the influence of the DDR&E depends largely on the man himself and his relation to the Secretary of Defense. The first DDR&E under Secretary McNamara, Harold Brown, was given ample latitude to demonstrate the potential of his office.

An idea for a new or improved military item or system may originate in one of the services, in industry, or within the Department of Defense. As the department is now organized under Secretary McNamara, a prospective major program must pass three tests. First, it is sent to the Office of the Comptroller for a cost, manpower, and material requirements analysis, based on the five-year program concept. The Joint Chiefs of Staff are asked for comments on the need for the weapon. The Secretary of Defense then decides whether or not to send it to the office of the DDR&E for technical evaluation. Final approval or disapproval is the prerogative of the Secretary of Defense. If a program is approved, one of the services is authorized to issue requests for proposals to industry. One effect of this procedure is that by the time an idea finally emerges in requests for proposals it may bear little resemblance to its original form.[45]

Defense contractors interviewed by *Missiles and Rockets* in 1963 were highly critical of both the organizational structure just de-

45. An excellent summary of the organization and policies of the Department of Defense under Secretary McNamara is found in *Missiles and Rockets*, XII (March 25, 1963). The entire issue is devoted to this topic.

scribed and of the individuals involved, especially Harold Brown and Comptroller Charles J. Hitch. The flow of ideas has been reversed, they maintained, and is now coming mainly from the office of the DDR&E to industry. Advanced planning by a contractor, according to one, is now essentially "trying to figure out what recommendations the DOD comptroller's office and the office of the Director, Defense Research and Engineering are going to make." Thus, time and talent that should be used in creating new concepts are wasted in second-guessing the customer. According to another man interviewed, imaginative and risky projects are discouraged: "We are beginning to get well-costed, mediocre systems because industry tailors its programs to get past Comptroller Hitch. It no longer thinks of how advanced a system it could produce, because it won't get funds." [46] A little earlier, *Missiles and Rockets* had commented on its editorial page, "Roaring free-wheeling private enterprise is going the way of the wooden prop, the helmet and the white scarf. Something rather more frightening is taking its place. Great pools of brainpower in the industry now must be devoted to figuring out what the government is *going* to do, rather than what it *ought* to do." [47]

It may well be that ideas flow from the office of the DDR&E to industry mainly because current advances, although their costs may be substantial, are adding only marginally to the nation's defense. In such a situation there is surely merit in having the Department of Defense in a position to make its own informed judgments as to its needs and so to advise its contractors. As noted in the previous chapter, Secretary McNamara has acknowledged that a development as important and novel as the ballistic missile would be handled differently.[48] The real test of whether the present Department of Defense system and its top-level personnel are unduly cost conscious and unreceptive to new ideas from outside must wait for a major and unanticipated technological breakthrough in an important area such as nuclear propulsion, antisubmarine warfare, or defensive missilery.

There is undoubtedly waste in assigning too many industrial scientists and engineers to efforts to anticipate the Department of

46. *Ibid.*, pp. 63, 66.
47. XI (Aug. 6, 1962), 46. Italics in original.
48. *Supra*, p. 93.

Defense when the best of them could otherwise be contributing to significant technological advancement. But waste of technical talent is an inevitable by-product of technological competition coupled with an absence of price competition. The more poorly informed the customer, the greater would be the competitive pressures on a contractor to assign his very ablest scientists and engineers to preparation of proposals and to selling efforts. Internal competence in the Department of Defense simply tends to replace brochuremanship by second-guessing. Still another unavoidable result of the competitive situation in the defense market is duplication of research. The basic issue is not whether the Department of Defense should develop internal technical competence, but whether the gains of technological competition among contractors outweigh the costs of the resulting lavish use of scientists and engineers.

While top levels of the Department of Defense approve major programs and program changes, agencies within the services issue requests for proposals, negotiate with and select contractors, and manage projects. There is, therefore, a need for technical competence available to the services. The three services have met this need in various ways in the face of two significant developments—the rise of the weapon system with its problems of interdependence and co-ordination of components, and the decline of the traditional arsenal system. Differences among the services are based in part upon historical accident and in part upon differences in current patterns of procurement.[49]

For many years the Army has owned and managed arsenals which prior to World War II conducted R & D, tested weapons and equipment, and engaged in manufacture. Under the old arsenal system peacetime procurement from civilian markets was primarily limited to civilian-type items and to materials and components which were assembled in the arsenals. Today, the arsenals have largely evolved into laboratories. As described in 1963 by Finn J. Larsen, Assistant Secretary of the Army for Research and Development, "If we examine the history of our arsenals, we find that they were established to manufacture weapons and equipment. Through the years, and especially since World War II, a trend has developed so that at

49. The following discussion comparing managerial systems in the Army, Air Force, and Navy draws very heavily on various issues of *Armed Forces Management*.

present most of the production is done by industry. As this trend evolved, our laboratories assumed a greater role in research and development." [50] Larsen went on to testify that Army laboratories now perform more basic research than is contracted to industry and do most of the Army's test and evaluation work. The arsenals also act as systems managers in weapon systems procurement, even if there is a single prime contractor, and prepare procurement packages. However, as late as 1959 there was still strong support within the Army for the older view that the role of civilian industry should be primarily as a reserve, confined to production of weapons in time of war or national emergency. This view was expressed by Frank Higgins, Assistant Secretary of the Army for Logistics, at the end of testimony lauding the work done at the Redstone Arsenal in development of the Redstone and Jupiter missiles:

In our American system which rejects the institution of a permanent big munitions industry such as the Krupps and Skodas in foreign countries, a link is needed between the mighty productive force of private industry capable of converting to war production, and the rapidly forward moving stream of military research and development and new weapons concepts. The arsenals furnish this irreplaceable link.[51]

The Air Force has developed a quite different managerial approach to procurement of complex and advanced items. "We never really believed in the arsenal system," testified Assistant Secretary of the Air Force Joseph S. Imirie in 1963, "and prefer rather to rely on industry for development and manufacturing. We have followed this course, which I personally believe is a correct one. Industry has been an innovator in a great many cases, a developer in a great many cases, and almost invariably the manufacturer. In my opinion, this is the correct relationship." [52] The Air Force, set up as a separate service after World War II, had nothing resembling the arsenal system at its inception, and no provision for effective internal technological competence. Moreover, the Air Force was organized

50. U.S. Congress, Senate Subcommittee of the Committee on Appropriations, *Hearings: Department of Defense Appropriations for 1964*, p. 1259.

51. U.S. Congress, House Committee on Government Operations, Military Operations Subcommittee, *Hearings: Organization and Management of Missile Programs*, p. 330.

52. U.S. Congress, House Committee on Appropriations, Subcommittee on Department of Defense Appropriations, *Hearings: Department of Defense Appropriations for 1964, Part 5, Procurement*, p. 835.

to rely on the other two services, particularly the Army, for procurement of subsistence items, clothing, and medical supplies. Faced immediately with the immense technological problems of jet aircraft and later those of missiles, the Air Force was virtually forced to turn to private industry for scientific and engineering talent. As a result, the Air Force took the lead in developing the weapon system method of contracting and the system engineering and technical direction (SETD) contract as means of buying management from private industry. The Air Force has been thoroughly aware of conflicts of interest that may arise when a firm holding or seeking contracts other than SETD in a program is also the program's manager (the problems of Thompson Ramo Wooldridge in this respect were noted earlier). As a result, the Air Force has come to rely very heavily on non-profit organizations, such as the Rand Corporation, Lincoln Laboratories, the Mitre Corporation, and the Aerospace Corporation, all set up primarily to perform SETD and EDTR work for the Air Force.

The Navy, which emerged from World War II with its own shipyards, laboratories, and manufacturing facilities, created the Special Projects Office to manage the development of the Polaris missile and nuclear submarine weapon system. The office was set up under the command of a Navy officer, Rear Admiral William F. Raborn, who was explicitly designated as the weapon system manager. The Special Projects Office negotiated and awarded contracts, supervised selection of subcontractors, directed work done in naval shipyards, and acted as over-all co-ordinator for the project. This form of managerial organization, with a uniformed officer as project manager, has since been extended to all major weapon programs under the jurisdiction of the Bureau of Naval Weapons and has also been adopted by the Army Material Command.

The starkest confrontation of alternative managerial systems occurred in the fifties during the parallel development of medium-range ballistic missiles by the Army at Redstone Arsenal and by the Air Force using Thompson Ramo Wooldridge as SETD. Since 1959, a common pattern has begun to emerge. Air Force General Bernard A. Schriever, who had been in charge of the Thor medium-range missile program and who later became director of the Air Force Systems Command, has stated that the Air Force should perform more research and test work internally and must upgrade its technical competence for this purpose.[53] Less than two weeks before his retirement in 1961, Herbert F. York, DDR&E during the Eisenhower Administration, testified that "one of the most important things we could do" would be to improve government laboratories. He later stated that he would much prefer internal research capability to use of the non-profit organizations. He noted, however, that these organizations were no longer actually managing programs, but were serving as advisers to managers from the uniformed services.[54] Shortly after taking office, Secretary McNamara reaffirmed York's opinion of the importance of military laboratories, commenting, "The in-house laboratories shall be used as a primary means of carrying out Defense Department programs. They shall provide scientific and technical advice in the exercise of Government responsibility for development and acquisition of new weapons." [55] In 1963, the Department of Defense issued a directive extending Air Force practice to all services by prohibiting firms with SETD contracts from bidding on systems components in the same program.[56] Despite the emphasis on internal competence and the shift of management responsibility to uniformed directors of project offices, reliance on the non-profit organizations has continued. The reason customarily given for their establishment and maintenance is the impossibility of competing for large numbers of technically able people under civil service pay scales and regulations.

Spokesmen for defense contractors have, not surprisingly, been highly critical of the downgrading of the role private profit-seeking business formerly played in weapon system management. In summarizing a 1962 survey of "defense-oriented" firms, *Armed Forces Management* noted that the non-profit groups were expanding from their original activities of research and advice-giving into the fields of design and development. Contractors, quite correctly in my opinion, made little distinction between government agencies and the

53. "In-House R & D Capabilities," *Armed Forces Management*, IX (Sept., 1963), 9–21.
54. U.S. Congress, House Committee on Appropriations, Subcommittee on Department of Defense Appropriations, *Hearings: Department of Defense Appropriations for 1962, Part 4, Research, Development, Test, and Evaluation* (Washington: Government Printing Office, 1961), pp. 25, 64–66.
55. "DOD In-House Labs Win 'Primary' Role," *Missiles and Rockets*, IX (Oct. 30, 1961), 17.
56. Department of Defense Directive 5500.10, dated June 1, 1963.

non-profit organizations; and those interviewed considered their competition with private enterprise as an unwarranted encroachment by government.[57] Members of industry fear a "new" arsenal system. "I'm afraid Aerospace will stretch out like an octopus until it becomes an arsenal type of operation, conceiving, designing, building and testing," stated the vice president of one corporation as quoted in a *Wall Street Journal* article.[58] Members of both industry and the Congress have expressed concern that the non-profit organizations, free from civil service restrictions and those of the market alike, will have little incentive to economical operation; and as a symptom of such extravagance it has been frequently pointed out that non-profit organizations have hired men away from private industry by offering salaries and working conditions which private profit-seeking contractors cannot match.[59]

In contrast to such opinions, Secretary McNamara has stated that he is not only quite satisfied with the operation of the non-profit groups but believes that the Department of Defense would benefit from an expansion of their services.[60] General Schriever sought to reassure Congress by stating that the non-profit organizations are "under closer Air Force supervision than any contractors in the history of Air Force–industry relationships."[61] In defending the creation of the Aerospace Corporation, General Schriever testified:

An across-the-board staff competence of this level and scope is most difficult to maintain either in Government or in any single industrial company, and even the larger hardware contractors would find it difficult to preserve such staff stability through the various phases of planning, development, and production effort, let alone in the give and take of system contract competition."[62]

57. VIII (Feb., 1962), 14.
58. Dec. 4, 1961, p. 14.
59. *Ibid.* See also questioning of Harold Brown by Subcommittee Chairman Mahon in U.S. Congress, House Committee on Appropriations, Subcommittee on Department of Defense Appropriations, *Hearings: Department of Defense Appropriations for 1964, Part 6, Research, Development, Test and Evaluation; Appropriation Language; Testimony of Members of Congress, Organizations, and Interested Individuals*, pp. 141–143.
60. *Ibid., Part 1, Secretary of Defense*, pp. 458–459.
61. *Ibid., Part 6, Research, Development, Test and Evaluation; Appropriation Language; Testimony of Members of Congress, Organizations, and Interested Individuals*, p. 599.
62. *Ibid.*, p. 602.

In 1964 the non-profit groups, particularly the Aerospace Corporation, came under renewed congressional investigation and criticism, culminating in a report from the House Committee on Armed Services which indicted Aerospace for excessive fees, unwarranted expenditure of these fees on public relations, excessive construction of new facilities, frivolous use of outside consultants, and lavish salary and other personnel benefits. The report also charged lax management and accused the Air Force of wilful failure to support its own auditing and contracting personnel who were attempting to "bring order out of the chaos in the contracting situation." Yet the committee's recommendations, following a bitterly critical analysis, did not include any definite proposal for eliminating non-profit organizations or for curtailing their activities. But it was recommended, pointedly, that the Air Force should reappraise the management concept which had led to the formation of non-profit organizations. Other recommendations were confined to fee policy and Department of Defense control over the private corporations it had created.[63]

The investigation by the House Armed Services Committee did not include any attempt to evaluate Aerospace's performance of the tasks assigned to it by contract with the Air Force. Yet in light of harsh criticisms from contractors and their concern over encroachment, it is only to be expected that the non-profit operations will be subject to continuing scrutiny.

The efforts to build up within the Department of Defense the competence necessary for efficient selection of weapon systems and informed dealings with contractors have placed the department in direct competition with private industry. This development appears to be an inevitable result of the limited supply of scientists and engineers in the nation, the great technological demands of both customer and suppliers, and the blurring of distinctions among research, development, and production. Throughout the economy, competition for factors of production crosses industry lines; but such competition between buyers and sellers is rarely as direct and obvious as that between the Department of Defense and defense contractors for technical talent. Once the military establishment had built up research and advisory capabilities, whether in military labora-

63. U.S. Congress, House Committee on Armed Services, Subcommittee for Special Investigations, *The Aerospace Corporation: A Study of Fiscal and Management Policy and Control.* The quotation is from p. 1.

tories or in non-profit organizations, there were obvious economies to be considered, similar to those giving an EDTR contractor an advantage in ensuing production work, in contemplating full-scale development and possibly production work in government facilities and by non-profit organizations. Contractor fears of a new arsenal system therefore seem to be perfectly logical.

In a careful study of the armed services' efforts to develop aircraft engines between 1919 and 1939, Robert Schlaifer concluded that the government's role in research was essential, since private firms were not interested in performing research of benefit to the entire industry and because the government could justify facilities, such as wind tunnels, beyond the means of private firms. Schlaifer also observed that public laboratories faced less pressure for measurably profitable results and for this reason provided an atmosphere favorable to creative research. But Schlaifer found that in the interwar period the military services were incapable of actually developing a finished product as complex as an aircraft engine.[64] Today, the situation is in many ways reversed. Private firms can certainly be induced to compete with each other for research awards which will benefit their competitors if EDTR contracts are made financially attractive in their own right. The Department of Defense, under Secretary McNamara, has become thoroughly cost conscious; and, ironically, industry is now criticizing the government for stifling creative research. Large firms, almost entirely dependent on defense orders and in many cases occupying government-owned facilities, possess buildings and equipment as good as or superior to those found in government laboratories.[65] Yet the Army succeeded, brilliantly in the opinion of some, in developing a ballistic missile at an arsenal.[66]

The Department of Defense shows no inclination to produce fairly standard items such as trucks, tanks, and uniforms, is attempt-

64. Robert Schlaifer, *Development of Aircraft Engines* (Boston: Graduate School of Business Administration, Harvard University, 1950).

65. "I think our best equipped laboratories probably do not match the best equipped industrial laboratories or the better industrial laboratories," testified Brockway McMillan, Assistant Secretary of the Air Force for Research and Development, in U.S. Congress, House Committee on Appropriations, Subcommittee on Department of Defense Appropriations, *Hearings: Department of Defense Appropriations for 1964, Part 6, Research, Development, Test and Evaluation; Appropriation Language; Testimony of Members of Congress, Organizations, and Interested Individuals*, p. 592.

66. Testimony heard by the House Military Operations Subcommittee in 1959 indicated that the Army's Jupiter missile was more reliable than the Air Force's Thor, and in addition was more rugged and mobile. The nose cone for the Jupiter was developed at a cost of $22 million in contrast to $300 million for the nose cone of the Thor, and the Army's nose cone principles were applied to the intercontinental

ing to dispose of its industrial facilities, and is shutting down some of its naval shipyards. At the same time it has become a large-scale actual and potential competitor of private enterprise in technically advanced portions of its market, where competition among firms is already intense. The Department of Defense's make or buy options are vastly heightened in importance by one of the most obvious features of the defense market, the fact that there is only the one customer. It has already been argued that technological rivalry, unless supplemented by the discipline of price competition, tends to become more wasteful as it intensifies. And there seems to be little if anything the Department of Defense can do to increase price competition in complex weapon system procurement, no matter how efficient and technically competent it becomes and no matter how successfully it controls internal proliferation in its own laboratories and among its non-profit organizations, unless the basic priorities of time and performance over cost change drastically.

E. Defense Technology and the Civilian Economy

A final set of problems is posed by the effect of technological advance in defense on the rest of the nation. The issue was expressed bluntly in the following brief exchange between Assistant Secretary of the Navy for Research and Development James H. Wakelin, Jr., and Congressman Melvin R. Laird:

> Mr. WAKELIN. I would say that we are rapidly approaching the period when the Government is going to dominate all areas of R. & D., industrial, academic, and other areas of our society, Mr. Laird.
> Mr. LAIRD. Do you think that is good?
> Mr. WAKELIN. No; I do not.[67]

---

ballistic missile program. Some officers from both the Army and Air Force believed it was easier to train troops to operate the Jupiter. The Jupiter flew shortly before the Thor. However, the contest was not strictly between an arsenal operation and a comparable program by industry, since there were several contractors at Redstone Arsenal. Further, the Army had the use of experienced German technologists. U.S. Congress, House Committee on Government Operations, Military Operations Subcommittee, *Hearings: Organization and Management of Missile Programs.* Earlier, in 1958, Senator Estes Kefauver had noted the superiority of the Jupiter and had stated that the Army's arsenal system, in contrast with the Air Force's use of industry for SETD, "cuts lead time very substantially" (*Aviation Week and Space Technology,* LXVIII [Jan. 13, 1958], 32).

67. U.S. Congress, House Committee on Appropriations, Subcommittee on Department of Defense Appropriations, *Hearings: Department of Defense Appropriations for 1964, Part 6, Research, Development, Test and Evaluation; Appropriation Language; Testimony of Members of Congress, Organizations, and Interested Individuals,* p. 408.

Military R & D has long been defended on grounds of "spillover" into civilian uses. But this external economy has, in the authoritative opinion of Jerome B. Wiesner, Director of the Office of Science and Technology, dwindled into insignificance as military technology has become more specialized and more widely divergent from civilian developments.[68] Similar pessimism was expressed by the *Wall Street Journal*:

When the Government was creating the old piston-powered warplanes, for instance, this technology could be easily and profitably translated into commercial airliner designs. When the military moved on to jet planes, the translation became far more difficult and costly—as the financial plight of both manufacturers and airlines currently testifies. The supersonic military jet has thus far defied any commercial translation at all, and the Government now debates whether it is worth pouring tax money into subsidizing creation of a supersonic airliner. As for commercial transport application of a moon rocket, it defies even day-dreaming.[69]

Military requirements for technically trained personnel inevitably have had unfavorable effects on the civilian economy. Among those most concerned with these effects is Seymour Melman, professor of industrial engineering at Columbia University. In 1963 testimony, Melman estimated that from two-thirds to three-fourths of all engineers and scientists in the United States were working directly or indirectly for the Department of Defense. Such concentration, he continued, had led to inadequate progress in design of civilian products and production systems. The machine tool stock of the United States, he noted, was older than that of any other industrialized nation. He expressed the opinion that the nation's balance of payments difficulties had resulted from lack of technical growth in civilian industry, citing instances in which foreign advances had so outspaced domestic industry that they had led to great increases in imports. Industries he specifically mentioned in this connection were steel, various types of machinery and motors, typewriters, and sew-

---

68. U.S. Congress, Senate Select Committee on Small Business, Subcommittee on Monopoly, *Hearings: Economic Aspects of Government Patent Policies*, p. 326.
Aviation Week and Space Technology, LXXVII (Aug. 6, 1962), 28, and LXXVIII (April 22, 1963), 103–105.

69. May 6, 1963, p. 14.

ing machines.[70] Melman's position was summed up in the following words:

We submit that the security of the United States is not promoted by a pattern of economic weakness that is developing at the base of the industrial system. The depletion of technological personnel and of productive capital is wrecking the basis of our industrial system by depriving manufacturing firms of technological talent and capital for investment.[71]

Judgments are necessarily imprecise concerning alternative employment opportunities for scientists and engineers or the contributions they might have made to the civilian economy if not engaged in military work. Melman's estimate of the proportion of the nation's scientists and engineers involved in the defense effort may be excessive.[72] His concern is certainly well founded, however, since it would be absurd to believe that a majority or even a substantial minority of the nation's technological talent could long be devoted to weaponry without any sacrifice of progress in civilian sectors of the economy. Melman has, in addition, made a plausible case that he has identified some of the specific areas in which the sacrifice has been felt.[73]

70. U.S. Congress, House Committee on Appropriations, Subcommittee on Department of Defense Appropriations, *Hearings: Department of Defense Appropriations for 1964, Part 6, Research, Development, Test and Evaluation; Appropriation Language; Testimony of Members of Congress, Organizations, and Interested Individuals,* pp. 897–902.

71. *Ibid.,* p. 899.

72. Murray L. Weidenbaum has estimated that 52 per cent of the engineers and scientists engaged in research and development work in American industry in 1963 were working on projects financed by defense or space programs. Although adjustments would have to be made for industrial scientists and engineers engaged in company-funded R & D oriented toward defense, for production engineers, and for scientists and engineers outside private industry who were working on defense projects, it seems highly doubtful that Weidenbaum's estimate could be reconciled with Melman's. U.S. Congress, Senate Committee on Labor and Public Welfare, Subcommittee on Employment and Manpower, *Hearings: Nation's Manpower Revolution, Part 9* (Washington: Government Printing Office, 1964), p. 3146.

73. See also *Our Depleted Society.* In this book Melman not only repeats his observations about the impact of defense spending on civilian industry but also notes the longer-run effects of channeling talent into careers in defense-related technology rather than, for example, into teaching.

VII. ENTRY INTO AND EXIT FROM THE DEFENSE MARKET

A. Influence of Entry and Exit Barriers on Market Structure

In Chapters II and III it was argued that the figures on turnover of firms included in the various lists of the 50 and 100 largest prime contractors give no support to the view that the defense market is a particularly unstable one, although in the absence of meaningful contrasts I have been careful to avoid labeling the market as exceptionally stable. The rank and product-moment correlations in these chapters suggest that stability within the lists was relatively constant or even slightly increasing during the period under study; and the correlation coefficients presented in Chapter IV indicate that the aircraft and electronics groups, both comprised of firms heavily committed to the defense market, experienced a greater degree of stability in contract awards than did the other large contractors that were less reliant on military sales. In part, these findings may be explained by characteristics of the defense market discussed in Chapters V and VI, notably the absence of serious fluctuations in the Department of Defense's demand since the cutback at the end of the Korean War and the likelihood that an initially successful EDTR contractor will remain in a program through several follow-on contract awards. But both these features would be consistent with high turnover during the entire period under discussion. A stable level of or rise in over-all market demand does not preclude turnover or shifts in relative position among individual firms. Non-price competition for awards in new programs has been sharp; and although the stickiness in follow-on awards in existing programs might dampen year-to-year shifts among firms, no reasons have yet been offered to explain why current contractors should have any advantages over potential entrants in competition for new awards. The period from FY 1955 to FY 1964 seems long enough to have shown heavy influences by new programs. Conditions of entry into the defense market are, therefore, evidently of importance to the market's structure. Of equal importance, it will be argued in this chapter, are factors which influence the exit of defense firms.

Barriers to entry are of various types. Some are inherent to an industry under any pattern of behavior and are not removable by reasonable public policies. Such a barrier would be found, for example, in an industry whose sales at competitive prices would absorb the output of only a very small number of firms of the minimally efficient size.[1] Other barriers are the result of firms' behavior or of public policy. A firm might gain the power to exclude competitors through acquisition of all available sources of supply for an essential raw material or through exclusive dealing agreements with its customers. The patent system is an obvious illustration of a barrier raised by government. Still other barriers are both inherent and consciously erected at the same time, so that any such distinction as "natural" and "artificial" becomes blurred, as in the case of an industry whose product is by nature subject to differentiation and sale by brand name, and in which the advertising practices of existing firms have established consumer preferences that an entrant could overcome only by an expensive selling campaign. Barriers to entry into the defense market result both from policies and practices of the Department of Defense and from certain basic aspects of the market. In part, the former stem from the latter, and it is impossible to make a clear and mutually exclusive distinction between the two types. Nevertheless, procurement policies and practices which hinder entry into the defense market will be reviewed first. Next, there will be a discussion of underlying features of the market which would hamper entry under any set of procurement rules and in the light of which the Department of Defense's policies must be evaluated. Finally, barriers to exit from the defense market will be noted.

---

1. A case of this sort of barrier in the defense market is indicated by the following exchange:

Mr. MINSHALL. Earlier in your statement you said there were only two steel manufacturers able to produce the steel for the submarines?

Admiral JAMES. United States Steel, and Lukens Steel Co.

Mr. MINSHALL. I understand it is specialized. Why cannot the others do it?

Admiral JAMES. The others might if there was an economic outlet for the greater tonnages of this type steel than the Navy orders. The Navy constitutes the sole customer today for this steel. It is just a pure matter of economics.

U.S. Congress, House Committee on Appropriations, Subcommittee on Department of Defense Appropriations, *Hearings: Department of Defense Appropriations for 1963, Part 4, Procurement*, p. 261.

B. Procurement Policies and Practices Impeding Entry

Entry into the defense market involves far more than an agreement to deliver certain goods to a defense agency or to perform specified services according to a predetermined schedule for a given price or fee. When a business firm signs a contract with a procurement agency it binds itself to all the complexities of the Relationship for the lifetime of the contract, and even beyond the termination date in some respects. It becomes subject to audit by the General Accounting Office for three years after the date of final payment. It must agree not to practice discrimination in its personnel policies for the lifetime of the contract. If the contract is a large one, if it is other than firm fixed-price, or if it calls for anything other than the delivery of standard commercial-type items, a firm must meet other requirements involving subcontracting procedures, security measures, advertising, record-keeping, and agreement to accept possible retroactive renegotiation of "excessive" profits.

Entering the defense market may be an exceptionally costly way of increasing sales unless the potential entrant intends to stay in the market for some time. "It has not always been clear," a vice president of a contracting firm stated, "that servicing the military would not fundamentally change the nature of any company." [2]

The overhead costs of entry, or the costs which may be spread over a number of contract awards, are substantial and tend in particular to discourage entry by small firms and temporary entrance. Defense contracts, which include a large number of standard clauses prescribed by the *Armed Services Procurement Regulation*, are long and complicated, and a firm without its own legal staff may not be in a position to understand its rights and obligations under a contract. A firm seeking cost reimbursement contracts will be required to set up an accounting system meeting government standards, a requirement which may be particularly onerous to a small firm. Arrangements for security precautions, fair employment practices, and provisions for subcontracting to small business and in labor surplus areas may all require organizational changes and additions to the staff.

2. *Armed Forces Management*, V (Feb., 1959), 29.

A 1960 article in *Armed Forces Management* cited the observations of one executive on the question of small business entry, with specific reference to subcontracting:

Many responsible small businessmen say it is "folly" to enter defense work because the government "imposes conditions both confiscatory and destructive to small business," according to Denham Scott, Assistant to the President of the Garrett Corp.

Testifying recently before the House Small Business Subcommittee, Scott said existing rules and specifications governing defense procurement policy deprives [sic] small business of proprietary rights. Scott said that it is a popular misconception that the government pays for all development of weapon systems and other defense programs.

He said the small businessman working on defense contracts "must inescapably become contractually obligated to conform to a bewildering maze of regulations, specifications, contractual clauses . . . and 'what nots' . . . all of which stem from the government with whom he has neither a contract nor a contact." [3]

In a 1960 report prepared by seven representatives from defense contractors and two staff members of the Government Procurement Subcommittee of the Senate Small Business Committee, it was noted that regulations on reports and record-keeping vary from one procurement agency to another, even within the same service. The requirements of these regulations appear burdensome enough to discourage many potential entrants. Not only may these requirements necessitate changes in a firm's basic operating procedures, but they inevitably add to the cost of doing business with the government. The ten largest members of the Aerospace Industries Association, according to the report, estimated that they spent over $100 million a year on administrative reports to the military services.[4] The approximate accuracy of the figure was later confirmed by Secretary McNamara, who testified in 1963 that required administrative and technical reports cost defense contractors an estimated total of $300 million per year.[5] To the extent that such requirements relate to cost reimbursement contracts, the contractor is able to pass on the burden and possibly a little more to the customer. Even on firm fixed-price contracts the bulk of the record-keeping and reporting

3. VI (May, 1960), 36.
4. Military Procurement Advisory Committee, *Report to Senator George A. Smathers,* pp. 34–40.
5. U.S. Congress, House Committee on Armed Services, *Hearings on Military Posture and H.R. 2440,* p. 511.

costs are ultimately borne by the Department of Defense, given the assumption of generally inelastic demand conditions in the defense market. Nevertheless, a contractor must have substantial manpower and capital tied up in keeping special records, gathering information, and preparing reports. A firm already in the defense business, especially one which has been in the market long enough to see the system evolve, has an advantage over a potential entrant both in the efficiency with which it can meet paper-work requirements and in its ability to estimate their costs in preparing bids or proposals. Finally, to the extent that factors other than pure profit maximization influence decisions, the red tape might appear annoying enough to discourage a potential entrant even if the firm felt that it could operate profitably in the defense market.

Security restrictions may bar or hinder entry by companies of all sizes. A firm's eligibility to receive contracts in many procurement areas is subject to delay while the clearance procedure is under way, and establishment and maintenance of required security measures can be costly and time consuming. A more important barrier to entry posed by security considerations appears to be the difficulty of obtaining the information needed to make informed bids in certain programs. Two examples, both involving large firms, may be cited. In the 1959 hearings on the missile program, there was discussion of an unsuccessful attempt by Du Pont to get into the solid propellants program. A Department of Defense official stated that Du Pont was given all the information about the program and its requirements necessary to make a responsive bid, but was refused access to classified materials which pertained to execution of the contract and which were presumably needed by Du Pont in order to estimate its performance costs.[6] In hearings on the 1962 Department of Defense appropriations, it was pointed out that Pan American had a virtually complete monopoly on its Cape Canaveral management contract because security restrictions prohibited any potential competitor from obtaining information necessary to make a bid. In reply to this observation it was conceded that the contract was a sole-source negotiated contract; but the arrangement was defended on the ground that the contract was renegotiated annually on the basis

6. U.S. Congress, House Committee on Government Operations, Military Operations Subcommittee, *Hearings: Organization and Management of Missile Programs,* pp. 499–500.

of a "definitized work statement," which was subject to rigorous cost analysis by the National Aeronautics and Space Administration and by all the service agencies concerned with programs at Cape Canaveral. The problem of barred entry was not pursued further by members of the committee.[7]

Still another illustration of the difficulties facing even a very large firm, related in this instance to the customer's demand for certain organizational structures rather than to security, is the failure of American Motors to win defense awards after it had set up a Special Products Division exclusively for this purpose. In announcing the shutdown of the division in 1958, American Motors' President George Romney stated:

We hired a nucleus of competent missile people and tried for three years to obtain a contract worthy of the name. . . . We contacted every known procurement agency. We had the excellent plant and production facilities of the Hudson Motor Car Co. to offer. It is my firm conviction that we were bypassed because of an unfounded lack of confidence in our stability as an organization.[8]

Any defense procurement contract can be terminated, prior to completion, for the convenience of the government. The Military Procurement Advisory Committee of the Senate Small Business Committee noted, on this point:

It is not uncommon for the time period required to settle a termination claim to exceed the delivery schedule specified in the contract and in some instances the time required for settlement continues for several years. This can impose a serious financial hardship on both prime contractors and subcontractors, particularly small business, who do not have adequate finances to cover the terminated inventories for the extended period of time involved in the settlement.[9]

The single most important aspect of the Relationship in terms of inhibition of entry into the defense market is embodied in Department of Defense policies regarding rights to data. "Many a small company," testified Chauncey Brooks of the National Small Business Association, "faced with loss of patent rights, trade secrets, and per-

---

7. U.S. Congress, House Committee on Appropriations, Subcommittee on Department of Defense Appropriations, *Hearings: Department of Defense Appropriations for 1962, Part 4, Research, Development, Test, and Evaluation,* pp. 501–510.

8. *Aviation Week and Space Technology,* LXVIII (Jan. 27, 1958), 65.

9. Military Procurement Advisory Committee, *Report to Senator George A. Smathers,* p. 31.

haps pirating of personnel from profitable commercial business, will refuse to deal with the Government. Other small firms will not deal with the Government because of the intricacies of contracting, and the difficulty of finally getting paid on a contract." [10] In drawing the legal implications from a case study and survey of relevant procurement regulations, H. I. Forman concluded that "if a contractor wishes to conceal its previously developed proprietary information from the Government as well as its commercial competitors, or from just its commercial competitors as in the above case study, it should neither seek nor accept a government contract." [11] The Department of Defense's policies in regard to patents and proprietary information have been reviewed in Chapter VI. The right of audit, in addition, gives defense officials access to virtually all cost data pertaining to a firm's performance under a military contract. A firm accepting a prime contract must be prepared to surrender to the government its privileges of maintaining the secrecy of its technical and cost data, and in addition must be willing to have such information made available to competing contractors. The *Armed Services Procurement Regulation* specifies that proprietary data and licenses under patents received from contractors are to be revealed or used only for public purposes, but Forman noted that a firm had no legal recourse against the government when it found that its proprietary data had been put to unauthorized commercial use.[12]

While the loss of rights of a prime contractor in matters of industrial secrecy has been considered unacceptable by some firms, the position of subcontractors in this area appears to be even more objectionable to the business community. The policy of the Department of Defense in this matter, as stated in response to an inquiry from the Senate Small Business Committee in 1961, is as follows:

> The acquisition of data from a subcontractor shall be governed by the nature and circumstances of the subcontract, it being the intent of the Department of Defense that in obtaining data originating with subcontractors, the contractor shall, insofar as carrying out his obligations under a prime contract is concerned, be guided by the same policies and procedures as if the subcontractor were contracting directly with the

10. U.S. Congress, Senate Select Committee on Small Business, Subcommittee on Monopoly, *Hearings: Economic Aspects of Government Patent Policies*, pp. 92–93.
11. "Proprietary Rights in Research and Development Contracting—A Case Study," *Research and Development Procurement Law*, p. 312.
12. *Ibid.*

Government and should not request unlimited rights in "proprietary data" where such rights are not required by the Government under the prime contract.[13]

Entry into the defense market through subcontracting is evidently affected by demands for data even more strongly than is entry through award of a prime contract. In 1959 the Military Procurement Subcommittee of the Senate Small Business Committee charged that prime contractors were requesting detailed technical data from subcontractors and then using the data, without authorization or offer of compensation, in their own production operations. According to a staff member, the subcommittee regarded this practice as posing one of the most serious problems the Department of Defense faced in its small business program.[14] In 1961, *Missiles and Rockets* called attention to cases of patent infringements by major contractors against their subcontractors.[15] And according to testimony given during hearings on the 1964 Department of Defense appropriations, prime contractors had shown little concern over requirements which had only recently been put into full effect that dealt with submission of certified cost data. There had, however, been several complaints from subcontractors who objected to furnishing prime contractors with similar information for fear of having trade secrets revealed.[16]

Procurement agencies have, at times, added to the tensions arising between contractors and subcontractors over the data issue. For example, in 1959 *Aviation Week and Space Technology* reported an indignant response from industry when the Air Force sought to require recipients of prime contracts to hold open competitions for subcontracts. Formerly, the Air Force had been willing to accept bids from "teams" of prime contractors and previously selected subcontractors. A spokesman for one firm commented, "In the future, we'll keep our good ideas to ourselves until after the prime contractor has been selected. Otherwise we may find our novel ideas disclosed in

13. Military Procurement Advisory Committee, *Report to Senator George A. Smathers*, p. 19.

14. *Armed Forces Management*, VI (Dec., 1959), 42.

15. IX (Dec. 11, 1961), 50.

16. U.S. Congress, House Committee on Appropriations, Subcommittee on Department of Defense Appropriations, *Hearings: Department of Defense Appropriations for 1964*, Part 5, *Procurement*, pp. 479–480.

the specifications to which we and our competitors are asked to bid for the subcontract." [17]

It is certainly understandable that many firms should find it unacceptable to be required to furnish confidential information to other firms even though they would be perfectly willing to supply the same data to the government. The requirement would be particularly discouraging to a firm which hoped to get into the defense market as a subcontractor and later, after some experience and perhaps growth, compete for prime contracts against the firms it would first be required to supply with confidential technical and cost data. In the previous chapter it was pointed out that the objective of the Department of Defense in its demands for proprietary data and transferable patent licenses is to increase the potential for price competition in procurement actions beyond the EDTR stage, and it has been argued above that this goal could be achieved only through some reduction in the incentives for non-price technical competition. To the extent that demands for data inhibit entry and weaken the potential for subcontractors to compete at the prime contract level, the long-run effects of the Department of Defense's demands for data and their use in procurement packages tend to make the policy a self-defeating one in the area of price competition as well.

The Department of Defense has attempted, for many years, to reduce barriers to the entry of small firms. Under the department's Small Business Program, an Office of Small Business has been established within each military department, and the post of Director of Small Business has been established at the Department of Defense level. A small business specialist is assigned to each major procurement center. Close working relationships have been established between the Department of Defense and the Small Business Administration. The Small Business Administration may assign a representative to any purchasing agency at its own discretion. These Small Business Administration representatives, when given proper security clearance, are permitted to have access to whatever procurement actions they wish to examine, and may make recommendations on procurements they consider suitable to small business, including suggestions as to specific potential contractors. Rejected recommen-

17. LXXI (July 6, 1959), 26–27.

dations may be appealed to the Secretary of the service involved. The Small Business Administration is authorized to certify any small firm to the Department of Defense for competence and credit capacity. Procurement agencies are required to restrict suitable purchases through total or partial set-asides for small business. "To the maximum extent possible," all non-classified proposed procurements, whether advertised or negotiated, are to be reported to the Department of Commerce for publication in the *Commerce Business Daily*. In all contracts of over $5,000, the contractor must accept a clause by which he agrees to accomplish the maximum amount of subcontracting with small business which is consistent with efficient performance of the contract. Contracts of over $500,000 contain a standard clause requiring the contractor to set up a prescribed program for small business participation, to maintain proper records and submit certain reports, and to notify the contracting officer of every proposed subcontract of over $10,000 for which no small business firms are to be solicited.[18]

Yet in at least two respects, Department of Defense procurement policies appear to have hindered entry into the defense market by small business. In 1952, J. P. Miller wrote:

> I do not wish to minimize the importance of the military establishment improving policies and procedures designed to facilitate the flow of contracts directly to willing small businesses. But I have a strong suspicion that the bulk of our small business concerns would prefer a subcontract of a given volume at a given time to a prime contract of the same amount at the same time. The administrative complications of government contracts are sufficient in many cases to dictate such a preference.[19]

Miller's words must now ring ironically in the ears of small business subcontractors. Today, subcontractors as well as prime contractors have been drawn deeply into the Relationship, with all its "administrative complications," through means of a clause in the prime contract which requires the contractor to insert numerous standard clauses in all of his subcontracts. The subcontractor is faced with fair employment requirements, security restrictions, submission to audits

18. *Armed Services Procurement Regulation*, 1963 edition, paragraphs 1–700 to 1–708, 1–1002.3, and 1–1003.1 (a).
19. "Military Procurement Policies: World War II and Today," *American Economic Review*, XLII, 471.

and inspections by both procurement agency and prime contractor representatives, demands for records and reports, cost certification, and participation in small business and labor surplus area programs to almost the same extent as a prime contractor. His situation is worse than that of a prime contractor in at least one very important respect in that he has no direct contract with a defense agency and hence no legal recourse against the government. Thus, in many respects other than through demands for data, barriers have been raised to entry along the route which is often most suitable to small business by the Department of Defense's procurement policies in regard to subcontractors.

Second, the small business program has been carried out under great political pressure and is the result of some wishful thinking based on erroneous premises. A 1962 survey of eighty-three "defense-oriented" firms by *Armed Forces Management* indicated that a majority of the respondents thought that the problem of small business participation in the defense market was political and that the program did not provide economic advantages for either the Department of Defense or the small business community.[20] The program is manageable, according to one Department of Defense official, only because in the postwar period the military agencies have not, and under current legislation and regulations cannot, pay a premium price in order to award a contract to a small business firm or to a firm in a labor surplus area. An example of confusion which was very likely the result of an effort to make facts conform to desired political objectives is found in the following exchange between Senator Proxmire and Assistant Secretary of Defense Morris during 1961 hearings:

> Senator PROXMIRE. History has been that small business gets almost 50 percent of advertised bidding and only about 20 percent of negotiated bidding; is that correct?
> Mr. MORRIS. I believe that is correct, sir.
> Senator PROXMIRE. One of the reasons why small business has done less and less and less well with the Defense Department is because there has been less and less advertised bidding and more negotiated bidding; is that right?
> Mr. MORRIS. We have had a very level situation.

20. VIII (Feb., 1962), 14–15.

Senator PROXMIRE. These things are together. Small business just coincides with the taxpayer interest, at least to the extent that the taxpayer interest is served by competitive bidding.

Mr. MORRIS. The two programs correlate very directly, sir, the breaking out of components from large systems, the conversion from sole source to competitive buying contributes directly to the small business program.[21]

It would appear that Senator Proxmire, like many people concerned with the implications of military procurement and at the same time desirous of promoting procedure in accordance with the letter of the law, would have liked to see advertised bidding used wherever possible instead of negotiated procurement. Advertised bidding reduces the likelihood of improper influence or pressures on procurement officials and opens procurement opportunities to all qualified firms on an equal basis. Further, Senator Proxmire indicated his interest in expanding small business participation in the defense market. It does not seem unfair to Senator Proxmire to suggest that he therefore hoped and certainly implied in his questions that the two objectives went together in the sense that advertised bidding favored small business, perhaps because of a belief that the more competitive the bidding the better the small firms' chances. Unfortunately, Senator Proxmire was wrong. Advertised bidding, as was noted earlier, is not necessarily more competitive than competitively negotiated procurement, nor does it favor small business. With some evident embarrassment, the Department of Defense later submitted a statement for the record to supplement the testimony of Assistant Secretary Morris:

While the answer given by Mr. Morris is essentially correct, it is also pertinent to consider the following facts. With respect to procurements that have been determined to be within the capabilities of known small firms, small business has fared better on negotiated types of procurement than on advertised. Thus, in fiscal year 1960, small business received 65 percent of the total negotiated small business potential of $3.5 billion, as opposed to 48 percent of the total advertised small business potential of $2.4 billion. Two-thirds of the total dollars small business firms received resulted from negotiated contracts, while only one-third came from advertised contracts.[22]

21. U.S. Congress, Joint Economic Committee, Subcommittee on Defense Procurement, *Hearing: Progress Made by the Department of Defense in Reducing the Impact of Military Procurement on the Economy*, pp. 34–35.

22. *Ibid.*, p. 34.

Whatever may be the source of the myth that emphasis on advertised bidding and the small business program supplement each other, it is evident that those most immediately affected know better. A 1961 survey of small defense firms indicated their clear preference for negotiated procurement over advertised bidding.[23]

C. Inherent Barriers to Entry

It seems beyond dispute that some of the barriers to entry to the defense market have been raised by the customer's procurement policies. There are other barriers which are inherent in the nature of the market. Only after some discussion of these more fundamental barriers will it be feasible to assess the effects of procurement policies on entry.

The most pervasive barriers to entry, and in many cases the most impenetrable, result from the complex and advanced technology typical of much of the defense market. The advantage an EDTR contractor has in obtaining follow-on production contracts is one such barrier. Economies of scale in research and, more importantly, in developmental work may effectively exclude smaller firms from entering at the earliest stage by competing for EDTR contracts. Technologically determined economies of scale and barriers to entry by small business into the more technically advanced procurement programs are suggested by Table VII-1 below, which indicates quite clearly that the shares of procurement dollars going to small business vary inversely with the levels of technology embodied in the procurement programs.

David Novick and J. Y. Springer, in a 1958 Rand Corporation study, noted several aspects of military technology which pose grave problems for small business in the defense market.[24] In order to maintain an effective national defense, technological improvements in weaponry must be made rapidly and must utilize the most recent of scientific and engineering advances. In the jargon of the defense market, new weapons must "push the state of the art" in order to

23. Military Procurement Advisory Committee, *Report to Senator George A. Smathers*, pp. 11–12.

24. *Economics of Defense Procurement and Small Business* (Santa Monica: Rand Corp., Aug 15, 1958). See also by the same authors, "Economics of Defense Procurement and Small Business," *Law and Contemporary Problems*, XXIV (Winter, 1959), 118–131.

stay abreast of potential enemies. In weapon programs which push the state of the art, large research and development organizations are essential to keep a contractor informed of and competent in new developments in science and technology, to relate these developments to the customer's needs, to perform research and to translate research findings into feasible processes of production. Few firms, Novick and Springer observed, could meet delivery schedules for new high-priority weapons unless they had participated in the underlying R & D. Pushing the state of the art requires that the prime contractor have a clear understanding of precision standards, material specifications, and process requirements covering all aspects of the program before production commences. R & D experience is the best or only way to gain such understanding. In addition, there are great uncertainties in a weapon program, which can best be met by a large organization. The procurement agency cannot really understand what contributions to the nation's defenses it will be acquiring until performance tests can be made. The decision to continue, cut back, expand, or cancel a program is reviewed by the procurement agency's branch of service, the office of the Secretary of the service, the Department of Defense, and

Table VII-1: Awards to small business by procurement program, FY 1960–64

Procurement program	Percentage of total prime contract awards going to small business, fiscal year				
	1960	1961	1962	1963	1964
Missile systems	1.2	1.2	1.4	1.6	1.6
Aircraft	2.6	2.9	3.2	2.8	3.2
Ships	8.7	8.6	12.8	9.5	10.2
Electronics & communication equipment	7.8	8.3	10.0	11.7	10.4
Tank-automotive	14.6	10.5	14.0	6.9	10.4
Ammunition	9.9	9.1	11.3	11.2	15.2
All business firms for work in U.S.	16.1	15.9	17.7	15.8	17.2
Fuels & lubricants	20.6	24.3	22.0	20.2	22.8
Services	21.4	24.7	34.2	21.1	22.9
Weapons	19.0	30.2	38.5	21.7	27.3
Miscellaneous hard goods	38.7	37.0	37.9	32.0	29.1
All actions of less than $10,000	64.5	63.9	64.6	53.6	51.5
Subsistence	57.3	55.8	57.4	51.3	53.0
Construction	50.0	53.6	47.8	51.5	56.4
Textiles, clothing & equipage	67.8	55.9	61.9	62.5	67.1

Source: OSD, *Military Prime Contract Awards and Subcontract Payments, July 1963– June 1964*, p. 22.

the Bureau of the Budget; and change orders must be expected. Delays are inevitable, and in order to minimize them the contractor must be able to maintain contacts with offices and individuals at several levels of the defense organization. The weapon system concept, Novick and Springer noted, had been blamed for limiting entry and tending to exclude small business, since it concentrated prime contracts in the hands of fewer firms and gave the prime contractor responsibility for the total system. Novick and Springer argued, however, that the weapon system merely recognized the needs of development and production of advanced weapons. Since 1958, the associate contractor system has expanded and weapon system management has shifted from contractors to military agencies. The views of Novick and Springer have been borne out in that there has been no significant increase in small business participation in weapon programs, nor is entry evidently easier, despite the fact that decisions are being made by presumably impartial government officials rather than by large prime contractors with high financial stakes in the programs.

Novick and Springer concluded that there was little if anything that the government could do to increase small business participation in the procurement of specialized military equipment other than reduce uncertainty by establishing a long-run federal procurement program with minimum annual procurement levels set for perhaps ten years. Writing in 1958, they were, I believe, more influenced than one should be today by the great fluctuations in defense spending during the Korean War and the subsequent cutback. But aside from the stability of over-all defense procurement relative to other manufacturing sectors of the economy from 1955 through 1964, there has been no development in the defense market which would call into question their view of the necessarily limited role of small business in modern weaponry.

Jacoby and Stockfisch, noting the high degree of specialization of skills and facilities which characterizes defense industries, commented:

The emphasis on quality of personnel skills can also launch "non-defense" firms into the defense business. For example, railroad car builders and truck-trailer manufacturers have acquired a large share of the missile ground-handling equipment business. As the "hardening" of missile systems gains key importance, architectural firms find themselves coping with the problems of silo design and construction. As anti-submarine warfare becomes increasingly vital, institutes of oceanography will thrive and perhaps even "spin off" some new firms. And who knows what the rising interest in chemical and bacteriological warfare may do for insecticide firms? [25]

G. A. Busch, in the same volume, observed that changing postwar technology has encouraged entry into the preserves of the airframe industry by firms from the chemical, electrical products, business machine, and rubber industries.[26] But the examples cited by Busch, as well as those of Jacoby and Stockfisch, simply highlight the contention that entry into advanced sectors of the defense market is virtually confined to large firms, preferably already research-oriented, and to those smaller firms which have previously developed exceptionally high degrees of technical proficiency in fields related to military technology.

It could be argued that the intense and sustained demand for technical proficiency has promoted entry by small firms with particular skills. One is readily reminded of numerous instances in which scientists and engineers, often moving directly from college and university faculties or graduate schools, have established business concerns based on the skills and sometimes the inventions of their founders. But the mortality rate of these firms has been high, both from outright financial failure and from highly profitable merger.[27]

The limited number of scientists and engineers available in comparison with the demand for them, coupled with pressures on contractors to "hoard" their technical staffs in order to strengthen their competitive chances in new programs, should be viewed as establishing a barrier to entry similar to that posed by the limited availability of a vital raw material.

The writing of specifications for components of weapon systems and for spare parts also raises entry problems. An item may be described in requests for bids or proposals by either design or performance specifications. Most specifications for complex items are a

25. *Planning and Forecasting in the Defense Industries,* p. 18.
26. "Some Emerging Developments in the Airframe Industry," *ibid.,* pp. 175–191.
27. An excellent study of such firms is Albert H. Rubenstein, *Problems of Financing and Managing New Research-based Enterprises in New England,* Research Report to the Federal Reserve Bank of Boston, No. 3, 1958.

combination of the two types. A performance specification gives greater scope for non-price competition, but does not allow for interchangeability or ready price comparison among proposals. In procurement of items intended for a common use or expected to have a long period of utilization, and in which additional purchases are therefore anticipated, design specifications are usually desirable or necessary. Design specifications may limit procurement to a single source when patents, proprietary data, or exclusive know-how are involved.[28] In addition, the information on which specifications are based or procurement orders placed must often be drawn from technical manuals. Because the developer of an item and the prime contractor in a weapon system project possess indispensable knowledge, these firms play an important role in the preparation of technical manuals. Even though the manuals are partly written, reviewed, and approved by military personnel, the contributions of contractors may deliberately or inadvertently heighten barriers to entry or perpetuate sole-source positions. Finally, because of lack of time or excessive cost of analysis of an item, specifications are occasionally written by citing the manufacturer's designation or the catalogue number of the item and adding, "or the equivalent thereof."

There have been recent shifts in the composition of the Department of Defense's demand pattern in two significant procurement areas. In one case the shifts should hinder entry while in the other they could conceivably facilitate it. The first set of shifts involves the procurement of major weapon systems. With the end of the missile build-up and the decline in reliance on manned aircraft, procurement of advanced weapons has come to emphasize the development of very complex devices—such as the manned orbiting laboratory—which are subsequently to be ordered in very small quantities. When weapon systems are slated for eventual production in some volume, Secretary McNamara has made it very clear that the pressures on the services for standardization will be severe, as in the TFX controversy. "We should not develop two aircraft," he has

28. Specification problems are discussed in a statement submitted by the Air Force in U.S. Congress, House Committee on Appropriations, Subcommittee on Department of Defense Appropriations, *Hearings: Department of Defense Appropriations for 1959, Procurement, Supply, and Surplus Operations of the Department of Defense*, pp. 436–439.

stated, "or two missiles or two of anything where one can do the job." [29]

The greater stress on advanced and specialized technology and the relative decline of production orders should further differentiate military and civilian industries and should make entry from one to the other more difficult. In like manner, emphasis on development and insistence on standardization will reduce opportunities for a type of subcontracting described by J. S. Day in his 1956 study of the airframe industry. There were, Day found, very real cost advantages in large-scale production of certain components used by several prime airframe contractors; examples given were special aircraft bolts and optically perfect plexiglass.[30] If economies of scale are denied to such subcontractors by a market for only a few items, or if the demand for components is limited to the production run needs of only one standardized weapon system, the specialized subcontractors' advantages will be eliminated and prime contractors might see no disadvantage in producing the components internally. Standardization also obviously tends to concentrate prime contracts in the hands of a few firms.

The second demand shift has been a result of the build-up of the Army ground forces and supporting units in order to increase the nation's capacity to fight limited wars. In testimony on 1964 defense appropriations, Secretary of the Army Cyrus R. Vance stated:

The Army is continuing to place emphasis on research and development to enhance our capabilities in the special warfare field—that is, unconventional warfare, psychological operations, and counter-insurgency.

The severalfold increase in effort since 1961 is aimed at assuring that items of equipment peculiar to these types of operations are provided to using units as soon as possible. Expedited development projects are under way in many fields—weaponry, demolitions, air and surface mobility, intelligence, communications, surveillance, psychological operations, and combat support. Some of these projects require considerable effort in terms of time and money—for example, the development of a powerful base radio station and a psychological warfare broadcasting system. Other projects are concentrating on much smaller, though certainly essential, items. Included in this category are such items as

29. U.S. Congress, Senate Subcommittee of the Committee on Appropriations, *Hearings: Department of Defense Appropriations for 1964,* p. 19.
30. *Subcontracting Policy in the Airframe Industry,* pp. 116–119.

simple security devices, lightweight weapons, and improved individual equipment needed to give our soldiers an additional edge in jungle operations.[31]

The strengthening of the ground forces involves increased procurement of items of equipment, clothing, weaponry, and vehicles which can be supplied by firms in related civilian industries. While Secretary Vance's statement indicated the Army's demand for innovation and new developments in such fields as small arms, field communication devices, and air and surface transport, the technological bases for advance in limited war capabilities appear to call more on ingenuity and originality than on very advanced scientific concepts and costly laboratories. Despite earlier predictions that the build-up would be completed in FY 1964, the increasing commitment of the United States in Vietnam makes it seem, as this is being written, that procurement expenditures for limited warfare will not level off and certainly not decline for some time. But through FY 1964, as noted in Chapter IV, the strengthening of the ground forces was not of so much benefit to small business or to entrants as it was to large contractors, especially those outside the aircraft and electronics fields. An article in the New York *Times* of March 14, 1965, suggested that the effect of the Vietnamese involvement will be similar. The article discussed the Department of Defense's counter-insurgency (COIN) program. Two small firms which had been awarded prime contracts under the COIN program were mentioned; but the article then went on to describe other COIN awards made to North American Aviation, Philco, Minneapolis-Honeywell, General Electric, General Motors, Cutler-Hammer, Union Carbide, Hallicrafters, R.C.A., Westinghouse, Ling-Temco-Vought, Fairchild-Hiller, Ryan Aeronautical, Curtiss-Wright, Bell Aerospace, and Lockheed, all familiar names in the defense field, and all firms of substantial size.[32]

There are also barriers to entry inherent in the relationships between contractors and subcontractors. Many of the large prime contractors are also major subcontractors and may be competing with each other for potential awards while simultaneously collaborating

31. U.S. Congress, Senate Subcommittee of the Committee on Appropriations, *Hearings: Department of Defense Appropriations for 1964*, pp. 457–458.
32. Pp. F1, F14.

on existing programs. Firms which compete may later find themselves in a buyer-seller relationship in the program for which they
competed. For example, after the Air Force awarded a prime
contract to McDonnell Aircraft for the F-4H fighter aircraft and
canceled its contract with Republic Aviation for the F-105, Republic
received a large subcontracting position in McDonnell's program.
Without imputing any wrongful intent or action to either company
in this case, it can be pointed out that the potential for abuse was
obvious in such a situation. Business reciprocity may also foreclose
potential entrants. A defense executive, Clarence O. Nelson, wrote
quite frankly on this point:

> Procurement and Engineering should coordinate fully prior to
> selecting prospective sources of supply for the new or major purchases.
> In this industry it is not infrequent that the Seller and Buyer role may
> be reversed in many instances. The complete reciprocal or competitive
> factors that may be applicable should be fully recognized.[33]

Members of the House Subcommittee on Department of Defense
Appropriations, especially Representative Daniel Flood of Pennsylvania, have been concerned about the problem of "satellite" subcontractors and have put sharp questions to Department of Defense
witnesses on this problem on several occasions. In hearings on the
1960 appropriations, Flood and Chairman Mahon pointed out that
many nominally independent small firms enjoyed established relationships with prime contractors. In some cases, Flood noted, subcontracting firms are actually created or assisted in their formation
by major prime contractors. "I am not questioning quality, integrity,
performance," said Flood. But he continued, "You are headed for
a closed corporation." Air Force Lieutenant General C. S. Irvine,
in reply to Flood, commented that "it is a little difficult to go into a
man's plant and run it for him." But General Irvine did remark that
the Air Force had occasionally vetoed a prime contractor's selection
of a subcontractor, and that there were firms which had begun by
doing almost all their work for one prime contractor and had later
competed for and won subcontracts from other major prime contractors.[34]

33. *Missile and Aircraft Procurement Management*, p. 59.
34. U.S. Congress, House Committee on Appropriations, Subcommittee on Department of Defense Appropriations, *Hearings: Department of Defense Appropriations for
1960, Part 5, Procurement*, pp. 536–540.

Three years later Flood, joined this time by Representatives Ford and Sikes, questioned Assistant Secretaries Morris and Imirie on the emphasis being given to directed subcontracting by Secretary Mc-Namara and his colleagues. The Department of Defense, according to the testimony, was making an intensive study of prime contractors' purchasing systems and practices, and was frequently requiring prime contractors to subcontract on a competitive basis. The testimony led to the following exchange:

Mr. FLOOD. You will not have this old racket of the "mother hen," where the prime contractor gets a lead from the Pentagon that the following bids will be made, and he spends 6 months touring the country getting prices from a whole flock of subcontractors, and they from sub-subcontractors.

Then when he gets the bid because of that series of operations then those are the jokers who get the subs and the sub-subs.

Mr. IMIRIE. You asked me that same question last year. I said I assumed not. I answer it this year and I say "I know not." [35]

There are, in summary, substantial barriers to successful entry into the defense market, entirely apart from the Department of Defense's procurement policies and practices, which lie behind the relative stability found over periods of time in the lists of the largest prime contractors. While it is impossible to make an incontrovertible assertion on the point, it seems reasonable to assume that the Department of Defense would have only a minor effect on conditions of entry even if it were to change its policies so drastically as to remove all the discretionary barriers posed by the contractual Relationship. Nevertheless, the procurement policies reviewed earlier do add, if only marginally, to entry barriers in the defense market.

D. Effects of Procurement Policies on Conditions of Entry

A clear distinction should be made between conditions of initial entry into the defense market from outside, and the facility with which firms already defense-oriented can enter into competition for

35. U.S. Congress, House Committee on Appropriations, Subcommittee on Department of Defense Appropriations, *Hearings: Department of Defense Appropriations for 1963, Part 4, Procurement*, p. 586.

positions in various new procurement programs. In regard to the former, most of the procurement policies and practices which might discourage civilian-oriented firms from entering the defense market—such as audit and inspection, security restrictions, enforced fair employment practices, paper-work requirements, renegotiation, and the small business and labor surplus area programs—are designed to serve fairly obvious military and social purposes. They do, undoubtedly, make temporary entry into the defense market more difficult and may impose basic, often drastic organizational changes on an entering firm. A firm does not, in all probability, contemplate only temporary entry into the defense market if it has acquired the facilities, the technological skills, and the effective contacts with procurement offices or prime contractors which are highly desirable if not essential to its success. A firm which has overcome these fundamental structural hurdles should find the additional hindrances posed by the customer relatively trivial nuisances. The basic issue here is not one of hindrances to entry so much as the question whether the military and social objectives achieved are worth the additional costs imposed on defense firms and ultimately on the government. Such problems as the military value of security and the social value of non-discriminatory employment practices pose questions far beyond the scope of this study.

Because of the highly specialized nature of military technology, Department of Defense policies on patent licenses and disclosure of proprietary data probably have their greatest effect on firms which are already in the defense market. While there have certainly been cases in which firms have refused to enter the defense market because of a reluctance to reveal secrets relating to their civilian-market products and processes, these instances should dwindle in importance if Jerome Wiesner and others who have noted the widening gulf between military and civilian technology are correct in their assessments. The degree of competition among firms already in the market is, to the customer, the most important aspect of the conditions under which contractors seek new awards. The Department of Defense has sought to reduce barriers to entry and thus increase competition in follow-on production awards by making the results of EDTR work as readily available as possible. But in the process, the incentives for intense non-price competition among prime EDTR contractors have been reduced. Also, by extending the disclosure requirements to subcontractors, potential competition from subcontractors hoping to become prime contractors has been discouraged and the enthusiasm for innovation among subcontractors may have been dampened. I must conclude that the untoward effects on competition in the long run are most likely to outweigh the short-run advantages gained on individual contracts and that the current demands for disclosure should be discontinued. An excellent substitute for the present policies is available in the proposal made by R. F. Lanzillotti and L. E. Preston before the Subcommittee on Monopoly of the Senate Small Business Committee and discussed in the previous chapter, that firms negotiating for EDTR contracts be permitted to make two offers, one in which they propose to retain rights to patents and proprietary data, and another granting the Department of Defense the rights it now demands.[36] Contractors should be free to conduct similar negotiations with their subcontractors. An exception should be made permitting the Secretary of Defense to compel disclosure when he determines that such action is essential to the nation's defense and is not merely cost saving. Negotiations on the price differentials between the two contracts should protect the government's rights to discoveries for which it has paid and at the same time reduce the unfavorable effects brought about by contractors' reactions to compulsory disclosure.

As a converse to the proposition that procurement policies and procedures which hinder entry have had only marginal effects, it appears that efforts by the Department of Defense to reduce barriers to entry have been rather ineffectual. The two most important attempts at easing entry have been made through the small business program and directed subcontracting. In 1955 the Hoover Commission staff maintained that it was a "fair assumption" that without any special programs or assistance from the Small Business Administration, small business would get its "fair proportion" of the quite limited number of defense contracts actually suitable for small business.[37] And in 1964 Albert N. Schrieber concluded that small busi-

36. U.S. Congress, Senate Select Committee on Small Business, Subcommittee on Monopoly, *Hearings: Economic Aspects of Government Patent Policies*, pp. 120, 244.

37. U.S. Commission on the Organization of the Executive Branch of the Government (1953–1955), Task Force on Procurement, *Five Staff Papers Prepared for the Task Force on Procurement*, pp. C–38, C–39.

ness was in fact getting its fair share of defense contracts, or was at least faring relatively as well in defense as in civilian sales. Schrieber's findings were made on the basis of careful analysis of data pertaining to the share held by small business in civilian markets compared to its share of defense programs.[38] The small business program is, by its very definition, subject to weakness in that a successful contractor or subcontractor will grow, and a firm that no longer qualifies as a small business may face problems resulting from the loss of whatever advantages it had gained from its small business preference. Further, the small business preference, while it may channel awards to small defense-oriented firms rather than to equally qualified larger rivals, can never be a real inducement to entry from outside the defense market so long as payment of a price premium to small firms is prohibited. Still, the fundamental determinants of limited small business participation in the defense market appear to be market and technological factors which the small business program or a more intense effort such as Operation Booster can do only little to influence.

Directed subcontracting subjects the purchasing systems of prime contractors to inspection and military approval, requires prime contractors to subcontract specified work, and provides that in designated purchases subcontractors must be obtained on a competitive basis. It is too early to assess the actual effect of directed subcontracting, which has been stressed only under Secretary McNamara, but in Chapter III reasons were given for doubting that any such program will have as much effect on the volume of subcontracting as it will on the placement pattern. Directed subcontracting could no doubt disrupt and virtually eliminate "satellite" subcontracting if such were the desire. But the satellite relationship, while a barrier to entry, is defensible as conducive to the freest possible flow of voluntary information between a contractor and his subcontractors. Recalling that it was required competitive subcontracting which evoked the response, "In the future, we'll keep our good ideas to ourselves until after the prime contractor has been selected," it seems that the Department of Defense would be wise to limit its use of directed subcontracting.

38. "Small Business and Government Procurement," *Law and Contemporary Problems*, XXIX (Spring, 1964), 390–417.

E. Barriers to Exit

Because of their potential significance to the nation in the event of disarmament, barriers to exit of firms from the defense market have been of great concern to Department of Defense and other government officials, businessmen, and interested outside observers; and a great deal more has been said and written about problems of moving out of defense and into civilian production than about barriers to entry into the defense market. Primarily as a result of dependence on increasingly specialized technology and methods of production, barriers to exit are becoming higher for defense firms.

In a 1963 statement before the Senate Subcommittee on Employment and Manpower, Assistant Secretary of Defense (Comptroller) Charles J. Hitch contrasted current conditions with those at the end of World War II and during the reduction in defense spending after the Korean War.[39] The adjustment at the end of World War II, Hitch noted, involved a reconversion by firms which had previously converted from civilian to war work and a "sharp contraction" by specialized defense contractors. The problems of postwar reconversion in the forties were eased by several factors. Most important was the great pent-up demand for civilian goods. Also, conversion had been largely financed by the government and contractors could leave defense work simply by discarding government-owned plant and equipment; the government's termination procedures were "prompt and liberal"; and the government very quickly put a large volume of usable equipment, facilities, machinery, and materials into the civilian economy through its surplus disposal program. In one important respect the situation at the end of the Korean War was similar, since the brunt of reconversion fell on normally civilian-oriented firms. General Motors, Ford, and Chrysler, Hitch noted, received nearly $10.9 billion in defense contracts from FY 1951 through FY 1953, and only about $500 million in the three following fiscal years. "All in all," Hitch stated, "the readjustment following the Korean war was accomplished without any major dislocations in the economy. Some individual firms, communities, and workers were

39. U.S. Congress, Senate Committee on Labor and Public Welfare, Subcommittee on Employment and Manpower, *Hearings: Nation's Manpower Revolution, Part 9*, pp. 3067–3077.

adversely affected but, in most cases, only temporarily. Large, well diversified corporations had little difficulty adjusting to even the very large post-Korean war cutbacks in military work." [40] The problems of today's contractors are more formidable, although less serious to the nation in the sense that defense spending is a much smaller fraction of the gross national product than it was in either 1945 or 1953. In Hitch's words:

> Admittedly, the situation today is quite different than it was, even at the end of the Korean war. While the defense effort now accounts for less than 10 percent of the gross national product (compared with about 14 percent during the Korean war), an important part of the resources now committed to defense work is highly specialized. As we have seen, the proportion of nonproduction workers in the defense-related industries has increased substantially in the last 10 years. Included among these nonproduction workers are the scientists, engineers and other technical personnel. Similarly, highly specialized research and development and production facilities have been constructed during this period. That much of these specialized resources is readily transferable to other scientific and engineering efforts, such as the NASA civilian space program, has been well demonstrated in recent years. But it seems reasonable to conclude that it will not be a simple matter to transfer such resources to strictly commercial-type work.
>
> Nor does the experience of specialized defense contractors since the end of World War II provide much confidence that they, as individual companies, can successfully convert to commercial work. In the past, these companies have survived principally by adjusting promptly to major changes in the size or character of the defense program. For example, with the exception of civilian transports, the specialized aircraft manufacturers have had very little success in the commercial field, and even the civilian transport business has not proved to be very profitable in the last 5 or 6 years.[41]

Secretary Hitch was drawing on a discouraging set of experiences when he observed that, with the exception of commercial aircraft development, specialized defense contractors had had very little success in civilian markets since World War II. The history of the aircraft industry's diversification efforts is illustrative. Murray L. Weidenbaum, in reviewing this history, noted that aircraft companies had at least a small measure of success after World War II in manufacturing such products as aluminum canoes, stainless steel

40. *Ibid.*, p. 3071.
41. *Ibid.*

caskets, and prosthetic devices, in subcontracting to produce radio and television tubes, automobile parts, cabinets and casings, musical instruments, and plumbing fixtures, and in using retained wartime earnings to acquire civilian-oriented firms. But when the Korean War broke out, these adventures were abandoned or de-emphasized. The most important reason, Weidenbaum observed, was "the overriding desire of the aircraft companies to build aircraft rather than canoes or wheelbarrows." Attempts to diversify again after the Korean War were much less successful in the absence of a great pent-up demand.[42]

These problems, Weidenbaum and others have observed, are based on defense firms' specialized equipment, their comparative advantages in high quality and precision coupled with a relative lack of skill in volume production at low cost, the virtual absence of marketing and distributing organizations and experience suited to civilian markets, the lack of transferability to civilian applications of the knowledge of scientific and professional personnel in defense industries, and the attitudes engendered among executives by the defense environment. Leaders of the defense industries have been charged with a lack of concern for costs, a conviction that there will be no major reductions in defense spending or only temporary cutbacks, and an almost irresponsible attitude toward their firms' financial structures.[43]

Spokesmen for defense firms have also taken a pessimistic view of the possibilities of diversification into civilian markets. H. Igor Anshoff of Lockheed was quoted as saying, "To be sure, no one can bend aluminum like we can bend aluminum in our industry, but advanced manufacturing skills have very little to do with success in consumer industries. Success depends on merchandising: distribution channels, competitive pricing, and aggressive product promotion. And the firms which were trying to sell aluminum skis, coffins,

42. "Product Diversification in the Aircraft Manufacturing Industry," *Analysts Journal*, XV (May, 1959), 51–56.
43. Problems noted here are discussed in the following:
Murray L. Weidenbaum, "The U.S. Aircraft Industry," *Financial Analysts Journal*, XIX, 49–53, and "Industrial Impact of Disarmament," *American Journal of Economics and Sociology*, XXII (Oct., 1963), 513–526.
"Industrial Adjustments to Shifts in Defense Spending," U.S. Congress, Senate Committee on Labor and Public Welfare, *Selected Readings in Employment and Manpower*, II, 697–708.
U.S. Arms Control and Disarmament Agency, *Economic Impacts of Disarmament*, Economic Series 1, Jan., 1962 (Washington: Government Printing Office, 1962).

canoes, and wheelbarrows had none of these skills." [44] The attitude is shared by firms in other branches of the defense market. David Packard, president of Hewlett-Packard, stated, "The hope . . . that our industry can and should become less dependent on military work is sheer wishful thinking that borders on irresponsibility.

It will be the continuing task of the electronics industry to add to our military strength for many years. . . ." [45]

An official of the Department of Defense, in commenting on the testimony of Secretary Hitch cited above, voiced the opinion that the best way for a firm which was losing defense orders to hold losses to its stockholders to a minimum would be to reduce its size promptly and ruthlessly. Diversification into civilian products, he believed, increased losses more often than it helped the situation.

Weidenbaum has suggested two ways in which the Department of Defense and other government agencies could alleviate the problem. First, the government could help firms to diversify by awarding contracts for commercial R & D to defense firms, by expanding its purchases of civilian-type goods from these firms, and by treating diversification planning costs as allowable costs under military contracts. Second, the government could facilitate the transfer of technical resources and personnel from the defense market by giving commercial R & D more favorable tax treatment, by entering into cost-sharing R & D contracts in which the government would be reimbursed only if the R & D led to a commercial product, by stepping up technical assistance to firms seeking commercial applications for military research findings, and by leasing government-owned facilities to non-defense companies.[46]

Since Weidenbaum's suggestions were made, the *Armed Services Procurement Regulation* has been revised to permit certain costs of "generalized long-range management planning" for dislocations and alterations of markets to be regarded as allowable costs under procurement contracts. But no expenditure for actual R & D on new civilian products can be allowed. In 1965, the President's Committee on the Economic Impact of Defense and Disarmament noted that further aids to defense firms had been "frequently" suggested. But

44. *Missiles and Rockets*, VII (July 11, 1960), 19.
45. *Ibid.*, VII (Sept. 5, 1960), 16.
46. Murray L. Weidenbaum, "Utilizing Defense and Space Technology," *Research for Industry*, XVI (March–April, 1964), 2–4.

the committee took a cautious view of government assistance to defense firms in their efforts to diversify into civilian markets, pointing out that preparation for disarmament need not and should not involve discrimination against non-defense firms.[47]

In a 1963 issue of *Missiles and Rockets* a different solution was proposed. After pointing to the failures of defense-oriented firms in commercial markets, the article went on to observe that there were peacetime needs which could make good use of the scientific and engineering talents of defense contractors. Programs mentioned included salt water conversion, erosion and pollution control, development of transportation, communications and information systems, conservation, harbor engineering and development, ocean shipping, nuclear power, and weather forecasting. In most of these programs, the government would continue to be the principal customer, which *Missiles and Rockets* considered all to the good.[48]

The proposals made by Weidenbaum and *Missiles and Rockets* illustrate the drastic changes in policy and the high costs involved in public efforts to facilitate the transfer of resources out of the defense sector. At present, the costs and likely degree of success are both problematic. In the absence of a much-improved climate for disarmament it seems highly improbable that appropriate administrative and congressional action will be forthcoming; in the meantime exit from the defense market is hindered, along with entry, by substantial structural barriers.

Exit from the defense industry was eased after World War II by the fact that much of the plant and equipment used by firms for war production was government-owned. In this respect, defense firms still have an advantage in exit, but one which is more likely to be used in bargaining and in adjustment to short-run fluctuations in output. An example was given when Representative Mahon noted in 1961 that if Boeing lost its contract for the B-52 bomber it would have to shut down its Wichita, Kansas, plant. "It seems to me," Mahon observed, "that you could drive a pretty good bargain here." But Air Force Lieutenant General Mark E. Bradley, Jr., Deputy Chief of Staff for Materiel, responded that Boeing had little to lose

47. U.S. President's Committee on the Economic Impact of Defense and Disarmament, *Report of the Committee on the Economic Impact of Defense and Disarmament, July 1965* (Washington: Government Printing Office, 1965), esp. pp. 40, 50–51.
48. XIII (Dec. 2, 1963), 24–26.

even if the B-52 were awarded to some other firm and the Wichita plant were closed down. "There will be very little overhead there. It is a Government-owned plant." [49]

The one civilian market in which defense contractors have been successful, indeed dominant, is that for commercial aircraft. There appear to be two principal reasons for this success. First, there are greater technological similarities between military and civilian products and hence greater "spillover" in aircraft than there are between any other technically advanced procurement programs and civilian industries. These similarities have, in fact, resulted in some degree from defense policy. The Air Force has deliberately specified design characteristics in military transport aircraft which are intended to meet both military and civilian needs, in the hope that there will be a spillover and that the commercial carriers will purchase aircraft which will strengthen the nation's emergency airlift capacity.[50] Such purchases have been further stimulated by a Department of Defense policy of contracting with private air carriers for the transportation of both personnel and materiel in cases in which the cargo could just as well be carried by military aircraft. The civilian regulatory agencies have also encouraged the establishment of a civil reserve air fleet in the hands of the carriers. One of the major arguments for development of the B-70 supersonic bomber, or the RS-70 reconnaissance-strike plane as it has been redesignated, is that military development of this craft will assist in the development of a supersonic transport plane which will be able to compete with supersonic craft being developed abroad.[51] Second, the manufacturers of large military and commercial aircraft face no purely civilian-oriented competitors and are therefore not seriously disadvantaged by whatever limitations on marketing ability and low-cost production skills they may share with other defense companies.

49. U.S. Congress, House Committee on Appropriations, Subcommittee on Department of Defense Appropriations, *Hearings: Department of Defense Appropriations for 1962, Part 5, Procurement*, p. 442.

50. *Ibid.*, p. 458.

51. The program to develop a supersonic transport in this country raises an interesting issue in public policy. Why should not citizens of the United States benefit from the subsidization of such aircraft by the British and French governments by patronizing foreign airlines? In other words, why not let foreign taxpayers bear the cost of a service available to citizens of all countries? The burden of maintaining national prestige in this field and preserving the position of United States airlines in transoceanic routes is extremely heavy unless Air Force supporters of the RS-70 are correct in their assessments of the military need for such a weapon system.

The market for commercial aircraft appears to be buoyant. In early 1965 the New York *Times* noted that carriers are committed to spending $2.1 billion for new jet aircraft over the next five years,[52] and an article in the *Wall Street Journal* predicted that demand would remain strong into the eighties as short- and medium-haul subsonic jet service is extended to new cities in the United States and abroad.[53] Yet the commercial aircraft market is a risky one, and it offers opportunities for only a few very large defense firms. To date, General Dynamics, Boeing, and Douglas, and to a lesser extent Lockheed, have been the only large contractors producing commercial jet aircraft, while United Aircraft has played an important role in development and manufacture of jet engines. Opportunities for additional entrants from the defense market or elsewhere are limited by the size of the market and by the risk. Despite predictions of a boom, memories of the late fifties must still be fresh and must serve to dampen the enthusiasm of contractors for greater reliance on civilian orders. In the three-way competition to equip the airlines with transcontinental jets, only Boeing, with its 707, made a substantial profit. Douglas reported losses in 1959 and 1960 as a result of write-offs on the developmental costs of the DC-8, which eventually competed on nearly even terms with the 707 but which suffered by coming into the market a year behind the Boeing airplane. General Dynamics' jet program had cost the company a $425 million loss by the end of 1961.[54]

In a competitive market, exit may occur through failure as well as through the desire of successful companies to enter new fields. The policies of the Department of Defense serve, to an unknown extent, to limit this sort of involuntary exit. On numerous occasions, Department of Defense officials testifying before congressional committees have been asked whether procurement agencies have "bailed out" contractors by generous change orders or through awards channeled to firms threatened with financial difficulties or plant closings. In virtually every specific instance inquired into, witnesses have denied that a particular award was made to assist the firm in question, but I have not found any testimony denying that

52. April 11, 1965, p. F1.
53. Jan. 8, 1965, pp. 1, 16.
54. For an account of the experience of General Dynamics in the jet market, see Richard A. Smith, *Corporations in Crisis* (Garden City: Doubleday, 1963), pp. 63–96.

the practice occurs. On the contrary, hearings do contain at least two instances in which Department of Defense officials did describe, quite frankly, placement of procurement orders designed to keep contractors in business.

The first case involved the plight of three established parachute manufacturers who were faced in the mid-fifties with competition from apparel firms that had come into the market during the Korean War. Although the new entrants could underbid the older firms on a price basis, the Air Force feared loss of the "important technical capabilities" of the established manufacturers. As a result, procurement was limited to "three parachute firms having proven production records and established developmental and engineering staffs." To protect the Air Force, it was provided that "careful price negotiations should be conducted to obtain the lowest possible prices; that sustaining amounts should be kept to the very minimum; and that the judgement of the commander, AMC, would of necessity have to be relied upon as to what minimum sustaining amounts should be for each contractor." [55]

The second, more recent, instance involved a repeat purchase of observation helicopters and was described in the following testimony of Paul R. Ignatius, Assistant Secretary of the Army for Installations and Logistics:

> Yes. I testified on that point, Mr. Ford. What I testified was that in fiscal year 1962, Hiller was the low bidder and won the contract. On the basic 1963 buy, which was for 150, Bell was the low bidder and the contract was awarded to Bell. After we did this it appeared from our own knowledge, plus information that was conveyed to us from Hiller Aircraft that the ability of Hiller to continue in the production of helicopters might be placed in jeopardy. Accordingly, I asked the Chief of Staff if he would have undertaken a study of the impact on the Army of the failure of Hiller to continue in helicopter production in terms of two considerations: One, the support of those Hillers already in the system, and secondly, with regard to the mobilization base for observation helicopters.
>
> This study was undertaken and recommended that in terms of both those considerations, current support and mobilization capability, it would not be in the Army's interest should the company cease making helicopters and the study recommended that if the [deleted for security

55. U.S. Congress, House Committee on Appropriations, Subcommittee on Department of Defense Appropriations, *Hearings: Department of Defense Appropriations for 1957, Procurement Policies and Practices of the Department of Defense*, pp. 372-373.

reasons] in the program change be approved by the Congress, that these be awarded to the Hiller Co. The question, then, arose: At what price should they be awarded to the Hiller Co.? It seemed to me and to Mr. Vance, with whom I discussed this in some detail, that we should not pay any substantial premium over the price that had been demonstrated competitively. We concluded that an equitable way to do this, all things considered, was to establish the Bell price as the target price for Hiller. If Hiller came in under that target, the Government would share 50–50. If Hiller's costs were over that amount, the Government and the contractor would share 50–50 between the target price and the ceiling price. The ceiling was established as the Hiller price on the competitive proposal.[56]

F. Summary

There are barriers both to entry into and exit from the defense market which are undoubtedly of major significance in explaining the degree of stability found among lists of the largest prime contractors. Barriers further pervade the remainder of the defense market and thus affect subcontractors and smaller contractors. Finally, there is little that the Department of Defense can do through its procurement policies and practices to lower the most important barriers to entry without having harmful effects on other aspects of the performance of defense contractors, but there are actions that the department should at least consider which would reduce barriers to exit from the defense market.

56. U.S. Congress, House Committee on Appropriations, Subcommittee on Department of Defense Appropriations, *Hearings: Department of Defense Appropriations for 1964, Part 5, Procurement*, p. 306.

VIII. FINANCIAL PERFORMANCE AND STRUCTURE OF THE MAJOR DEFENSE CONTRACTORS

In order to round out and complete its depiction, the defense market may be viewed in still another way, in terms of the financial performance and structure of the major contractors. Of particular interest here is the question whether there are any substantial differences in financial data among the primary product groups and among the major contractors when they are subdivided according to the degree of specialization in defense sales.

Table VIII-1 shows after-tax rates of return on assets, equity, and sales for the large defense contractors in each of the primary product groups described in Chapter IV. Group I comprises firms which are classified as primary producers in aircraft and propulsion fields, Group II is made up of electronics firms, Group III contains industrial firms other than petroleum refiners, and Group IV includes petroleum refiners. The "average" figures were obtained by taking a simple unweighted average of the rates of individual companies; the "over-all" figures are the rates of return derived by summing total assets, net sales, owners' equity, net income after taxes, and fixed charges for the entire group and then calculating rates from these totals.[1]

Group II, electronics firms, is dominated by the American Telephone and Telegraph Company, which accounted for approximately two-thirds of the sums of both total assets and owners' equities of the group in both 1957 and 1962. This company also differs substantially from the others in Group II in having an extremely low

---

1. Most of the financial data were obtained from Standard & Poor's COMPUSTAT magnetic tape library of statistics on industrial corporations, through the courtesy of the Amos Tuck School of Business Administration at Dartmouth College. For several firms which are not included on the COMPUSTAT tapes, the data was obtained from *Moody's Industrial Manual.* An effort which I believe was in the main successful was made to collect the data from *Moody's* in forms similar to those used in preparing the COMPUSTAT tapes.

Percentage rates of growth and decline based on COMPUSTAT and Moody's data have been calculated by using the lower figure as a base, rather than always using the earlier. This permits comparability and averaging.

Table VIII-1: After-tax financial rates of return for publicly owned profit-seeking firms among the 50 largest prime contractors, by primary product groups, 1957 and 1962

Rate of return on	Average				Over-all				Over-all (omitting A.T. & T. and GM)			
	I	II	III	IV	I	II	III	IV	I	II	III	IV
Assets, 1957 *	7.56	6.30	7.44	9.08	8.17	6.23	9.57	9.68	8.17	7.49	8.08	9.68
Assets, 1962	6.72	6.26	6.83	7.37	6.64	6.63	10.31	7.81	6.64	7.33	7.01	7.81
Owners' equity, 1957 **	15.34	11.07	11.75	12.35	16.96	9.98	14.71	13.44	16.96	13.23	12.42	13.44
Owners' equity, 1962	14.02	9.73	10.08	9.58	12.67	10.09	16.06	10.51	12.67	12.07	10.77	10.51
Net sales, 1957 *	3.25	6.38	5.39	10.92	3.23	8.88	6.12	11.09	3.23	5.78	4.98	11.09
Net sales, 1962	3.03	5.66	5.17	10.05	2.87	10.13	7.52	10.17	2.87	6.03	5.32	10.17

* Based on net income plus fixed charges.
** Based on net income excluding fixed charges.

ratio of sales to assets and therefore an extremely high rate of return on net sales, despite the fact that its rates of return on assets and equity are among the most modest found within the group. Similarly, over-all figures for Group II are heavily influenced by General Motors Corporation, which accounted for around one-third of that group's total assets, owners' equities, and net sales in both years, and whose rates of return, especially in 1962, were all substantially higher than those of any other firm in the group. Sales for defense purposes of both American Telephone and Telegraph and General Motors were less than 10 per cent of their total sales in 1957 and 1962. It therefore seemed advisable to add a third set of figures to Table VIII-1, showing over-all rates of return for Groups II and III which omit the amounts for these two large and atypical firms.

Table VIII-1 shows a general decline in all three rates of return between 1957 and 1962. On an average basis and on an over-all basis omitting American Telephone and Telegraph and General Motors, the rates of return on assets and equity fell for all four groups. Indeed, while profits in defense contracting were commonly viewed as excessively high in 1957,[2] in 1963 Secretary McNamara stated:

> I, too, feel we are not getting enough for our defense dollar, but I do not believe it is because private corporations on the average are receiving profits in excess of what is reasonable on Defense business. Quite the contrary, as a matter of fact. The profit rate is too low today on Defense contracts on the average to induce the type of effort and the assignment of the type of resources which we need to achieve some of the objectives Mr. Ford was referring to a moment ago, namely the application of our most advanced scientific and engineering talent to our weapons systems developments.
>
> The average profit as a percent of sales on defense work, for example, is something on the order of 3 percent plus. This is far too low a rate in

2. See, for example, testimony of Thomas Coggeshall, Chairman of the Renegotiation Board, who noted in 1960 that great amounts of excessive profit resulted from the sudden expansion of defense purchasing associated with and following the Korean build-up. From 1957 on, Coggeshall stated, "we see the results of improved contracting." U.S. Congress, Senate Committee on Armed Services, Procurement Subcommittee, *Hearings: Procurement Study*, p. 126.

In hearings on alleged overcharges on Navy and Air Force contracts from February of 1957 through March of 1961, Comptroller General Joseph Campbell testified that $1 billion in total overcharges on negotiated procurement by the Department of Defense would not be an unreasonable estimate for the period. U.S. Congress, House Committee on Armed Services, Subcommittee for Special Investigations, *Hearings: Overpricing of Government Contracts* (Washington: Government Printing Office, 1961), pp. 14–15.

relation to the investment required to draw to this Defense business the most efficient resources in terms of human abilities and equipment.[3]

Yet the rates of return shown on assets and owner's equities, even in 1962, hardly appear low, nor is the decline from 1957 to 1962 out of line with general business experience. The over-all after-tax rate of return on assets for all United States manufacturing corporations, except newspapers, was 7.09 per cent in 1957, and it fell to 6.30 per cent in 1962. The over all after-tax rate of return on stockholders' equity for the same group fell from 11.0 per cent in 1957 to 9.8 per cent in 1962.[4] It should be noted that only the rates of return for Group I are rates earned primarily on defense business, as was indicated in Table IV-14.

Two related aspects of defense contracting are highlighted by comparisons between Group I and the other groups shown in Table VIII-1. First, it can be seen that the rate of return on sales is much lower for the aircraft firms, whose defense sales are about 80 per cent of their total sales, than it is for any of the other three groups. Second, the aircraft firms had the highest rates of return on owners' equities in both years, whether measured on an average or an overall basis (provided that General Motors is excluded for 1962). Rates of return on total assets for the aircraft group, on the other hand, are fairly similar to those of the others and in fact are somewhat on the low side in 1962. Normally, a high rate of return on owners' equity coupled with a low rate on assets suggests a levered capital structure, and owners' equity does turn out to be a substantially lower percentage of total assets for the aircraft group than it is for any of the other groups. A comparison of over-all equity/asset ratios for the four groups indicates that Group I is the most highly levered, with a 1962 ratio of 43 per cent, down very slightly from 44 per cent in 1957. The next lowest 1962 ratio is that of Group II, 55 per cent (51 per cent with American Telephone and Telegraph omitted), followed by Group III's 61 per cent (60 per cent with General Motors omitted) and Group IV's 70 per cent.

3. U.S. Congress, House Committee on Appropriations, Subcommittee on Department of Defense Appropriations, *Hearings: Department of Defense Appropriations for 1964, Part 1, Secretary of Defense,* pp. 326–327.

4. U.S. Federal Trade Commission and U.S. Securities and Exchange Commission, *Quarterly Financial Report, United States Manufacturing Corporations, 4th Quarter, 1957,* p. 30, and *4th Quarter, 1962,* p. 34.

A very low rate of return on sales coupled with a more normal rate of return on assets implies that the ratio of sales to assets is quite high. Nineteen reporting aerospace firms surveyed in the Stanford Research Institute study, *The Industry-Government Aerospace Relation,* had a distinctly higher sales/assets ratio than that for a cross-section of manufacturing firms.[5] One reason for the very low ratio reported to Stanford Research Institute and implied in Table VIII-1 is that only a fraction of the assets employed by defense-oriented firms are owned by them and listed on their balance sheets. Both the Stanford Research Institute report and the Arthur D. Little study, *How Sick Is the Defense Industry?,* note that defense firms still make very substantial use of leased and government-furnished plant and equipment. Often the two are identical, since government-owned facilities are rented to contractors or operated by them on a fee basis. However, when it is to the advantage of the government to do so, government-owned facilities may be furnished to a contractor without charge.[6] Defense contractors have an incentive to rent property and equipment from private sources as well as from the government, rather than purchase needed assets, since under existing Department of Defense cost principles lease and rental payments are allowable costs while interest and costs of financing are not.[7] The Arthur D. Little report makes an effort to estimate the real rate of return on over-all assets employed, reflecting a reasonable valuation of and fair rental payments for government-owned assets, and concludes that the actual rate of return on assets employed in defense production is much lower than rates indicated by published financial statements.[8] The Stanford Research Institute study shows that total assets employed by major aerospace firms replying to a questionnaire were approximately two-thirds larger in value than the total reported assets of the firms.[9]

An adjustment which makes the rate of return on assets in defense industries look lower, at the same time makes the apparent leverage of Group I appear to be even more serious. Thus the Arthur D. Little report describes the composite debt/equity ratio for fifty-one

5. II, 113.
6. *Armed Services Procurement Regulation,* 1963 edition, paragraph 13–407.
7. *Ibid.,* paragraph 15–205.17.
8. *How Sick Is the Defense Industry?,* pp. 60–66.
9. *The Industry-Government Aerospace Relationship,* II, 124.

aerospace companies as "unheard of in normal business practice for a manufacturing company (except some textiles) ." [10] But leverage is dangerous to shareholders only to the extent that the firm is saddled with excessively high fixed interest charges and onerous requirements for repayment or refunding of debt, and it is unprofitable only in the event that the rate of return earned on total assets dips below the rate paid for borrowed funds. A great portion of the owned assets of defense contractors above and beyond the value of owners' equity is not supported by interest-bearing debt but by financial assistance from the government. Purchasing agencies make advance payments on contracts, representing non-interest-bearing liabilities to the recipients; they also make progress payments, which reduce the need for owned capital to be tied up in work in progress under defense contracts. Further, the government aids defense contractors in their financing and reduces interest charges levied by private lenders by guaranteeing loans made from commercial sources.

During the period from 1957 to 1962, however, the absolute and relative level of governmental financial assistance to defense contractors declined sharply. Under the direction of Secretary Mc-Namara the Department of Defense engaged in a vigorous effort to dispose of government-owned plant and equipment and encouraged contractors to expand and modernize their own facilities. In 1963, Assistant Secretary of Defense Morris described Department of Defense policy as "dedicated to the preservation and strengthening of a free enterprise economy." He noted that "no commercial or industrial activities within the United States will be started or continued in operation under military control unless a clear determination is made that established reasons such as national security, requirements for the training of personnel, commercial unavailability, or other compelling reasons necessitate exceptions to this policy." In addition, he stated that periodic reviews of existing facilities were required, and that in the first two years of the Kennedy Administration fifty-five government-owned, contractor-operated plants had been sold to private industry.[11] The government's effort to divest itself of these facilities had begun under the

10. *How Sick Is the Defense Industry?*, p. 67.

11. U.S. Congress, House Committee on Appropriations, Subcommittee on Department of Defense Appropriations, *Hearings: Department of Defense Appropriations for 1964, Part 5, Procurement,* p. 162.

Eisenhower Administration. In 1960, Air Force Major General W. E. Davis advised a congressional committee that "we are not making an effort to fully utilize Government facilities as they stand as of last year or any particular time. We are making an effort to get rid of the Government facilities, actually." [12] A little earlier, General Davis, who was Director of Procurement and Production, Air Materiel Command, had told the committee that "all other things being equal, the man without the Government facility will get the award." [13]

Not only was the Department of Defense reducing the availability of government-owned facilities, but it was also cutting back the level of financial support given to contractors. The Arthur D. Little report shows that, from 1957 to 1962, the outstanding balance of advance payments, guaranteed ("V") loans and progress payments declined from $4.47 billion to $2.56 billion, or from 21.3 per cent of total procurement to 9.1 per cent. [14]

Table VIII-2 indicates percentage growth for each of the four primary product classes from 1957 to 1962. Whether the basis is average growth, over-all growth, or over-all growth eliminating the two very large and atypical firms, it can be seen that the electronics firms of Group II had the greatest rates of growth in assets, sales, net income, and net income plus fixed charges.

The rapid growth of the electronics firms is not surprising. As shown in Table IV-14, the reporting firms of Group II made about 50 per cent of their sales to the Department of Defense or government on an unweighted average basis, and somewhat over 20 per cent when the average was weighted by total sales. The electronics field has been characterized by rapid and sweeping innovations and by high and growing demand in civilian as well as military markets. Yet it does not appear from Table VIII-2 that the aircraft firms of Group I have been too severely damaged by the inroads of the electronics firms and the rather unrestricted intergroup competition which characterized the missile program during this period. On all three bases of measurement shown in Table VIII-2 the aircraft firms

---

12. U.S. Congress, House Committee on Armed Services, Special Subcommittee on Procurement Practices of the Department of Defense, *Hearings Pursuant to Section 4, Public Law 86–89*, p. 358.
13. *Ibid.*, p. 357.
14. *How Sick Is the Defense Industry?*, p. 56.

Table VIII-2: Percentage of growth in assets, sales, and after-tax income for publicly owned profit-seeking firms among the 50 largest prime contractors, by primary product groups, 1957 to 1962

Percentage growth in	Unweighted average				Over-all				Over-all (omitting A.T. & T. and GM)			
	I	II	III	IV	I	II	III	IV	I	II	III	IV
Net sales	62.19	138.63	25.25	20.11	28.62	40.29	15.48	21.62	28.62	39.36	3.92	21.62
Total assets	69.92	70.09	30.48	36.45	41.40	50.21	31.56	38.22	41.40	48.63	27.91	38.22
Net income	54.58	74.00	5.02	7.80	3.05	56.08	41.94	9.65	3.05	41.92	8.62	9.65
Net income plus fixed charges	50.69	88.08	15.60	10.70	14.25	60.06	41.78	11.60	14.25	45.58	10.99	11.60

had a greater rate of growth in sales and assets than did the other industrial firms of Group III or the petroleum refiners of Group IV. And when General Motors is omitted, the growth of net income plus fixed charges for the aircraft group compares favorably with that for Groups III and IV.

Over-all net income for the aircraft firms rose very little between 1957 and 1962, by only 3.05 per cent, while net income plus fixed charges for Group I as a whole rose by 14.25 per cent. During this period the Department of Defense was reducing its financial commitments and assistance to defense contractors. Rather than rely on increased retention of earnings or new equity issues, the aircraft firms in turn assumed substantially higher fixed charges in order to meet the increased financial burdens, to support a greater volume of owned assets, and in some cases to adjust to heavy losses growing out of civilian ventures.[15] It can be seen that the larger firms of Group I underwent the greatest relative increase in fixed charges, since on an unweighted average basis net income for Group I actually showed a greater percentage growth than did net income plus fixed charges. General Dynamics, the largest of the aircraft group in terms of assets in both 1957 and 1962, saw its ratio of net worth to total assets drop from 39 per cent to 26 per cent between 1957 and 1962, while its fixed charges rose from $2.53 million to $11.99 million. Over the same period General Dynamics' net income rose from $44.28 million to $52.86 million. Boeing, the second largest in terms of assets in both years, experienced an increase in its equity/asset ratio from 36 per cent to 42 per cent, but an increase from $2.00 million to $6.29 million in fixed charges and a decline in net income from $38.16 million to $27.15 million. United Aircraft, which ranked third in both years, went from an equity/asset ratio of 56 per cent to one of 54 per cent, with fixed charges growing from zero to $6.32 million and net income declining from $51.37 million to $18.11 million. Only four firms in Group I—Fairchild, Garrett, Lock-

---

15. Debt financing may have been inevitable. The Arthur D. Little study made an estimate of the rate of return on owners' equity in major defense firms on the assumption that equity capital be substituted for government financing of assets. The conclusion was that the adjusted rate of return was extremely low, well below the all-manufacturing average (*How Sick Is the Defense Industry?*, p. 68). Deterioration of the equity/asset ratio for some of the aircraft firms was inadvertent and unrelated to their defense business, resulting from heavy losses in the commercial jet transport market between 1957 and 1962.

heed, and McDonnell—actually reduced their fixed charges during the period, and all four enjoyed increases in net income. Of these four, only Lockheed has assets greater than the average for the group.

An additional interesting aspect of Table VIII-2 is revealed by the fact that the unweighted average growth figures for Groups I and II are all substantially higher than the corresponding over-all figures. This indicates greater growth in both size and earnings for the smaller firms in the two most defense-oriented groups. Differential growth rates may be illustrated dramatically by comparing the smallest firms in the two groups with the largest. The Group I firm with the lowest assets in 1957 was Thiokol, a contractor primarily associated with development and production of missile propellants. Thiokol's rates of growth from 1957 to 1962 were 728 per cent in sales, 552 per cent in assets, 341 per cent in net income, and 380 per cent in net income plus fixed charges. In the electronics group, the smallest firm in 1957 was Litton Industries, an electronics firm notable for its active merger history and entry into the shipbuilding field. Rates of growth for Litton during the same period were 1400 per cent in sales, 502 per cent in assets, 904 per cent in net income, and 959 per cent in net income plus fixed charges. By way of contrast, the largest firm in the aircraft group, General Dynamics, had rates of growth of 21 per cent, 15 per cent, 19 per cent, and 39 per cent in sales, assets, net income, and net income plus fixed charges, respectively; while General Electric, the largest firm in the electronics group other than American Telephone and Telegraph, had corresponding increases of 11 per cent, 20 per cent, 7 per cent, and 6 per cent.

Many of the differences among the primary product groups are evidently accounted for by differences in the degree of specialization in defense sales. Tables VIII-3 and VIII-5 break down rates of sales made to the Department of Defense or government and by changes in these percentages.

In showing the over-all rates of return in Table VIII-3 it did not seem desirable to separate General Motors, American Telephone and Telegraph, or any other firm. Both General Motors and American Telephone and Telegraph are in the 1 to 9 per cent groups in both 1957 and 1962, a position they share with several other very large companies, including the nation's second largest industrial firm,

Standard Oil of New Jersey. Therefore, no one firm dominates the group.

The most obvious feature of Table VIII-3 is the increase in rates of return on sales as specialization in the defense market declines. There does not appear to be any distinct or meaningful relationship between rate of return on assets and the mix between civilian and military sales. Rates of return on equity in 1957 were, in a very general way, higher for firms with high percentages of sales in the defense market than they were for those with lower percentages going to the military. The general decline in rates of return on both assets and owners' equity from 1957 to 1962, as shown in Table VIII-1, is also evident in Table VIII-3, but inspection of the 1962 rates shown in Table VIII-3 certainly does not indicate that rates of return on equity for firms selling primarily in the defense market were depressed below the levels prevailing among firms which made the largest portion of their sales in civilian markets. In this connection, a point made by J. S. Bain is highly relevant. Bain noted that if a risk premium is justified by actual risk, some of the risk-takers should lose. There should be losses or subnormal profits to offset the high

Table VIII-3: After-tax financial rates of return for publicly owned, profit-seeking firms among the 50 largest prime contractors, by degree of specialization in defense sales, 1957 and 1962

Percentage of total sales for defense	Average rate of return on			Over-all rate of return on		
	Assets	Owners' equity	Sales	Assets	Owners' equity	Sales
1957: 90–100	7.32	16.20	2.98	8.10	18.01	2.71
80–89	7.19	13.88	3.08	8.69	18.04	3.38
70–79	7.42	15.99	3.72	6.18	13.91	3.09
60–69	6.60	11.32	3.96	6.16	10.69	3.91
50–59	7.42	12.03	3.61	7.42	12.03	3.61
40–49	5.62	8.90	4.12	5.46	8.47	4.26
30–39	8.42	13.61	6.77	8.48	13.67	6.82
20–29	7.57	13.63	5.97	9.56	17.45	6.51
10–19	6.69	10.12	4.68	6.24	9.35	4.40
1–9	7.75	11.56	9.27	8.01	12.02	8.97
1962: 90–100	6.28	11.22	2.93	6.48	12.80	2.72
80–89	6.86	15.08	2.88	6.27	12.08	2.54
70–79	6.42	11.56	3.34	6.07	11.32	3.29
60–69	6.96	11.58	3.48	7.49	12.43	3.70
50–59	6.62	12.21	4.13	6.64	11.75	4.07
40–49	5.44	7.18	3.88	4.78	6.52	3.46
30–39	5.84	8.73	5.10	5.93	8.96	4.55
20–29	6.95	10.20	4.57	7.78	11.79	5.01
10–19	7.47	12.19	8.90	8.00	13.75	8.72
1–9	7.46	10.63	9.27	8.22	12.14	10.61

gains of those who were favored by fortune; average profit rates in truly risky industries should not be far from the average rates in safer industries.[16] But one would expect, following this line of thought, that the dispersion of profits would be greater in more risky industries. Although Bain quite rightly made his argument only in terms of long-run profits, it is nevertheless of interest to inquire whether variations from one firm to another in rates of return are related to the various percentages of sales made for defense purposes in any one year. The firms were classified by primary product groups to investigate this question, mainly because the primary product classes contain larger numbers of firms than do some of the percentage-of-sales classes, and because the primary product groups probably comprise more comparable collections of firms. Table VIII-4 shows coefficients of variation computed from individual rates of return on total assets for the various primary product groups.

The figures in Table VIII-4 indicate a greater relative variation in profit rates among the aircraft and electronics firms than within Group III in 1957, but the 1957 coefficients for the two defense-oriented groups are quite similar to that for the petroleum refiners of Group IV. The coefficient for the aircraft firms in 1962, presumably after the worst of the adjustment to the missile age had been endured, is surprisingly low in comparison with the others. Certainly Table VIII-4 does not suggest a substantially greater variation in profit rates from one firm to another in Group I than in the other groups, although Group I is by far the most dependent on the defense market.

16. J. S. Bain, *Industrial Organization,* pp. 374–376.

Table VIII-4: Coefficient of variation for average rates of return on assets for firms among the 50 largest prime contractors, by primary product groups

Group	Coefficient of variation	
	1957	1962
I	32.4%	25.9%
II	34.6	35.0
III	27.4	45.1
IV	32.2	35.1

The figures in Table VIII-5 represent an attempt to compare the success, in terms of growth in size and profitability, of firms which reduced their dependence on the defense market with those whose specialization in defense sales increased.

It is difficult to interpret Table VIII-5 because of some of the substantial differences between the unweighted "typical firm" averages and the corresponding over-all growth figures. Furthermore, it is impossible in most cases to adjust for distortions caused by firms dominant in their classes without revealing information which responding firms submitted on a confidential basis. Fortunately the most extreme divergence—that between the net income figures for firms whose defense sales as a percentage of total sales decreased by 1 to 4 per cent—can be partially explained and adjusted. This class, comprising ten firms, contains both General Motors and American Telephone and Telegraph. From 1957 to 1962 General Motors' net income increased by 72.96 per cent, while American Telephone and Telegraph's net income rose by 67.29 per cent. In both years the combined net income of these two firms accounted for roughly 80 per cent of the total net income of the class. Figures on the defense sales of both General Motors and American Telephone and Telegraph are not confidential, but are published by the firms in their annual reports.

With the elimination of General Motors and American Telephone and Telegraph from the over-all figures of Table VIII-5, one clear and not particularly surprising finding emerges. Firms which either increased or decreased their degree of specialization in defense sales by 10 per cent or more enjoyed greater growth in terms of all four indicators and on either an average or over-all basis than did those whose mix between military and civilian sales remained more constant. There are two closely related reasons for expecting this result. First, firms may have increased the percentage of sales made in civilian markets by a substantial increase in the absolute volume of these sales rather than through a cutback or a sluggish increase in their defense business. Similarly, the percentage of sales made in the defense market may have risen through successful penetration of a new market rather than as a result of failure to achieve and maintain a satisfactory rate of growth in civilian sales. Second, the flexibility demonstrated by substantial shifts in markets is very likely

Table VIII-5: Percentage of growth in assets, sales, and after-tax income for publicly owned profit-seeking firms among the 50 largest prime contractors, by change in percentage of sales made to DOD or government, 1957 to 1962

	Increase of 10 per cent or more	Increase of 5–9 per cent	Increase of 1–4 per cent	No change	Decrease of 1–4 per cent	Decrease of 5–9 per cent	Decrease of 10 per cent or more
Unweighted average percentage growth in:							
Net sales	120.23	68.87	38.36	10.84	52.63	32.88	64.39
Total assets	98.93	46.07	42.20	30.42	62.05	51.18	80.71
Net income	74.29	-.88	24.20	31.84	-3.49	8.36	86.44
Net income plus fixed charges	78.85	31.59	27.24	16.12	20.31	29.92	103.75
Over-all percentage growth in:							
Net sales	63.54	15.68	18.65	20.98	32.68 (22.36)*	17.56	61.12
Total assets	52.45	45.90	29.84	31.57	43.52 (29.25)*	47.94	84.34
Net income	51.92	-4.83	6.30	5.00	57.99 (2.94)*	41.75	120.29
Net income plus fixed charges	52.79	14.47	7.92	8.39	59.68 (6.67)*	46.32	118.34

* Figures in parentheses are those calculated after omitting General Motors Corp. and American Telephone and Telegraph Co.

to be an attribute of the more progressive and dynamic firms.

The figures of Table VIII-5 suggest another finding which it was not so reasonable to anticipate. The six firms which decreased their dependence on defense sales by 10 per cent or more had a much greater percentage increase in profits, whether viewed as net income or net income plus fixed charges, than did the ten firms whose percentages of defense sales increased by 10 per cent or more.[17] Both the average and over-all percentage increases in profits for the six whose diversification was into civilian markets clearly exceeded their percentage increases in total assets, representing an increasing rate of return on total invested capital, which was not true for the ten which increased their relative dependence on defense sales. However, it should be pointed out that five of the six whose emphasis on civilian markets increased still made more than 50 per cent of their sales in the defense market in 1962.

It is dangerous and possibly seriously misleading to interpret the financial data presented here and to arrive at definite conclusions from the interpretations. Only two years are involved, although the two were chosen to reflect recent changes in the defense market and to avoid showing the results of presumably non-recurrent losses in civilian ventures incurred by some of the aircraft firms. Interfirm comparisons based on financial statements inevitably suffer from well-known difficulties with accounting figures, such as the valuation of fixed assets at historic cost, different methods of depreciation and inventory valuation, alternative methods of computing and reporting profits, and allowances for different types of contingencies. In addition, the comparisons made here are not within a single industry with similar accounting problems and conventions, but are among firms in quite disparate industries. The petroleum firms of Group IV have problems connected with the depletion allowance and treatment of exploration costs which are not encountered by the companies in any other group. Asset valuations are unequally influenced by provisions for rapid write-offs of essential plant and equipment. Group III comprises a very heterogenous collection of "other in-

17. The number of firms whose percentage of defense or government sales increased by 10 per cent or more is one less than that shown for firms in this class in Table IV-11. The discrepancy is explained by the absence of financial figures for Hughes Aircraft, which is in this class. Hughes Aircraft furnished figures on the distribution of its sales without requesting that they be kept confidential.

dustrial" firms. Group II contains two public utilities with accounting and reporting requirements and conventions which are quite different from those of the industrial firms in the group. The aircraft firms of Group I have, in general, a much larger stake in government-owned, contractor-operated facilities than do the firms in the other groups. The extent to which development costs can be and are treated as current expense will differ from firm to firm.[18] Nevertheless the data are suggestive, and two somewhat negative inferences may be formulated.

Defense contracting is characterized by an absence or minimization of certain risks typical of commercial civilian operations. At the same time, other risks, which either do not exist or are very slight in non-defense business, face the defense contractor. Short-run selling risks in the defense market are minimized by advance contracting under which sale is guaranteed before production is commenced. Even if a contract is canceled, the defense contractor is almost invariably reimbursed for his outlay. When cost reimbursement contracts are used the only risk of actual loss arises from the possibility that certain costs will not be allowed by the government. Even when firm fixed-price contracts are used, the risk on a given production run is normally far less than that facing a firm which must produce in advance of sale, often without any foreknowledge of the level of the ultimate selling price or, in extreme cases, without any assurance that the product can be marketed at any price. The defense-oriented firm faces very real risks in its efforts to obtain new contract awards. Competition is intense at the level of negotiation and submission of bids, and a contractor's ability to compete at this stage of the marketing process is determined in the main by its real or reputed technological know-how and its past success in developing and maintaining a skilled research and development organization. This factor has become particularly important in recent years, as contracts calling for the development and subsequent production of only a few extremely expensive and complex prototype units have tended to replace long production runs. Yet firms in cer-

18. A financial analyst commented, "One of the crosses the aircraft analyst must early learn to bear is the difficulty of analyzing the income statement. No two are alike or even roughly comparable. The approaches taken by the various managements in accounting for their stewardship are as individual as their design concepts for new aircraft and often as bewildering" (James J. Quinn, "Aircraft," *Investing in American Industries*, ed. Lester V. Plum [New York: Harper, 1960], p. 328).

tain civilian markets, such as for electronic devices, engage in very severe competition in technological change and new products. Statutory renegotiation of profits is a risk clearly setting defense contractors apart from manufacturing firms selling to either private customers or to non-defense agencies of government. However, comparisons among the levels of and variations in growth and profits do not indicate that risks typical of the defense market have had substantially different impacts on defense-oriented firms than normal commercial risks have had on firms with much lower degrees of reliance on military sales.

The greatest risk faced by a firm which depends on defense sales is not reflected in the financial figures for the past few years: a substantial reduction in the level of defense spending, whether caused by a thaw in the cold war, an arms limitation agreement, or any other reason. This risk is somewhat similar to that borne by other firms which depend on only one customer, but the threat of virtually complete loss of its market is undoubtedly of greater importance for the defense contractor than it is for most of those engaged in civilian business enterprises. Yet the thin equity structures of the aircraft firms, which are dependent on the Department of Defense for some 80 per cent of their sales, as well as the rise in fixed charges which these firms have assumed in recent years, suggest that the financing of the group as a whole is becoming less rather than more appropriate to an industry whose very survival is subject to risk. The significance of this deterioration in protection for creditors and owners is heightened by the low true rate of return on total assets employed in defense production and by the growing necessity for private financing of these assets.[19]

19. I am indebted to Professor Daniel Marx, Jr., for making available some unpublished material dealing with the various types of risk in defense contracting.

IX. PROJECTED STRUCTURAL TRENDS AND PROCUREMENT POLICIES

A. Structural Trends in the Defense Market

In discussing the increase in concentration of defense contracts, the relative stability of market shares, the slight apparent increase in this stability, and the decrease in concentration within the select group of the 50 largest prime contractors, I scrupulously refrained from use of the word "trend." The period from 1955 through FY 1964 is too short to justify such a term, and it could be argued that the data might be unduly influenced by very significant but non-recurrent events such as the shift from manned aircraft to missiles and the administrative changes instituted under Secretary McNamara. Similarly, no forecasts of the future were made from the finding that stability in contract awards was greater among the aircraft and electronics firms than among the mixed "other" firms which, as a group, had a much lower percentage of total sales made in the defense market. Nor were measures of comparative financial performance projected. As indicated by the title of this chapter, I have now abandoned caution. It is quite conceivable that projections made and "trends" described at time of writing will appear simply ludicrous when this or any study treating the future is read in that future. But the chance should be taken, since the findings of any industry or market study ought to be given some relevance to future problems and policies.

My opinion, bolstered by the previous predictions of virtually everyone who had commented on the issue in public forums before the Vietnamese build-up, is that the observed increase in concentration is part of a trend and can be expected to continue. The FY 1965 decline in over-all concentration must, therefore, be viewed as only a temporary reversal. As noted earlier, the shift from manned aircraft to missiles and the subsequent missile build-up are now completed. Barring a dramatic and unpredicted technological breakthrough or a sudden and drastic change in the international climate, the bulk of missile contracts in the next few years will be for replacements, spare parts, and the phasing in of newer and more sophisticated missiles at a measured pace in a non-crisis atmosphere. Standardization of weapon systems will lead to fewer but larger contracts on those occasions when volume production is contemplated. Further, standardization and the space programs are breaking down a distinction among contractors in which, for example, Grumman and McDonnell were known as "Navy" contractors while Northrop and Republic were considered "Air Force" contractors. Firms will, in the future, be less content and less able to make the bulk of their sales to one service. The effect of the cutback in missile procurement is evident in the figures for FY 1965. While overall concentration of prime contract awards fell, concentration within Group I, aircraft, rose between FY 1964 and FY 1965. The Gini coefficient for Group I increased from .41 to .43, and the Herfindahl index increased from .105 to .114, although in both years there were the same number of firms, fifteen, from Group I among the 50 largest prime contractors.

In 1961, Deputy Secretary of Defense R. L. Gilpatric, while defending the tri-service fighter concept in a talk made to the Aerospace Industries Association, noted that "there simply is not enough volume in the offing to justify a large number of different types, and we cannot afford to pay the high premium on short production runs of very complex aircraft." [1] Secretary of the Air Force E. M. Zuckert stated quite clearly, in the same year, that consolidation would be an inevitable result of these changes. Representative Otis G. Pike of New York put the following question to Secretary Zuckert:

I also sympathize completely and agree completely that, as you said in your opening statement, that you want these contracts to be awarded on a competitive basis, wherever possible.

My conclusion, however, is, How are you going to keep the airframe industry competitive when one by one the companies are going out of business, and where Bell is gone, Curtiss-Wright is gone, and Republic is apparently going?

I just don't know whether the net result to our defense posture is going to be served by this kind of attrition.[2]

1. *Aviation Week and Space Technology,* LXXIV (June 19, 1961), 109.
2. U.S. Congress, House Committee on Armed Services, *Hearings on Military Posture and H.R. 9751,* p. 3734.

Secretary Zuckert replied:

> Now, on your question of what happens to the industry, this is a tough one, when you consider that the TFX, and perhaps the VAX, which follows it, are perhaps—not the last airframe contracts we will see, but perhaps close to the last.
>
> What happens to the industry after that I can't say. There certainly is going to be need for some consolidation of the industry.[3]

Consolidation could result entirely from differential growth rates, with the expansion of some firms being financed by retained earnings or recourse to capital markets for new investment funds, and with less favored firms somehow liquidating their investments in specialized plant and equipment and moving out of the industry. But a more typical method of consolidation in industry has been through merger. Merger has been and is most likely to continue to be the predominant factor in increasing concentration of the defense market.

The recent experience of the electronics industry provides an illustration. In the middle and late fifties the outlook for military electronics seemed exceptionally promising, and a large number of small firms entered the industry. But the anticipations of many of the smaller entrants proved excessive. In 1958, during the period of great optimism, *Missiles and Rockets* reported on a survey of the reasons given for mergers in the aerospace field under the caption, "Missile Mergers: Brains Are Target." According to the survey, the most important factor underlying aerospace mergers at the time was the need among established defense contractors for new technical knowledge, especially in areas of electronics. The history of the missile industry, the article continued, accorded with a familiar business pattern in beginning with a large number of small firms entering the industry on the strength of particular capabilities in some specialized aspects of the new technologies involved, followed by a period of merger and consolidation. The only unique feature of the missile industry's evolution, the article concluded, was the remarkable rapidity of the process.[4] And in 1961, when much of the excessive optimism regarding the future of the electronics market

3. *Ibid.*, p. 3735.
4. IV (Oct. 27, 1958), 12–13.

had faded, the magazine *Aircraft and Missiles* commented on the "trend" toward the growth of large diversified electronics firms and the disappearance of smaller specialized manufacturers of electronic components. Even in 1959, the article stated, 64 per cent of sales in the electronics industry were being made by twenty firms.[5]

The forces which evidently underlay the consolidation of the electronics industry during the fifties are undoubtedly common throughout the defense market. A merger between a small firm with an exceptional capability in some branch of a new technology and a large established defense contractor with adequate resources and experience in the ways of selling to the military brings together complementary strengths and may be highly advantageous to both firms. Major contractors must diversify in the sense of maintaining facilities and abilities in new fields of interest to the customer in order to maintain their competitive positions in the defense market, and the best or sometimes only way to do so may be through "buying brains." Small firms may be unrealistically optimistic in their evaluation of the chances for successful entry into the defense market, especially when spurred on by widespread but inevitably uncertain predictions of a booming market in specific new and conceptually advanced fields, and they may therefore later become prime candidates for acquisition.

More recently, as defense firms began to feel the actual impact of the end of the missile build-up and of the Department of Defense's successful introduction of standardization, the concern about overcapacity and the predictions of increasing concentration became more emphatic. In its 1963 issues, *Aerospace Management* (formerly *Aircraft and Missiles*) devoted several articles to problems of existing overcapacity in the aerospace industry and to interviews with executives of defense companies, all of whom agreed not surprisingly that there was, indeed, excess capacity. In its issue of June, 1963, *Aerospace Management* said in an editorial, "Both [a vice president of General Dynamics and the president of Grumman Aircraft] go on to explain that the overcapacity is in facilities and technical talent. The recent record in proposal response is further substantiation. There are at least seven or eight companies bidding on each

5. IV (Aug., 1961), 17.

project—there is only one winner. And each bidder is carefully screened before the invitation to bid." [6]

The views of industry executives on this subject do not appear to be unduly colored by their unavoidable lack of objectivity, since their concern about overcapacity is supported by more disinterested observers. F. T. Moore, writing in 1964, noted the problem of excess capacity, which he attributed to the decline in expenditures on new major weapon systems, the decline in long production runs, and the growing needs for specialized R & D organizations. The most likely response to overcapacity, Moore believed, would be merger. But, he continued, such mergers could be expected to lead to economics of combination which might well benefit the Department of Defense and might, conceivably, even increase the degree of effective competition in the defense market. Competition, Moore pointed out, is not merely a function of numbers of firms in the defense market or even in a sector such as aircraft or missiles. Grumman and Republic, he observed, do not really compete with General Dynamics and Boeing, although all four manufacture aircraft.[7] The existence of fewer larger firms with widespread capabilities might broaden the competition for both EDTR and production contracts in any given weapon system program.

Also in 1964, Arthur D. Little published its second study of the defense market, entitled rather ominously *Strategies for Survival in the Aerospace Industry*.[8] In this study it was noted that the aerospace firms' market environment had changed in three ways during the past decade. The market is no longer a growth market and, indeed, can be expected to decline somewhat over the coming five years.[9] R & D are now more important factors in the market, in terms of dollar expenditure, than is production. Finally, the Department of

6. VI (June, 1963), 9.

7. "Efficiency and Public Policy in Defense Procurement," *Law and Contemporary Problems*, XXIX (Winter, 1964), 3–18.

8. Thomas G. Miller, Jr., *Strategies for Survival in the Aerospace Industry* (Cambridge: Arthur D. Little, Inc., 1964).

9. The Arthur D. Little report has been criticized for undue pessimism in regard to the predicted decline in defense spending. Forecasters at Lockheed Aircraft have projected a gradual rise in defense spending after 1969, the terminal date of the Little prediction. Lockheed's criticisms are contained in two speeches by company executives reprinted in *Aerospace: Two Predictions of Profitability and Long-term Growth* (Burbank, Calif.: Lockheed Aircraft Corp., 1965).

Defense is no longer concerned with maintaining a mobilization base, assuming that large wars requiring aerospace weapons will be fought with what is on hand; consequently the government's concern with the preservation of individual aerospace companies is a thing of the past. The report recommends three corporate strategies for maintaining stability in the coming years (the idea of "survival" is not stressed in the report, despite its title) : first is adaptation to the new emphasis on R & D; second is specialization in a limited number of technical areas and products; third is *"diversification through acquisition outside of the aerospace industry."* [10] The report emphasizes the past difficulties and failures of defense firms in attempts to diversify internally. Successful diversification, the author suggests, will more often than not require merger with a non-defense firm in order to acquire necessary management skills.

Events have confirmed the analyses of Moore and the Arthur D. Little report. Following the merger of Hiller Aircraft and Fairchild-Stratos, the new firm of Fairchild-Hiller entered into negotiations with Republic Aviation which, at time of writing, had led to a merger proposal approved by the stockholders of both corporations. Republic had suffered a substantial loss in 1964 after termination of its major prime aircraft contract, failure to develop non-defense business in replacement, and absorption of excessive costs on subcontracting activities for McDonnell.[11] It had slipped badly as a prime contractor, falling from a rank of 15 in FY 1962 to 30 in FY 1963 and 51 in FY 1964. Several cases of diversification through acquisition of non-defense firms have been reported in the *Wall Street Journal* in 1964 and 1965: Litton Industries acquired the materials handling equipment firm of Hewitt-Robins, became the largest stockholder of the Dictaphone Corporation, acquired Royal-McBee, a business machine firm, and entered into "active discussions" with the management of Universal Controls, which manufactures race-track and toll-booth equipment; General Dynamics sought to merge U.S. Instrument Corporation, a manufacturer of telephone equipment, into its Stromberg-Carlson Division; Avco acquired Delta Acceptance Corporation, a Canadian-based finance company which accounted for 16 per cent of Avco's earnings in the first six months of

10. *Strategies for Survival in the Aerospace Industry,* p. 6. Italics in original.
11. *Wall Street Journal,* April 1, Aug. 11, and Sept. 30, 1965.

1965; Thompson Ramo Wooldridge (now renamed TRW, Incorporated) and McNeil Corporation, a manufacturer of vulcanizing and other industrial equipment, agreed to merge; ITT has acquired several finance and insurance companies, Avis Rent-A-Car, and a mutual fund; and Raytheon, after a formal review of its diversification-through-merger objectives, made ten acquisitions for this purpose during the following two years.[12]

From FY 1963 to FY 1964 the Gini coefficient shown in Table II-8 rose from .45 to .47, reversing a downward movement which had indicated a steady increase in equality of prime contract awards among the 50 largest prime contractors from FY 1958 through FY 1963. There are influences operating in the defense market today which would tend to perpetuate this reversal and cause an increase in concentration within the ranks of the top 50 as well as an increase in over-all concentration of defense awards. Total procurement awards in FY 1964 were well below those of FY 1963, and a reduction in defense spending might be expected to have its greatest relative effects on smaller contractors, even those within the top 50, as well as on those less specialized in defense. The FY 1964 cut had its greatest effect on the missile systems program category, in which awards were reduced by $1,110 million. But this cutback was more than half offset for the aerospace firms as a group by a rise of $558 million in aircraft awards. The other program categories which suffered the most serious reductions, totaling $799 million, were ships, tank-automotive, ammunition, and fuels and lubricants, all of which are predominantly made up either of smaller contractors or of firms which are primarily civilian-oriented.[13]

Increased procurement and renewed emphasis on the strengthening of ground forces, resulting from heightened efforts by the United States in Vietnam, have once again reduced concentration within the ranks of the largest contractors for a time. The Gini coefficient for the 50 largest prime contractors fell from .47 to .45 between FY 1964 and FY 1965. But this procurement effort may, hopefully, be temporary. Further, the policy of developing and producing fewer multi-service standardized weapon systems will not only serve to in-

12. *Ibid.*, Nov. 23, Dec. 1, and Dec. 2, 1964; July 30, Sept. 3, Oct. 25, and Oct. 28, 1965.
13. OSD, *Military Prime Contract Awards and Subcontract Payments, July 1963–June 1964*, p. 22.

crease over-all concentration but will also benefit some major contractors and hurt others; to repeat an observation of the Arthur D. Little report, differences among these contractors will in all probability not be ameliorated by deliberate spreading of contracts in order to preserve and strengthen the industrial base of defense. The extent of inequality of contract awards among the 50 largest prime contractors, and the increase in this inequality from FY 1963 to FY 1964, may be seen in Table IX-1 as well as in the rising Gini coefficient. As still another indication, Lockheed, the largest prime contractor, received awards 20.1 times as great as those of the fiftieth firm in FY 1963; while in FY 1964, Lockheed, again first on the list, was shown with awards 21.1 times the dollar volume of those going to the fiftieth firm.

If Lockheed, Boeing, General Dynamics, and North American, the contractors at the very top of the recent award lists, were to acquire defense firms, particularly from those now among the 50 largest prime contractors, the result quite obviously would be to increase intra-group concentration. On the other hand, mergers such as that of Fairchild-Stratos, Hiller, and Republic serve to establish larger, more viable firms with greater degrees of diversification of technical skills in the middle and at the lower end of the list of 50 largest prime contractors. Thus, increased merger activity could either increase or decrease the inequality of award distribution among the major defense contractors. Mergers within the defense market are far more likely to take place among the smaller contractors and thus reduce inequality of distribution even while increasing over-all concentration. Companies such as the four giants of the defense market mentioned above, while primarily aerospace firms, are producers not only of various aircraft and missile systems and

Table IX-1: Percentage distribution of contract awards among the 50 largest prime contractors, FY 1963 and FY 1964

Rank	FY 1963	FY 1964
1–10	51.9	54.5
11–20	20.2	18.5
21–30	12.8	13.4
31–40	9.5	8.6
41–50	5.7	5.1
1–50	100.0*	100.0*

* Totals do not add because of rounding.

components, but have already diversified even farther into such fields as shipbuilding and electronic systems. In addition, these largest firms possess research staffs and facilities which are more capable of adapting to the new emphasis on advanced research and low-volume development projects than are those of their smaller rivals. The largest contractors are not, therefore, under the same intense pressure to merge with other defense firms as are contractors of lower rank; at the same time the largest contractors are more vulnerable to hostile public opinion, congressional criticism, antitrust prosecution, and disapproval from the Department of Defense if they increase their shares of the market by merger. It seems more probable that significant acquisitions by the very largest contractors will be in non-defense areas unless such mergers are actively discouraged through public policy. One recent exception must, however, be noted. In 1963 General Dynamics purchased Bethlehem Steel's shipyard at Quincy, Massachusetts. Bethlehem Steel then fell from 52 on the FY 1963 list of prime contractors to 85 on the FY 1964 list, representing a decline in prime awards from $68.4 million to $30.7 million.

Just below the largest aerospace firms, but still within the ranks of the ten largest prime contractors on every list from FY 1957 through FY 1965, are General Electric and American Telephone and Telegraph. These two firms, possessing extensive and nationally famous laboratories, having a relatively small proportion of their sales in the defense market, and ranking among the very largest firms in the nation, are most unlikely to acquire defense firms. They have even less incentive and more to fear from antitrust action than do the largest aerospace firms.

There are, then, forces at work in the defense market operating both for and against a more equal distribution of awards within the ranks of the major contractors. There seems to be no basis on which to predict future Gini coefficients through selection of the set of forces more likely to prove the stronger.

Both concentration through merger and changes in Department of Defense procurement policies are influences which tend to stimulate turnover and which might conceivably reduce year-to-year or period-to-period stability in rank and size of contract awards. Nevertheless, it seems reasonable to assume that stability among the major contractors will increase rather than decrease over the next few years, since the rate of change would have to be accelerated in order to reduce stability as it is defined and measured in this study. The period for which indexes of stability have been shown, from FY 1955 through FY 1964, was one in which concentration increased and in which there were several dramatic mergers. Even if the defense market continues to become more concentrated, concentration would have to increase at a growing rate in order to cause a reduction in stability. To lessen stability, future merger activity would have to more than rival in intensity the effects of such events as Textron's absorption of Bell's defense business, Ford's acquisition of Philco, the formation of Ling-Temco-Vought, and the rise of Litton and General Telephone and Electronics through merger. New Department of Defense policies, while they will undoubtedly have an impact on the structure of the market, do not at this time seem any more likely to contribute to instability than such past occurrences as the transition from manned bombers to missiles, the replacement of fixed fee contracts by incentive awards, the procurement cutback of FY 1960, and the reductions in both the amount of financial assistance to contractors and the amount of government-owned facilities made available to contractors.

B. Impact of Defense Spending on the Structure of Civilian Markets

One more aspect of structure must be considered, beyond the defense market proper. There has been continued concern about the spillover effects of military spending on the structure of industry in the civilian economy. Thus the 1946 report of the Smaller War Plants Corporation expressed concern that the concentration of contracts in World War II, the large retained earnings carried over into peacetime from profits earned on war work, and the facilities for both production and research in the hands of large firms which had been financed by the government during the war would all tend to increase business concentration in the postwar period.[14] Over-all industrial concentration has in fact increased since the end of World War II, rising sharply from 1947 to 1954 and subsequently increasing at a much more gradual rate, as shown in Table IX-2:

14. Smaller War Plants Corporation, *Report to the U.S. Senate Special Committee to Study Problems of American Small Business: Economic Concentration and World War II.*

A good part of the increase in over-all concentration between 1947 and 1954 is accounted for by the postwar rise in defense spending associated with the Korean War, and in particular by large aircraft firms. There were fifteen entrants to the list of the nation's 50 largest manufacturing firms, ranked by value added, between 1947 and 1954, and seven of these fifteen were aircraft firms. Indeed, Ralph L. Nelson, in a study of concentration data which included unpublished material made available by the Bureau of the Census, noted that changes between the two lists were predominantly the result of the rise of the aircraft companies and a sharp increase in concentration in the motor vehicles and parts industry.[15]

Curiously, while over-all concentration rose sharply between 1947 and 1954, concentration within individual industries stayed, on the average, virtually constant. One possible explanation would be that the largest firms and the entrants grew faster than did the economy as a whole, but grew through diversification so as not to increase, on the average, their shares of particular industries. Nelson found that this explanation was not valid for the nation's 50 largest firms. Three four-digit aircraft industries increased their aggregate value of shipments 571 per cent between 1947 and 1954, in contrast to an increase of 51 per cent for manufacturing as a whole. This increase put seven aircraft firms into the ranks of the nation's 50 largest manufacturers, while concentration within the aircraft industries declined, as shown in Table IX-3. The total shares of the seven entrants in the aggre-

15. *Concentration in the Manufacturing Industries of the United States* (New Haven: Yale University Press, 1963), pp. 101–102. See also testimony by Nelson and M. A. Adelman in U.S. Congress, Senate Committee on the Judiciary, Subcommittee on Antitrust and Monopoly, *Hearings: Economic Concentration, Part 1, Overall and Conglomerate Aspects* (Washington: Government Printing Office, 1964), pp. 227–241, 263–277.

Table IX-2: Share of value added by manufacture, accounted for by 200 largest manufacturing companies, 1947–1962

Company rankings in respective year	Percentage of value added by manufacture			
	1947	1954	1958	1962
Largest 200 companies	30	37	38	40
Largest 150 companies	27	34	35	36
Largest 100 companies	23	30	30	32
Largest 50 companies	17	23	23	24

Source: Reproduced from U.S. Congress, Senate Committee on the Judiciary, Subcommittee on Antitrust and Monopoly, *Hearings: Economic Concentration, Part 1, Overall and Conglomerate Aspects* (Washington: Government Printing Office, 1964), p. 388.

gated value of shipments by the three aircraft industries fell from 42 per cent in 1947 to 33 per cent in 1954.[16]

Concentration in the motor vehicles and parts industry rose sharply between 1947 and 1954. Thus the aircraft and automobile companies, through what Nelson noted as "disproportionate influence,"[17] contributed in different ways to the rise in over-all concentration. The effect of diversification, Nelson concluded, was "so small as to defeat attempts even to learn its direction."[18]

National defense undoubtedly had only a minimal and perhaps undetectable effect on over-all concentration between FY 1955 and FY 1964. During this period procurement expenditures were a roughly constant or slightly declining proportion of the gross national product, and concentration within the defense market itself rose at a moderate rate. A sharp increase in defense spending in the future would, in all likelihood, increase over-all concentration while decreasing concentration within the defense market; the effects of a substantial cutback should be the reverse.

Defense procurement may, in two important respects, have an effect on concentration within individual industries. First, military procurement may heighten concentration in civilian industries in which the Department of Defense makes most of its purchases from the largest firms. For example, General Electric is a much larger contractor and a far bigger company than is Westinghouse, and

16. *Concentration in the Manufacturing Industries of the United States*, p. 102.
17. *Ibid.*, p. 14.
18. *Ibid.*

Table IX-3: Share of aircraft industry shipments accounted for by largest companies, 1947 and 1954

| SIC Number | Industry and year | Percentage of value of shipments accounted for by | | |
		4 largest	8 largest	20 largest
3721	Aircraft			
	1947	53	75	97
	1954	47	76	96
3722	Aircraft engines			
	1947	72	88	98
	1954	62	81	93
3723	Aircraft propellers			
	1947	98	99	100
	1954	91	98	100

Source: U.S. Congress, Senate Committee on the Judiciary, Subcommittee on Antitrust and Monopoly, *Concentration in American Industry* (Washington: Government Printing Office, 1957), p. 216.

General Motors ranks well above its smaller rivals, Ford and Chrysler, on the lists of largest contractors. Second, defense firms may become important factors in civilian industries as a result of diversification. If procurement awards in a particular industry become more concentrated than total sales, the immediate result will be to increase the concentration ratio and at the same time reduce the specialization ratio.[19] The increased concentration will have no effect on the largest firms' share of the industry's civilian market unless they, like any defense firms considering diversification, decide to apply their defense earnings or know-how to expansion of their civilian businesses.

The problem cannot be dismissed merely by observing that earnings on defense work are moderate, as shown in Chapter VIII, or that defense know-how is becoming more specialized and less transferable to production of civilian goods. Sheer size and diversification give a firm advantages over smaller and more specialized rivals. A diversifying defense firm may have advantages over a specialized potential entrant to a civilian market even when spillover effects are negligible and when both are prepared to invest the same amount in the civilian industry under consideration. Corwin D. Edwards has stressed the advantages possessed by a large conglomerate firm entirely apart from whatever degree of monopolistic power it may have in any one market. Such a firm may subsidize losses in one market with profits from others, and sheer size may give it the ability to absorb very heavy losses in one area even without subsidization. Reciprocity becomes a possible market tactic: a defense contractor, for example, might place subcontracts for certain parts only with firms which in turn agreed or were expected to purchase equipment from the prime contractor's civilian products division. A large firm may have advantages in possessing legal and public relations staffs which can be used for litigation or lobbying activities on behalf of any of its divisions even though these

19. Strictly, this statement holds true only if the products produced for the defense market fall into a different product class than does the industry's primary product. The "specialization ratio" is defined as a measure of "the extent to which the plants in an industry specialize in making the product primary to that industry. It is derived by dividing the total output (both primary and secondary products) of the industry's plants into their output of products primary to the industry" (U.S. Congress, Senate Committee on the Judiciary, Subcommittee on Antitrust and Monopoly, *Concentration Ratios in Manufacturing Industry, 1958: Report Prepared by the Bureau of the Census* [Washington: Government Printing Office, 1962], p. 6).

staffs can only be sustained by contributions from all divisions. Large diversified firms may have access to credit on terms more favorable than those available to smaller rivals even if unjustified by the financial condition and prospects of the branch or division to which the funds are to be applied.[20]

Conglomerate power based on the defense market has probably not increased much if at all during the cold war period after adjustment to the end of the Korean War. At least, the survey of major contractors reported in Chapter IV noted a very slight increase between 1957 and 1962 in the average percentage of sales made in civilian markets by the firms covered, and absolutely no change in this percentage when it was weighted by the total sales of the individual companies. The constancy in the over-all degree of specialization did hide fairly sizeable changes in the composition of sales of certain firms, with seventeen out of fifty-six increasing or decreasing the percentage of sales made in the defense market by 10 per cent or more; but the simple proportional figures on civilian and military sales do not indicate the extent to which defense firms have cut back on military business or expanded into existing civilian markets, nor do they show whether growth through diversification was accomplished by merger or internal expansion. Although conglomerate power may often be a mutually reinforcing phenomenon, defense firms have typically sought to diversify in order to even out fluctuations in defense business, reduce the risk of disarmament, or avoid reliance on a single customer rather than because of a conviction that existing defense business would give them an advantage over civilian-oriented firms. Further, the most promising type of diversification which does take advantage of experience in the defense market may well be a movement into new fields with advanced technologies and no existing competitors. In 1964, for example, Martin Marietta and Thompson Ramo Wooldridge jointly established a new firm, Bunker-Ramo Corporation, to design and instal computerized assembly lines for industrial firms. The hope of the founders is for a billion-dollar corporation in the next decade making sales to both foreign and domestic industries.[21]

It is extremely difficult to draw up an appropriate public policy

20. *Maintaining Competition* (New York: McGraw-Hill, 1949).
21. *Time*, LXXXIII (Jan. 31, 1964), 65.

prescription for dealing with the impact of defense spending on the structure of the rest of the economy. From the point of view of easing the adjustment to disarmament, defense contractors should be encouraged to diversify and to lessen their reliance on the Department of Defense. While it is not self-evident that diversified defense firms could expand their civilian production and absorb men and resources released by disarmament any more rapidly and efficiently than could non-defense firms, there are reasons for presuming that prior diversification among the major contractors would facilitate the adjustment. If diversification through merger is controlled and restrained, defense firms are more likely to seek out new civilian markets, such as automation of assembly lines, in which their technological skills can best be applied. One of the major problems of disarmament will be the relocation of scientists and engineers, and defense contractors are the most likely candidates for production of civilian goods and services requiring the talents of this group. Use of the existing research organizations of defense contractors could in many cases lead to a quicker adjustment than one which involved non-defense firms in recruiting the technical personnel, equipping them, and establishing smoothly functioning organizations. Also, firms now engaged primarily in defense work could inject additional competition into civilian industries if they converted rather than dissolved. The alternative in some industries would appear to be that firms already dominant in their fields would account for the bulk of the increased civilian output. A significant side benefit of diversification might be a weakening of the military-industrial complex. A firm which makes only one-quarter to one-third of its sales in the defense market and which contemplates the possibility of a 50 per cent reduction in the corporate income tax as a result of disarmament would view the prospect with much less alarm than one entirely committed to military production. In my opinion, public objectives of a much higher priority than the control or reduction of defense firms' economic power in civilian markets today are the following: the greatest possible reduction in domestic resistance to disarmament and an economic structure prepared to adjust to disarmament with the greatest possible facility. There are, however, two suggestions which seem consistent with both sets of objectives.

First, defense firms should be encouraged to diversify through internal expansion or conversion of their own facilities rather than through merger with civilian-oriented firms. The initial effect of such entry into an existing market is to introduce a new competitor rather than merely replace one. Both the Department of Defense and the antitrust enforcement agencies would have roles to play in such a policy. The Department of Defense should give very serious consideration to the proposals of Murray L. Weidenbaum that contracts for commercial-type EDTR be awarded to defense firms, and that the government step up its purchases of civilian-type goods and services from defense contractors.[22] But it seems obvious enough that such contracts and purchases should not go to firms already dominant in civilian markets, and should probably be confined to firms that have specialized in defense production. Not only should planning costs be made allowable costs and hence reimbursable on contracts, as was done in part in 1964, but the government might with some justification subsidize the capitalizable portions of the necessary costs of putting a diversification plan into effect without merger. Such costs would include recruitment and training of management personnel and the establishment of marketing and distribution organizations, perhaps including the fees of management consulting firms. The treatment of patents and proprietary data recommended earlier is not inconsistent with this proposal. It does not seem unreasonable that defense contractors should be permitted and in some cases encouraged to use the patents and know-how acquired during work paid for by the government to facilitate entry into civilian markets as temporary monopolists or with great technical advantages, provided that in every case the government has had the opportunity to bargain for the full value of the advantages. Indeed, if the two proposals were to be viewed as a package, the savings to the government growing out of lower-priced contracts with no patent or rights to data clauses could, conceivably, be used to defray the costs of a program to encourage diversification.

The Antitrust Division of the Department of Justice and the Federal Trade Commission, on the other hand, should keep a careful watch on mergers involving defense firms, and these agencies

22. "Utilizing Defense and Space Technology," *Research for Industry*, XVI, 2–4.

should be quite ruthless in attacking those deemed to have anti-competitive effects in civilian markets. It is difficult to envisage a situation in which a defense firm could call for special treatment or exemption from antitrust prosecution in a contested conglomerate merger on the grounds that the merger would promote the national defense or public interest if the Department of Defense were to embark on a serious and substantial program to encourage diversification from within. The antitrust agencies and the courts have been concerned with the application to conglomerate mergers of Section 7 of the Clayton Act, which prohibits mergers "where in any line of commerce in any section of the country, the effect of such acquisition may be substantially to lessen competition, or to tend to create a monopoly." [23] Here I must hazard another guess, but it seems most likely that the Supreme Court will sooner or later interpret Section 7 in such a way as to make it fully applicable to conglomerate mergers whenever there is a reasonable probability that the contested merger will have the proscribed effect in any market.

Second, the Department of Defense could, as a matter of procurement policy, give preference to the smallest qualified bidder or to the proposal of the smallest qualified firm whenever the offers of two or more firms appeared equal in ultimate cost to the government and could not be distinguished on the basis of prospective performance and delivery time. Alternatively, such a preference might be expressed in terms of market shares, but the problems of classification of multi-product firms, of market definition, and of procedure when bidders were in different industrial classifications would appear to make size a preferable criterion and one which would ultimately lead to approximately the same results. There would have to be adequate safeguards, such as a strict prohibition against price premiums paid to the smaller firms; and there should be reasonable limitations, such as that the preference would apply only in procurement actions of over $50,000. But the policy could be administered as easily or more easily than the small business and labor surplus area programs if carefully formulated, and it has, I believe, a somewhat greater potential for social benefit.

23. 15 U.S.C. §18, 21 (1950).

C. Implications of Market Structure for Procurement Policy

Whether or not increasing concentration of contracts within the defense market proper should be of concern, and whether or not the Department of Defense should try to reduce such concentration, are questions that can only be answered in light of very basic procurement policy alternatives. It is certainly not clear a priori that a market functions best with a large number of firms and intense competition on the supply side when there is only one customer. Other nations have decided to the contrary and have sought to consolidate their defense industries. Great Britain's Ministry of Aviation, according to a 1959 report in *Aviation Week and Space Technology,* brought great pressure on British aviation firms to "regroup" into three aircraft groups and two engine firms. Pressures reportedly included stoppage of contracts.[24] In 1963, *Aviation Week and Space Technology* had a similar report on the West German Defense Ministry, which was seeking a "major reorganization designed to weld the nation's aerospace industrial complex into a single entity responsible for most research, development and production." The rationale, the article continued, was that "integrating the industry would simplify not only channeling and division of work on future multination production projects but also the Defense Ministry's coordination of these programs internally as well as externally."[25] Industry sources in the United States have raised the same issue. In 1959, W. M. Allen, president of Boeing, noted that consolidations similar to those in Britain were being attempted in the United States. He doubted that the Department of Defense would exert pressure "forcing consolidation by government fiat," but he felt that the economics of the defense market would be a compelling force. There were too many firms and not enough money in the defense budget to support all the programs being carried on within these firms. The result, Allen concluded, was that there were too many firms bidding on each Air Force competition.[26] Two years later, Donald W. Douglas, Jr., president of Douglas Aircraft, stated that

24. LXXI (Dec. 7, 1959), 35.
25. LXXVIII (March 11, 1963), 293.
26. *Ibid.,* LXXI (Dec. 28, 1959), 81.

"very large companies or groups of companies, and a narrowing of competition, may be an unavoidable part of maintaining a strong aerospace industry. Our British cousins seem to think it is, and have acted accordingly. Have we given this problem enough thought?" [27]

One can distinguish three fundamental approaches which might be taken by the Department of Defense in dealing with its suppliers. These are not entirely exclusive alternatives, since to some extent all three are present in the current Relationship. First, the Department of Defense might seek to intensify competition in the defense market and hope thereby to reduce procurement costs; second, the department might reduce its reliance on private industry by expansion of government-owned and operated arsenals and shipyards; and third, in recognition of special characteristics of the Relationship the Department of Defense might choose a course of positive regulation of the market, playing a role analogous to that of a public utility commission.[28]

Increased concentration within the defense market, in the sense of a rise in the proportion of total dollar volume of procurement awards going to the 50 largest prime contractors, is not inconsistent with a greater degree of competition. Many of the relatively smaller firms in this group are specialized to the extent that they can compete only in quite narrowly defined areas within procurement programs. If concentration occurs through consolidation and diversified growth of defense capabilities of contractors near the middle and bottom of the list, it may well result in a greater potential for competition across a wider range of projects. Consolidation, however, may prove to be of technological benefit to even the very largest contractors, faced as they are today with the Department of Defense's standardization policy and the demand for very complex systems. As an example of the demands of this complexity, only Boeing decided to "go it alone" in the TFX competition, while General Dynamics and Grumman teamed to submit the winning proposal. Other joint entries in the competition were Republic and Ling-Temco-Vought, and Douglas and McDonnell.[29] But increased con-

27. *Aerospace Management,* IV (Oct., 1961), 39.
28. These three policy alternatives have been distinguished long before this study. For a clear statement see F. T. Moore, *Military Procurement and Contracting,* p. 117.
29. The TFX competition is described in a well-written, summary fashion in *Corporations in Crisis,* pp. 171–204.

centration resulting from relative growth of the very largest contractors would tend to reduce rather than increase the Department of Defense's opportunities for competitive procurement of major weapon systems. Indeed, a reduction in competitive pressures is certainly what industrial spokesmen and the trade press have had in mind when they commented on overcapacity and referred rather pointedly to the efforts of the British and West German defense ministries to promote merger and consolidation.

In one obvious respect, its size, the defense market in the United States differs from those of Great Britain and West Germany. The fact or contention that mergers and regrouping of British and German defense firms would increase efficiency certainly does not mean that the very large contractors in this country are foregoing any similar economies of scale. As shown in Table IX-4, the awards going only to the four largest prime contractors in the United States are approximately equal to the total expenditure on defense of either Great Britain or West Germany. The defense expenditures shown for these two countries include non-procurement outlays and procurement of items other than aircraft and missiles, while all four largest prime contractors in this country have been aerospace firms in the years shown.

Secretary McNamara has placed a great deal of emphasis on shifting from non-competitive to competitive procurement, noting that the Department of Defense is able to reduce its procurement

Table IX-4: Total defense expenditures of Great Britain and West Germany, compared with awards to the largest prime contractors in the United States, 1961 to 1964 ($ billions)

Year*	Total defense expenditures		U.S. prime contract awards	
	Great Britain	West Germany	Largest contractor	Largest 4 contractors
1961	$4,469	$3,021	$1,461	$4,753
1962	4,724	3,995	1,420	4,781
1963	4,948	4,611	1,517	4,969
1964	5,018	4,946	1,455	4,997

* Years shown for Great Britain and the United States are fiscal years; years shown for West Germany are calendar years.

Sources: For Great Britain, Central Statistical Office, *Annual Abstract of Statistics, No. 101, 1964* (London: Her Majesty's Stationery Office). For West Germany, S. H. Steinberg (ed.), *The Statesman's Year-book, 1955–66* (London: Macmillan, 1965). Conversion to dollar figures made from exchange rates in International Monetary Fund, *International Financial Statistics,* XVII (Oct., 1965).

costs by 25 per cent, on the average, each time such a shift is made; but he has been very careful to point out that the potential for competitive procurement is limited. For example, in 1964 testimony he confirmed his previously announced target of raising competitive procurement to 40 per cent of the total, adding that studies were being made to determine if the objective could be raised. But just before mentioning the target figure, he stated:

As I indicated to you last year, there are limitations on the percentage of our purchases which can be made on a competitive basis. Where large engineering and tooling costs are involved, for example, and that is typically the case, as you know, in aircraft, missiles, and many other complex weapons systems, it is unlikely that any new source could compete successfully against the development contractor who had already incurred these costs, and therefore we have no alternative but to place the follow-on procurement contracts with that development contractor and this removes those contracts from the competitive category.

Nevertheless, we developed ways in which to expand the scope of competitive procurement, for example, by "breaking out" components or spare parts from the prime contract, so that these components or spare parts could be procured through competitive procedures.[30]

In the spring of 1965, the Department of Defense announced a new type of competition for the development and manufacture of the C-5A, a strategic transport airplane designed to carry three times the load of the largest present Air Force cargo craft, the C-141. In congressional testimony Lieutenant General James Ferguson, Air Force Deputy Chief of Staff for Research and Development, described the contract as follows:

We will use a new contracting approach for the C-5A, one in which we intend to use a single contract, at the beginning of development, for the entire life cycle procurement. This unique plan also has flexible incentive features designed to provide substantial cost savings for the Air Force and, at the same time, rewards commensurate with risks for the contractor.

By combining development, production, and support into a single contract, and by using competitively established cost and performance targets, we expect to (1) curtail "buy-in" bidding, (2) encourage production design from the beginning, and (3) motivate contractors to

30. U.S. Congress, Joint Economic Committee, Subcommittee on Defense Procurement, *Hearings: Impact of Military and Related Civilian Supply and Service Activities on the Economy* (Washington: Government Printing Office, 1964), pp. 7–8.

develop reliable and simple systems. We will implement this "total package" plan at the completion of the project definition phase, later this year.[31]

The "total package" contract is to be awarded only after competitive negotiation. It is to be used only in the case of weapon developments which rely mainly on existing technology, so that there is some assurance both to the Department of Defense and to the contractor that development can in fact lead to production. Contracts for new weapon systems that require major technological advances will still be awarded separately for the several stages.

Later in the year, the Department of Defense announced the award of a $2 billion contract for the C-5A to Lockheed, with the first of the new airplanes expected to be in operation in 1969.[32] The contract is extended beyond delivery dates to include a twelve-month maintenance guaranty.

Substantial use of such long-term contracts will require new adjustments by future users of the types of data supplied by the Department of Defense and relied upon in this study. Year-to-year shifts in contract awards and rankings will appear greater, the apparent concentration of awards in any one year will be heightened, and it will be necessary to use periods of more than three years to correct for distortions. Department of Defense statisticians will be faced with a problem of reporting competitive and non-competitive procurements on a basis comparable with that previously employed. In the past, a development contract such as that for the C-5A would have been classed as awarded by competitive negotiation, while the subsequent production and maintenance contracts, if negotiated only with Lockheed, would have been recorded as sole-source awards. If the entire $2 billion contract is considered a competitive award, and future total package contracts are treated in the same way, there will be a sharp but spurious rise in the amount and percentage of "competitive" procurement.

In light of the arguments made in Chapter VI, which maintained that efforts to obtain price competition in follow-on awards could

31. U.S. Congress, House Committee on Armed Services, *Hearings on Military Posture and H.R. 4016* (Washington: Government Printing Office, 1965), p. 1204. A report and description of the Department of Defense's announcement of the "total package" contract is in the *Wall Street Journal*, March 15, 1965, p. 3.

32. *Wall Street Journal*, Oct. 1, 1965, p. 2.

have unduly unfavorable effects on non-price competition at the EDTR stage, the total package contract appears to be a thoroughly commendable innovation and one which I am virtually forced to predict will prove successful.

Goods and services purchased by the Department of Defense may be divided into three main types, although admittedly it would be impossible to fit every item procured neatly and unambiguously into the classification scheme. The implications for competition seem to differ by type of item procured. First, there are items which are identical with or closely similar to civilian products. Fuels and lubricants, textiles, and much of military construction fall into this category. Second, there are products such as tanks and field artillery which are produced solely for the military market, but which make use of industrial techniques that rely on technological principles similar to those already in use throughout civilian industry. Third, there are strictly military products, usually costly and complex, which are the result of extensive research and whose development and production require very advanced, specialized, and often secret technology. Price competition is most appropriate in the first class, and there seems to be no reason the Department of Defense, in procurements of this type, should not seek to obtain the lowest possible prices by soliciting bids from as many firms as possible through formal advertising or negotiation. At the other extreme, in the third class, price competition has been and ought to be subordinated to non-price competition; it has been argued above that in most weapon systems programs the devices which have been used to promote price competition are inappropriate. But it would seem utterly essential to acceptable performance by weapon systems contractors that a high degree of non-price competition be maintained at the technological level. Following William Fellner's analysis,[33] a large number of firms is not a requirement for effective non-price competition, but it should be cause for serious concern if the structure of the defense market is at any time such that the Department of Defense has no alternative to sole-source negotiation in any major EDTR contract.

In general, the policies of the Department of Defense in regard to price and non-price competition appear to be developing along

33. *Supra,* p. 117.

proper and logical lines, but only if greater use is made of total package procurements in situations in which proposals can be obtained from several technically competent competitors. The attitude of the department toward the use of arsenals and other government-owned and operated facilities is, in my opinion, much less sound.

The Department of Defense has, admittedly, been under heavy and continuing criticism for fostering government "competition" with private enterprise. However, its reaction to criticism has failed to distinguish between the first two of the procurement classes just suggested. Thus, a 1963 congressional study noted:

In 1955, when the committee was considering a substantially similar bill, it had before it a statement of the then Director of the Bureau of the Budget which indicated that, as of 1952, the Government was engaged in the manufacture of rum, fertilizer, helium, rubber, lumber, electric power, sleeping bags, false teeth, spectacles, ice cream, maps, flags, paint, ammunition, clothing, aluminum, furniture, and ships. Other activities included rail, air, and marine transport, trucking, blueprinting, warehousing, operation of hotels and laundries, scrap processing, tire retreading, garbage collection, baking, furniture and typewriter repair, window washing, dry cleaning, salvage, and fur sealing. As will appear below, a considerable number of these activities have been terminated by administrative action.[34]

The great majority of the items listed are clearly civilian-type products well within our first class. The study noted that many of these activities had been discontinued; yet in a statement on compliance the Department of Defense described its efforts to reduce its commercial and industrial activities, citing as examples the closing of the Naval Gun Factory and of the ordnance plant operated by the Navy at York, Pennsylvania. Since that time, the Department of Defense has given much attention to disposal of arsenals and shipyards. In defending retention of other facilities, the Department of Defense statement noted:

The remaining 69 plants under military control are Government operated (not contractor operated), and include activities which predate World War II, such as the Army manufacturing arsenals at Rock Island and Frankford, the Navy shipyards at Philadelphia and Portsmouth; the Navy propellant plant at Indian Head; and other long established

34. U.S. Congress, Senate Committee on Government Operations, *Government Competition with Private Enterprise*, p. 3.

activities. Some plants in this GOGO group include those which are the sole source of classified and highly specialized material for which current production arrangements made continued Government ownership advisable. Others are engaged in military research and pilot production in the field of ballistics, torpedoes, and other areas in which a limited level of continued military participation has been found necessary.[35]

The Department of Defense appears to have been defending government operation of facilities for development and production of technically advanced weapon systems, but responding to concern over government "competition" with producers of civilian-type goods by disposing of facilities for production of strictly military but not particularly advanced goods.

The word "competition" has been put within quotation marks because the use of Department of Defense facilities has never really involved competition between government and private enterprise for sales to third parties. The question is one of determining the circumstances under which the government is justified in producing for its own use rather than procuring from private firms. It seems perfectly obvious that it is in the taxpayers' interests for the government to produce whenever the full additional costs incurred by doing so are lower than those of procuring from private firms.[36] It is difficult to see how the basic rationale or ideology of free enterprise is violated by allowing the government the option of producing for itself.

In general, it is doubtful that the government would have any advantage over private enterprise in the manufacture of civilian-type goods, although there are certain cases in which government production of even this class of goods is necessary or justified. First, producers of goods sold in civilian markets must adjust their prices

---

35. *Ibid.*, p. 11.

36. Relevant "costs of production" will depend on whether the work is to be done in existing facilities or will require the construction of new facilities. See pp. 107–108 *supra* for an argument that only incremental costs should be taken into account if existing facilities are to be used. There are, it must be noted, serious difficulties of estimating certain items of avoidable cost in cases involving new construction. Both confusion on this issue and some of the real difficulties are illustrated in the following 1965 statement of the Deputy Director of the Bureau of the Budget:

"We have been working principally on the question of trying to develop the cost basis for determining what true Government costs are, and this has been very difficult —as to, for example, how much you include for overhead, or whether you include in overhead an amount to carry the same total costs as a private corporation has to pay, in which case you would include in an allowance for cost of Congress, and the judiciary, and the Civil Service Commission, Budget Bureau, and all of the central agencies of Government.

to the possibility that some of their customers will produce for themselves. When the Department of Defense can purchase in such a market, it reaps the advantage of prices which are restrained by the power of other buyers to manufacture, even if the possibility is not open to the government itself. Second, the government cannot be expected to be as efficient as private firms in most commercial and industrial activities in which there is a potential for profit, since its organizational structure, personnel policies, and rules of procedure are geared to other purposes.[37] Also, public enterprise may be handicapped by political interference, manipulation, and criticism. Yet the Department of Defense may be thoroughly justified in occasionally undertaking production of civilian-type goods where there is a need to serve an isolated installation, for example, or where exorbitant prices are being charged because competition is absent and impossible to obtain, or where military needs are subject to extreme fluctuation and likely to strain or exceed private capacity to produce when the demand is urgent. Production of civilian-type goods should, however, be undertaken only very rarely by government agencies as an alternative to procurement, and then only if properly tested by the criterion of minimization of public expenditures.

Goods and services produced strictly for military purposes pose a different set of problems, even in cases in which the underlying technology is analogous to that of production of normal civilian

---

The difficulty here is whether or not we go beyond what we might regard as true costs of Government, in performing or carrying out a particular activity. Whether we include all of the costs that are incurred by private enterprise, if it produced the same item.

The reason it gets very complicated is whether or not, for example, would we be able to know in advance what State and local taxes are involved? We are dealing with, say, a prime contractor who may have subcontractors unknown at the time the prime contract is let" (U.S. Congress, Joint Economic Committee, Subcommittee on Federal Procurement and Regulation, *Hearings: Economic Impact of Federal Procurement*, pp. 320–321).

Whether an existing facility is to be used or a new one is to be constructed, "overhead" items such as the cost of Congress are irrelevant, as these costs will be incurred regardless of the decision and their magnitudes will not be observably affected by it. On the other hand, if construction of a new facility is contemplated, very difficult estimates of such items as hypothetical interest and taxes are properly involved.

37. The opinion is sometimes expressed that government personnel cannot manage any operation as efficiently as their counterparts in private industry, since they are not motivated by the prospect of profit and are unafraid of losing their jobs through discharge or bankruptcy of their employer. This contention is not, to my mind, persuasive.

goods. The most obvious contrast lies in the fact that if the Department of Defense is the only buyer there are no private customers whose make or buy policies act as a restraint on producers' prices. Simply to protect itself in such situations, the Department of Defense should have the option of engaging in production. Also, there may be economies of vertical integration in having a military product produced under the direct control of the branch of service which prescribes the specifications, makes field tests or shakedown cruises, and proposes modifications on the basis of experience in use. Government-owned and operated facilities producing only a portion of the output acquired by the Department of Defense may serve as a yardstick by which the performance of contractors can be judged; such facilities may also be used to test new production processes or modifications in the product before they are recommended to private firms. Private firms may hesitate to adapt their plants to production of strictly military goods, particularly if substantial investment in new or modified plant and equipment is required. Companies dislike being in a position of undue reliance on one customer, and the Department of Defense is viewed as a particularly unreliable customer, since its needs are likely to change suddenly through technological advances or changes in strategic planning, and since the added danger of disarmament or a cutback in military spending is always present. Private industry's aversion to uncertainty can be overcome by a substantial enough price premium, but the Department of Defense itself may be in the best position to assess the situation. If so, there may be substantial savings in having the brunt of possible fluctuations borne by public capital.

Finally, there is a political problem involved in having private firms engaged in the manufacture of armaments. Without any comparison with pre-World War II "merchants of death," it may be noted that exports of weapons are rising. In an article entitled "Traffic in Arms Again Rising," the New York *Times* reported:

Despite the Department of Commerce's report of $243 million in exports of firearms of war and ammunition thereof for 1964, private arms exports apparently have grown to more than $1 billion in 1964, including transshipments—compared with the Government's direct export sales amounting to $1.5 billion.

How does a foreign country buy American equipment? In the present campaign, if it is not ruled out for political or economic reasons, it may find an American salesman knocking on its door. To push its campaign, the United States provides credits to purchasing countries. It encourages defense contractors to scout Western Europe, in particular, for sales possibilities.

Some foreign defense ministers may initiate the deal in direct inquiries to a major United States defense contractor in an effort to compare quality and prices—a United States tank, for example, compared with one produced in Britain or Sweden; a United States jet plane compared with one produced in France.

Representatives of American firms are armed with pamphlets, films and other advertising materials that have been approved by Government authorities in Washington for security reasons. If the promotion succeeds, licensing is arranged.[38]

Although American defense firms must be licensed to sell weapons abroad, with licenses granted or withheld on grounds of foreign policy, there is the inevitable danger that private enterprise seeking sales abroad will bring inappropriate pressures to bear on those formulating foreign policy, especially in the event of a decline in domestic military procurement.

A good case could be made that private enterprise has encroached too far upon the legitimate activities of military agencies, and that this imbalance is in greater need of correction than is the reverse. In 1959, Herbert Roback, Staff Administrator for the House Subcommittee on Military Operations, put the following questions to W. F. Finan of the Bureau of the Budget:

Do you think it is inappropriate for contract personnel to set up the Air Force Thor overseas?

Is it an appropriate function for an airline company to operate a missile range?

Is it appropriate or inappropriate for a subsidiary of a utility company, a telephone company specifically, to operate, construct and operate the DEW line and collect telephone revenues from the Government?[39]

Mr. Finan, in reply, stated that he saw nothing inherently wrong with any of these arrangements. He added that he saw no reason, in an emergency, the government should not contract with private agencies for personnel investigations "ranging all the way down to

38. May 30, 1965, p. 6E.
39. U.S. Congress, House Committee on Government Operations, Military Operations Subcommittee, *Hearings: Organization and Management of Missile Programs*, pp. 590–591.

normal credit agencies." [40] There are perfectly reasonable standards under which the services of private enterprise are inappropriate for most of the activities just cited. A private firm should not be engaged, as an agent of the government, in overseas operations in which a mishap or an error in judgment could bring on a diplomatic crisis or even a war. The Department of Defense should never be dependent on a private firm for the day-to-day operation of an essential element of the nation's defense, since the potential for abuse during negotiations on contract renewal is all too evident. Without their free consent, government personnel should not be subject to investigation by a private agency which could disseminate or otherwise make use of the information in its later business with clients other than the government.

Evidence is mixed on the relative efficiency of government and private enterprise in weapon production. A 1963 study made a convincing case that private shipyards are more efficient than naval shipyards in shipbuilding, although the findings on repairs and maintenance were not so decisive and the Navy disputed other conclusions. [41] On the other hand, there is little doubt that the Army's Redstone Arsenal outperformed the Air Force's contractors in the intermediate-range ballistic missile program. But several contractors, notably Chrysler, played important roles in the Army's Jupiter development at Redstone Arsenal, and it can be argued that the Army's success had nothing to do with the relative merits of its organization but was the result of the historical accident that the Army rather than the contractors had the services of a number of German rocket engineers. In response to inquiries about difficulties in the manufacture of the M-14 rifle, Secretary McNamara testified that production schedules had slipped at commercial operators' plants but not at the Springfield Arsenal. [42] Military leaders have been harshly critical of contractors' performance. Air Force General Curtis E. LeMay stated in 1963:

Our problem is that the bulk of the aircraft industry, where we are spending our money, is really subsidized by the Government.

40. *Ibid.*, p. 590.
41. U.S. Department of Commerce, Office of Technical Services, *Bureau of Ships Analysis of Arthur Andersen and Company: Shipbuilding Cost Study*, Nov. 30, 1962.
42. U.S. Congress, House Committee on Armed Services, *Hearings on Military Posture and H.R. 9751*, p. 3203.

They haven't been subject to the dog-eat-dog competition of normal industry.

And from that standpoint, their managing is not as good as it probably should be.

When we give them a contract for a product, they really have us in a bad position because we must have a weapons system. And they know it.

If they get into trouble, pricewise or something, we always have to bail them out, because we just can't afford to drop what we have and go to someone else, because they probably couldn't build it in the first place, and even if they could we would lose a period of years probably before they could pick it up and do it.

So we really hire them to work for us. And if it is a cost-plus-fixed-fee contract, the more money they spend the more they make.

Now we have management teams, of course, trying to help them do a satisfactory job.

But we are not getting into the aircraft industry the keen competition that is in existence throughout all the rest of the industry of the United States.[43]

In the same year, Admiral Hyman G. Rickover was quoted as saying:

During the past few years hundreds of major conventional components, such as pressure vessels and steam generators, have been procured for naval nuclear propulsion plants. Less than 10 per cent have been delivered on time. Thirty per cent were delivered six months to a year or more later than promised. Even so, reinspection of these components after delivery showed that over 50 per cent had to be further reworked in order to meet contract specification requirements.

Time and time again I have found that management is reluctant to depart from outdated practices; that it is not informed of what is actually going on in the plant; that it fails to provide the informed and strong leadership necessary to bring about improvements in engineering and production.[44]

There is no need, in this study, to enter into further examination of the controversy surrounding the relative efficiency of private and government enterprise. The only point to be made in citing specific studies, instances, and testimony is that it is incorrect to assume on a priori grounds that private firms are inevitably more efficient, especially as producers of weapons, than are government-operated facilities. Further, government operation of facilities

43. U.S. Congress, House Committee on Armed Services, *Hearings on Military Posture and H.R. 2440*, p. 1203.
44. *Aerospace Management*, V (Dec., 1962), 66.

supplying only government needs, particularly in the area of national defense, does not appear to violate any meaningful principle of free enterprise. The Department of Defense's decision to make or buy should be based on careful and pragmatic comparison of costs. At present, such decisions appear to be based instead primarily on a partially misinformed and perhaps partially misconstrued political antipathy toward even economically justifiable government activities.[45]

The final type of basic procurement policy characterizing the defense market in the cold war is positive regulation. In previous chapters there has been discussion of various regulatory aspects of the Relationship, such as audit and inspection, control of wage rates, directed subcontracting, renegotiation, small business and labor surplus area preferences, preference for domestic goods, non-discriminatory employment practices, security, and rights to data. Some of these controls have been criticized in this study and elsewhere as unwise, unnecessary, and harmful to performance in the defense market; but others seem inevitable in light of the nature of military procurement. As a single customer the Department of Defense cannot escape assuming two of the major burdens of a public utility commission: it inevitably determines prices and profits and it permits or bars entry to the defense market through the fundamental act of procurement.

The Department of Defense has used its monopsonistic power as sole buyer to limit profits, but it has also acted "fairly" in its dealings with contractors so as to assure reasonable returns and the survival as defense producers of firms on which it depends. In his study of approximately three thousand contracts, F. T. Moore made the following findings:

When one looks at the arrays of profit rates presented in Section III of this report—arrays that are broken down in various ways by type of

45. One exception to this criticism is the Department of Defense's attitude toward support of the Civil Reserve Air Fleet through transportation contracts with private carriers. In 1965 Secretary McNamara testified that certain commitments had been made by his predecessors and that commercial carriers had acquired and modernized aircraft in reliance on business from the Department of Defense. These commitments, he continued, were probably a mistake but would nevertheless be honored. But as soon as possible, Secretary McNamara testified, "I want to move away from this use of commercial lift into the use of internal Department of Defense lift" (U.S. Congress, House Committee on Armed Services, *Hearings on Military Posture and H.R. 4016,* pp. 352–355).

contract, by product, by type of work, and so forth—the remarkable fact is not that they are so different, but that they are so similar. True, there are differences between average profit rates on CPFF [cost-plus-fixed-fee] and incentive contracts of approximately 2.5 per cent; within each type of contract one can observe that the range of profit rates is quite wide. For CPFF prime contracts the range is from zero to over 14 per cent, and for incentive contracts the range is from an actual loss to 18 per cent. The similarity might not seem great. But note that of the CPFF contracts 65 per cent have profit rates between 6 per cent and 8 per cent, and in incentive contracts 52 per cent have rates between 8 per cent and 11 per cent. Perhaps even more to the point is the fact that in the CPFF contracts for R&D work, two-thirds of the contracts had profit rates between 6 per cent and 8 per cent—exactly the same result as for total CPFF prime contracts. Reference may also be made to the figures cited previously on the similarity of average profit rates regardless of whether the work was for R&D, construction, or services. In short, there is stronger evidence on the bunching of profit rates than there is on their dispersion.[46]

Such "bunching" is undoubtedly an important factor not only in defense profits but also in the relative stability found among contractors.

In procurement areas where competitive restraints are necessarily weak or lacking, and those in which arsenal-type operations are impractical, the Department of Defense has little choice but to subject its contractors to some degree of positive regulation. Where competition can be obtained, particularly non-price competition for positions in new programs involving technically specialized and advanced weaponry, it should be encouraged to the utmost. Under some circumstances production should take place in government-owned and operated facilities. There is no inherent inconsistency in a procurement policy composed of a blend of competition, operation of arsenals, and regulation of contractors, but the appropriate emphasis differs with the nature of the item being procured and with the stage of the procurement cycle for advanced weapons.

The final question, which provides one of the most important justifications for a study of this sort, is whether the Department of Defense should take deliberate action to influence or alter the structure of the defense market through its procurement decisions. Measures of stability of rank and dollar volume of prime contract

46. *Military Procurement and Contracting*, p. 63.

awards, coupled with higher than average rates of return on investment among contractors, indicate that the Department of Defense can and should pay little attention to proposals for more generous treatment of contractors across the board because of alleged high risk and instability in the defense market. The financial structures of the major contractors, unfortunately, bear out the inference that there is little serious concern among them over the very real long-run risk to them and hope for the rest of us posed by the prospect of disarmament. Given the monopsonistic character of the defense market, the degree of regulation, the overwhelming importance of non-price competition, and the Department of Defense's current emphasis on research and on standardization, the present level of over-all concentration and even the apparent trend toward increased concentration of the market as a whole do not appear to be causes for concern. But it seems absolutely essential that the Department of Defense prevent concentration within the ranks of the largest contractors from increasing until non-price competition at the technological level is weakened or in some cases lost. In the interest of economic preparation for the eventuality of disarmament, contractors should be encouraged to diversify without acquiring non-defense firms. The power over market structure which is necessarily associated with the placement of contracts can be used to improve the performance of the defense market, hopefully along with other changes in procurement policy proposed in this study, and such use of power is herewith advocated.

Sources Cited

A. Books and Pamphlets

Abramovitz, Moses (ed.). *The Allocation of Economic Resources: Essays in Honor of Bernard Francis Haley*. Stanford: Stanford University Press, 1959.

Arthur D. Little, Inc. *How Sick Is the Defense Industry?* Cambridge: Arthur D. Little, Inc., 1963.

Bain, J. S. *Industrial Organization*. New York: Wiley, 1959.

Baldwin, William L. *Antitrust and the Changing Corporation*. Durham, N.C.: Duke University Press, 1961.

Berle, A. A. *The 20th Century Capitalist Revolution*. New York: Harcourt, Brace, 1954.

Berle, A. A. and G. C. Means. *The Modern Corporation and Private Property*. New York: Macmillan, 1932.

Caves, Richard E. *American Industry: Structure, Conduct, Performance*. Englewood Cliffs, N.J.: Prentice Hall, 1964.

Cook, Fred J. *The Warfare State*. New York: Macmillan, 1962.

Day, J. S. *Subcontracting Policy in the Airframe Industry*. Boston: Division of Research, Graduate School of Business Administration, Harvard University, 1956.

Edwards, Corwin D. *Maintaining Competition*. New York: McGraw-Hill, 1949.

Fellner, William. *Competition Among the Few: Oligopoly and Similar Market Structures*. New York: Knopf, 1949.

Galbraith, John K. *American Capitalism: The Concept of Countervailing Power*. Boston: Houghton Mifflin, 1952.

Hays, William L. *Statistics for Psychologists*. New York: Holt, Rinehart and Winston, 1963.

Hitch, Charles J. *Decision-Making for Defense*. Berkeley: University of California Press, 1965.

Hitch, Charles J., and Roland N. McKean. *The Economics of Defense in the Nuclear Age*. Cambridge: Harvard University Press, 1960.

Jewkes, John, David Sawers, and Richard Stillerman. *The Sources of Invention*. London: Macmillan, 1958.

Kaplan, A. D. H. *Big Enterprise in a Competitive System*. Washington: Brookings Institution, 1954.

Kaysen, Carl, and Donald F. Turner. *Antitrust Policy: An Economic and Legal Analysis*. Cambridge: Harvard University Press, 1959.

Lazure, Albert C., and Andrew P. Murphy, Jr. (eds.). *Research and Development Procurement Law*. Washington: Federal Bar Journal, 1957.

Lockheed Aircraft Corporation. *Aerospace: Two Predictions of Profitability and Long-term Growth*. Burbank, Calif.: Lockheed Aircraft Corp., 1965.

Melman, Seymour. *Our Depleted Society*. New York: Holt, Rinehart and Winston, 1965.

Miller, Thomas G., Jr. *Strategies for Survival in the Aerospace Industry*. Cambridge: Arthur D. Little, Inc., 1964.

Military Procurement Advisory Committee. *How to Improve Federal Procedures for Buying National Defense Materials: Report to Senator George A. Smathers Prepared by His Military Procurement Advisory Committee*, Aug. 18, 1961.

Moore, F. T. *Military Procurement and Contracting: An Economic Analysis*. Memorandum RM-2948-PR. Santa Monica: Rand Corp., 1962.

National Security Industrial Association. *Problems in Military Contracting: Papers Presented at NSIA's Ninth Annual Meeting, October 1, 1952*. New York: National Security Industrial Association, 1952.

Nelson, Clarence O. *Missile and Aircraft Procurement Management*. New York: Vantage Press, 1961.

Nelson, Donald M. *Arsenal of Democracy: The Story of American War Production*. New York: Harcourt, Brace, 1946.

Nelson, Ralph L. *Concentration in the Manufacturing Industries of the United States*. New Haven: Yale University Press, 1963.

Novick, David, and J. Y. Springer. *Economics of Defense Procurement and Small Business*. Santa Monica: Rand Corp., Aug. 15, 1958.

Peck, M. J., and F. M. Scherer. *The Weapons Acquisition Process: An Economic Analysis*. Boston: Division of Research, Graduate School of Business Administration, Harvard University, 1962.

Plum, Lester V. (ed.). *Investing in American Industries*. New York: Harper, 1960.

Price, Don K. *Government and Science*. New York: New York University Press, 1954.

Rubenstein, Albert H. *Problems of Financing and Managing New Research-based Enterprises in New England*. Research Report to the Federal Reserve Bank of Boston, No. 3, 1958.

Scherer, F. M. *The Weapons Acquisition Process: Economic Incentives*. Boston: Division of Research, Graduate School of Business Administration, Harvard University, 1964.

Schlaifer, Robert. *Development of Aircraft Engines*. Boston: Graduate School of Business Administration, Harvard University, 1950.

Schumpeter, Joseph A. *Capitalism, Socialism, and Democracy*. New York: Harper, 1942.

Smith, Richard A. *Corporations in Crisis*. Garden City: Doubleday, 1963.

Stanford Research Institute. *The Industry-Government Aerospace Re-*

lationship: Prepared for Aerospace Industries Association of America, Inc. 2 vols. Menlo Park, Calif.: Stanford Research Institute, 1963.

Steinberg, S. H. (ed.). *The Statesman's Year-book, 1965–66.* London: Macmillan, 1965.

Stockfisch, J. A. (ed.). *Planning and Forecasting in the Defense Industries.* Belmont, Calif.: Wadsworth, 1962.

Stocking, George W. *Basing Point Pricing and Regional Development.* Chapel Hill: University of North Carolina Press, 1954.

B. Periodicals

Aerospace Management, various issues.

Aircraft and Missiles, various issues.

Armed Forces Management, various issues.

Aviation Week and Space Technology, various issues.

Collins, N. R., and L. E. Preston. "The Size Structure of the Largest Industrial Firms." *American Economic Review,* LI (Dec., 1961), 986–1011.

Eisenhower, Dwight D. "Liberty Is at Stake: Farewell Address by Dwight D. Eisenhower, President of the United States." *Vital Speeches of the Day,* XXVII (Feb. 1, 1961), 229.

Fortune, Directory of the 500 Largest Industrial Corporations, July, 1962, 1963, 1964, and 1965.

Friedland, Seymour. "Turnover and Growth of the Largest Industrial Firms, 1906–1950." *Review of Economics and Statistics,* XXXIX (Feb., 1957), 79–83.

Hamberg, Daniel. "Size of Firm, Oligopoly, and Research: The Evidence." *Canadian Journal of Economics and Political Science,* XXX (Feb., 1964), 62–75.

Heyman, Victor K. "Government by Contract." *Public Administration Review,* XXI (Spring, 1961), 59–64.

International Monetary Fund. *International Financial Statistics,* XVII (Oct., 1965).

Miller, Arthur S. (ed.). "Administration by Contract: An Examination of Governmental Contracting-Out," *George Washington Law Review,* XXXI (April, 1963).

Miller, J. P. "Military Procurement in Peacetime." *Harvard Business Review,* XXV (Summer, 1947), 444–462.

————. "Military Procurement Policies: World War II and Today." Papers and Proceedings of the Sixty-fourth Annual Meeting of the American Economic Association. *American Economic Review,* XLII (May, 1952), 455–475.

Missiles and Rockets, various issues.

Moore, F. T. "Efficiency and Public Policy in Defense Procurement." *Law and Contemporary Problems,* XXIX (Winter, 1964), 3–18.

New York *Times,* various issues.

Novick, David, and J. Y. Springer. "Economics of Defense Procurement and Small Business." *Law and Contemporary Problems,* XXIV (Winter, 1959), 118–131.

Schrieber, Albert N. "Small Business and Government Procurement." *Law and Contemporary Problems,* XXIX (Spring, 1964), 390–417.

Time, LXXXIII (Jan. 31, 1964), 65.

Wall Street Journal, various issues.

Weiner, Neil S. "Multiple Incentive Fee Maximization: An Economic Model." *Quarterly Journal of Economics,* LXXVII (Nov., 1963), 603–616.

Weidenbaum, Murray L. "Utilizing Defense and Space Technology." *Research for Industry,* XVI (March–April, 1964), 2–4.

————. "Industrial Impact of Disarmament." *American Journal of Economics and Sociology,* XXII (Oct., 1963), 513–526.

————. "Product Diversification in the Aircraft Manufacturing Industry." *Analysts Journal,* XV (May, 1959), 51–56.

————. "The U.S. Aircraft Industry." *Financial Analysts Journal,* XIX (March–April, 1963), 49–53.

Worley, J. S. "Industrial Research and the New Competition." *Journal of Political Economy,* LXIX (April, 1961), 183–186.

C. Government Documents

Great Britain, Central Statistical Office. *Annual Abstract of Statistics, No. 101, 1964.* London: Her Majesty's Stationery Office.

U.S. *Armed Services Procurement Regulation,* 1963 edition.

U.S. Arms Control and Disarmament Agency. *Economic Impacts of Disarmament.* Economic Series 1, Jan., 1962. Washington: Government Printing Office, 1962.

U.S. Bureau of the Budget Bulletin No. 60–2, dated Sept. 21, 1959.

U.S. Commission on Organization of the Executive Branch of the Government (1953–1955). *Business Organization of the Department of Defense.* Washington: Government Printing Office, 1955.

U.S. Commission on Organization of the Executive Branch of the Government (1953–1955), Task Force on Procurement. *Five Staff Papers Prepared for the Task Force on Procurement,* 3 vols. (mimeographed, dated June, 1955).

————. *Report on Military Procurement.* Washington: Government Printing Office, 1955.

U.S. Congress. House. Committee on Appropriations, Subcommittee on Department of Defense Appropriations. *Hearings: Department of Defense Appropriations for 1957, Procurement Policies and Practices of the Department of Defense.* Washington: Government Printing Office, 1956.

———. *Hearings: Department of Defense Appropriations for 1958, Procurement Policies and Practices of the Department of Defense.* Washington: Government Printing Office, 1957.

———. *Hearings: Department of Defense Appropriations for 1959, Procurement, Supply, and Surplus Operations of the Department of Defense.* Washington: Government Printing Office, 1958.

———. *Hearings: Department of Defense Appropriations for 1960, Part 5, Procurement.* Washington: Government Printing Office, 1959.

———. *Hearings: Department of Defense Appropriations for 1962, Part 4, Research, Development, Test, and Evaluation.* Washington: Government Printing Office, 1961.

———. *Hearings: Department of Defense Appropriations for 1962, Part 5, Procurement.* Washington: Government Printing Office, 1961.

———. *Hearings: Department of Defense Appropriations for 1963, Part 4, Procurement.* Washington: Government Printing Office, 1962.

———. *Hearings: Department of Defense Appropriations for 1964, Part 1, Secretary of Defense.* Washington: Government Printing Office, 1963.

———. *Hearings: Department of Defense Appropriations for 1964, Part 5, Procurement.* Washington: Government Printing Office, 1963.

———. *Hearings: Department of Defense Appropriations for 1964, Part 6, Research, Development, Test and Evaluation; Appropriation Language; Testimony of Members of Congress, Organizations, and Interested Individuals.* Washington: Government Printing Office, 1963.

U.S. Congress. House. Committee on Armed Services. *Hearings Before the Special Subcommittee on Procurement: Waste in Defense Department Procurement Including Testimony on H.R. 1033, Cataloguing and Standardization and H.R. 7405.* Washington: Government Printing Office, 1952.

———. *Hearings on Military Posture and H.R. 9751.* Washington: Government Printing Office, 1962.

———. *Hearings on Military Posture and H.R. 2440.* Washington: Government Printing Office, 1963.

———. *Hearings on Military Posture and H.R. 4016.* Washington: Government Printing Office, 1965.

U.S. Congress. House. Committee on Armed Services, Special Subcommittee on Procurement Practices of the Department of Defense. *Hearings Pursuant to Section 4, Public Law 86–89.* Washington: Government Printing Office, 1960.

———. *Report Pursuant to Section 4, Public Law 86–89.* Washington: Government Printing Office, 1960.

U.S. Congress. House. Committee on Armed Services, Subcommittee for Special Investigations. *The Aerospace Corporation: A Study of Fiscal and Management Policy and Control.* Washington: Government Printing Office, 1965.

————. *Hearings: Overpricing of Government Contracts.* Washington: Government Printing Office, 1961.

U.S. Congress. House. Committee on Government Operations. *Organization and Management of Missile Programs, Eleventh Report by the Committee on Government Operations.* Washington: Government Printing Office, 1959.

U.S. Congress. House. Committee on Government Operations, Military Operations Subcommittee. *Hearings: Organization and Management of Missile Programs.* Washington: Government Printing Office, 1959.

U.S. Congress. House. Select Committee on Small Business. *Small Business and Government Procurement: A Report of the Select Committee on Small Business.* Washington: Government Printing Office, 1962.

U.S. Congress. Joint Economic Committee, Subcommittee on Defense Procurement. *Hearings: Impact of Military and Related Civilian Supply and Service Activities on the Economy.* Washington: Government Printing Office, 1964.

————. *Hearing: Progress Made by the Department of Defense in Reducing the Impact of Military Procurement on the Economy.* Washington: Government Printing Office, 1961.

U.S. Congress. Joint Economic Committee, Subcommittee on Federal Procurement and Regulation. *Hearings: Economic Impact of Federal Procurement.* Washington: Government Printing Office, 1965.

U.S. Congress. Senate. Committee on Armed Services, Preparedness Investigating Subcommittee. *Investigation of the Preparedness Program, Second Report, Report on Concentration of Defense Contracts.* Washington: Government Printing Office, 1955.

U.S. Congress. Senate. Committee on Armed Services, Procurement Subcommittee. *Hearings: Procurement Study.* Washington: Government Printing Office, 1960.

U.S. Congress. Senate. Committee on Government Operations. *Government Competition with Free Enterprise.* Washington: Government Printing Office, 1963.

U.S. Congress. Senate. Committee on the Judiciary, Subcommittee on Antitrust and Monopoly. *Concentration in American Industry.* Washington: Government Printing Office, 1957.

————. *Concentration Ratios in Manufacturing Industry, 1958: Report Prepared by the Bureau of the Census.* Washington: Government Printing Office, 1962.

————. *Hearings: Economic Concentration, Part 1, Overall and Conglomerate Aspects.* Washington: Government Printing Office, 1964.

U.S. Congress. Senate. Committee on Labor and Public Welfare. *Selected Readings in Employment and Manpower,* Vol. 2, Washington: Government Printing Office, 1964.

U.S. Congress. Senate. Committee on Labor and Public Welfare, Subcommittee on Employment and Manpower. *Hearings: Nation's Manpower Revolution, Part 9.* Washington: Government Printing Office, 1964.

U.S. Congress. Senate. Select Committee on Small Business, Subcommittee on Monopoly. *Hearings: Economic Aspects of Government Patent Policies.* Washington: Government Printing Office, 1963.

U.S. Congress. Senate. Subcommittee of the Committee on Appropriations. *Hearings: Department of Defense Appropriations for 1963.* Washington: Government Printing Office, 1962.

————. *Hearings: Department of Defense Appropriations for 1964.* Washington: Government Printing Office, 1963.

U.S. Congress. Senate. Subcommittee on Government Operations. *Government Competition with Private Enterprise.* Washington: Government Printing Office, 1963.

U.S. Department of Commerce, Bureau of the Census. *Annual Survey of Manufacturers,* 1959, 1960, 1961, and 1962. Washington: Government Printing Office, 1961, 1962, 1963, and 1964.

————. *1958 Census of Manufactures.* Washington: Government Printing Office, 1961.

————. *1963 Census of Manufactures, Preliminary Report, Summary Series: General Statistics for Industry Groups and Industries,* Dec., 1964.

————. *Statistical Abstract of the United States.* Washington: Government Printing Office, various dates.

U.S. Department of Commerce, Office of Business Economics. *Survey of Current Business,* various issues.

U.S. Department of Commerce, Office of Technical Services. *Bureau of Ships Analysis of Arthur Andersen and Company: Shipbuilding Cost Study,* Nov. 30, 1962.

U.S. Department of Defense Directive No. 4100.15, dated March 5, 1963.

————. Directive 5500.10, dated June 1, 1963.

U.S. Department of Defense, Office of the Secretary of Defense. *100 Companies and Their Subsidiaries [or Affiliates] Listed According to Net Value of Military Prime Contract Awards* (mimeographed, various dates; title varies slightly).

————. *Military Prime Contract Awards and Subcontract Payments, July 1962–June 1963; July 1963–June 1964;* and *July 1964–June 1965.*

U.S. Department of Justice. *Identical Bidding in Public Procurement: Report of the Attorney General under Executive Order 10936.* Washington: Government Printing Office, 1962; *Second Report,* 1964.

————. Press releases dated Aug. 29, 1963; Oct. 9, 1964; and May 11, 1965.

U.S. Federal Trade Commission and U.S. Securities and Exchange Commission. *Quarterly Financial Report, United States Manufacturing Corporations, 4th Quarter, 1957,* and *4th Quarter, 1962.*

U.S. National Science Foundation. *Research and Development in Industry 1960: Final Report on a Survey of R & D Funds and R & D Scientists and Engineers.* Washington: Government Printing Office, 1963.

U.S. President's Committee on the Economic Impact of Defense and Disarmament. *Report of the Committee on the Economic Impact of Defense and Disarmament, July 1965.* Washington: Government Printing Office, 1965.

U.S. Securities and Exchange Commission, Division of Trading and Exchanges. *Directory of Companies Filing Annual Reports with the Securities and Exchange Commission.* Washington: Government Printing Office, various dates.

U.S. Smaller War Plants Corporation. *Report to the U.S. Senate Special Committee to Study Problems of American Small Business: Economic Concentration and World War II.* Washington: Government Printing Office, 1946.

Worsley, T. B. *Wartime Economic Stabilization and the Efficiency of Government Procurement.* Washington: Government Printing Office, 1949.

Yoshpe, H. P., and M. V. Massen. *Procurement Policies and Procedures in the Quartermaster Corps during World War II.* Quartermaster Corps Historical Studies, No. 17. Washington: Government Printing Office, 1947.

Index